The Traitor and the Jew

In the same series :

A Mess That Deserves a Big NO, by Pierre Elliott Trudeau
The Last Cod-Fish, by Pol Chantraine
Zen and the Art of a Postmodern Canada, by Stephen Schecter
Seven Fateful Challenges for Canada, by Deborah Coyne

Canadian Cataloguing in Publication Data
Delisle, Esther, 1954-
 The Traitor and the Jew : anti-Semitism and extremist right-wing
 nationalism in Quebec from 1929 to 1939.
 (Food for thought ; 2)
 Translation of : Le Traître et le Juif.
 Includes bibliographical references.

 ISBN 1-895854-01-6

 1. Anti-semitism - Quebec (Province) - History - 20th century. 2. Groulx,
Lionel, 1878-1967. 3. Right and left (Political science) - Quebec (Province) -
History - 20th century. 4. Nationalism - Quebec (Province) - History - 20th
century. 5. Quebec (Province) - History - 1897-1936. 6. Le Devoir. I. Title II.
Series :
Food for thought (Montreal, Quebec) ; 2.

FC2924.9.N3D4413 1993   305.8'9240714   C93-096290-7

If you wish to receive our lists of forthcoming titles,
please send your request to the following address :
Robert Davies Publishing,
P.O.B. 702, Outremont, QC, Canada H2V 4N6

Esther Delisle

The Traitor and the Jew

Anti-Semitism and extremist right-wing nationalism in
Quebec from 1929 to 1939

*translated by Madeleine Hébert,
with Claire Rothman and Käthe Roth*

Preface by Ramsay Cook

ROBERT DAVIES PUBLISHING
MONTREAL – TORONTO

DISTRIBUTED IN CANADA BY

Stewart House,
481 University Avenue, Suite 900
Toronto, Ontario M5G 2E9

☎ *(Ontario & Québec) 1-800-268-5707*
(rest of Canada) 1-800-268-5742
Fax 416-940-3642

For Pierrette

"I took part in a meeting where I spoke a great deal about politicians and not much about Jews, although even that little was too much. We said terrible things that night. One of us went so far as to say that it was impossible to step on the Jew-bitch's tail in Germany without hearing barking all across Canada."

"At the same time as Hitler was preparing to kill six million Jews, the Jeune-Canada movement spoke very sincerely of a 'supposed mistreatment', 'imaginary persecution' that they contrasted with the oppression—'quite real in this case'— that the French Canadians suffered here. I can still see myself, hear myself bitching as loudly as I could during the meeting, while that same night, some poor German Jew must have been trying to save his family from death by leaving Germany..."

André Laurendeau: "No one is hostile. Why must we always mention the fact that someone is a Jew?", quoted from *Ces choses qui nous arrivent. Chronique des années 1961-1966,* **Montreal, HMH Publishers, Collection Aujourd'hui, 1970.**

Table of Contents

THE REMEMBRANCE OF ALL THINGS PAST

"What is a nation? It is an abstract idea. For me, there are groups of humans, changing, constantly in transformation, but whose characteristics nationalists wish to congeal."

Esther Delisle

HERE IS NO DOCUMENT OF CULTURE," the German cultural critic Walter Benjamin wrote in his "Theses on the Philosophy of History," "which is not at the same time a document of barbarism."[1] This was written as a warning against attempts to "historicize," to sanitize, the past. He might have had in mind those who wish to use the past, or rather a particular construction of it, to fabricate contemporary ideologies. Such attempts always distort the past and mislead the present. Benjamin, himself a victim of the anti-Semitic furies of Hitler's Germany, would not have been surprised either by the content of *The Traitor and the Jew* or by the controversy that it has aroused.

Esther Delisle's book, now translated into English, is a thoroughly documented account of the anti-Semitic and anti-liberal ideology of right-wing French Canadian nationalists during the decade leading up to the Second World War. The book began life as a doctoral thesis in political science at Canada's oldest institution of higher learning, Laval University in Quebec City. Returning to her home province after three years of study at the International Centre for the Study of Anti-Semitism in the Hebrew University in Jerusalem, she was well equipped to make a detailed analysis of Quebec history during a period in which it had long been known that anti-Semitic sentiments, expressed in both French and English, had existed. Most writers, however, had judged these sentiments marginal, almost eccentric.[2] Delisle's study did more than simply confirm the existence of random anti-Jewish remarks; it demonstrated extensive evidence of systematic *Judenhass* in the writings and teachings of some of the most important, and in nationalist circles revered, names from the recent past. And while Delisle made it clear that her study was confined to nationalists of the "extreme right," anyone who knew Quebec realized that to include the leading nationalist historian, *Abbé* Lionel Groulx, the leading nationalist daily newspaper, *Le Devoir*, the leading nationalist monthly, *l'Action nationale*, and the leading nationalist youth organization, *Jeune-Canada*, meant that the study focused on mainstream nationalist ideology in the 1930's.

Though Delisle was in search of a Ph.D., not a public scandal, both her subject and the rigour of her analysis ensured the latter and made the road to her academic goal problematic. First she faced an unusual number of bureaucratic mishaps when the time arrived for her to give the required oral defense of her research results before a board of experts. When word of her difficulties leaked out, the Quebec news magazine *l'Actualité* headlined its story *"le chanoine au pilori"* and immediately drew the connection between this "crucifixion" and the mountains, the schools, the CEGEP, and the Metro station that bore Groulx's name. It also reminded readers that shortly after coming to power, René Lévesque (who remembered preferring Groulx's racist novel *l'Appel de la race* to the "preachy" *Notre Maître, le passé*) had dedicated a plaque to the nationalist-priest's memory. The story might have added that in 1967, when Groulx died, debate on normal business in the Quebec National Assembly was adjourned so that members on both sides of the legislature could pay homage to perhaps the leading intellectual opponent of the Quiet Revolution. Though by then Groulx's *Chemins de l'avenir* led only to the past, he had once been a true keeper of the nationalist flame.[3]

Bureaucratic excuses and a public controversy left Delisle in limbo, still anxiously awaiting announcement of a date for her examination. Then came the Mordecai Richler explosion, caused first by his *New Yorker* article and then in the spring of 1992 by his rollicking diatribe against Quebec nationalism, *Oh Canada! Oh Quebec!*—a book which relied on Delisle's research for some of its information about anti-Semitism in Quebec. When the storm broke over Richler, some of the thunderbolts struck Delisle. To the charge that she had hitched her wagon to the Richler locomotive, Delisle replied: "My wagon advances very well by itself, and I have no need of anyone else's locomotive." Then she added, with characteristic courage: "I am not embarrassed to see my name coupled with Mordecai Richler's."[4] Delisle, though discouraged, refused to accept defeat. Her insistence on her right to an examination was finally recognized in September 1992. A normal waiting period would have been three to six months, but two years had passed before Delisle's examining committee finally convened. Three hours later, by a vote of three to two, the thesis was accepted. Those who rejected it, as well as critics in the public press, maintained that its argument was extreme, that it lacked context, that Groulx's remarks, while "regrettable" were nevertheless "marginal to his vast output."[5] Delisle's sin was her refusal to "historicize" anti-Semitism, preferring to reveal the "barbarism" of these "documents of culture."

The problem with Delisle's study, from the point of view of her critics, was that she had indeed successfully placed anti-Semitism in context, thus raising fundamental questions about the usable past, the essential narrative of modern Quebec nationalist discourse. In Delisle's view some of the creators of that past, most notably Abbé Groulx, expressed not only anti-Semitic sentiments but, more significantly, those sentiments formed an integral part of an ideology that rejected liberal democracy and advocated the transformation of Quebec into a "Fascist utopia" modelled on Franco's Spain, Salazar's Portugal, Mussolini's Italy and Dollfuss' Austria. Moreover, she argued that at the heart of extreme right-wing nationalism lay a fierce hatred of contemporary French Canadians, and a consequent belief that the French Canadian nation true to its past had yet to be constructed. As Groulx wrote in 1934: " this is the great affliction of the French Canadians, one must dare to say: *there are no* French Canadians." Rather than admiring their compatriots, Delisle implied, right-wing nationalists hated them, for having failed to follow nationalist teachings.

What *The Traitor and the Jew* had succeeded in doing was to remind Quebeckers that their past was less than perfect, a claim bound to disturb those whose ideology is founded on selective memory. Just as Groulx had insisted on the purity and homogeneity of the French and Catholic "race" that had founded New France, so too modern nationalists preferred that any blemishes on the past, such as "anti-Semitism" were "marginal" and should be ignored. Only a selective past can provide an adequate foundation for a nationalist future. Or as Ernest Renan observed in his famous essay *Qu'est-ce qu'une nation?*: "the essence of a nation is that all individual members have many things in common and also that all have forgotten many things...Every French citizen must have forgotten the St. Bartholemy Day massacre, and the massacres in the Midi in the XIII century..."[6]

For nationalists everywhere, forgetting the past is at least as important as remembering it. The scandal of Esther Delisle's book is its insistence on the remembrance of *all* things past.

RAMSAY COOK

Notes

1. Walter Benjamin, *Illuminations* (New York, 1969), 256

2. Pierre Anctil, *Le Devoir, les Juifs et l'immigration. De Bourrassa à Laurendeau* (Québec 1988) and Pierre Anctil, "Interlude of Hostility: Judeo-Christian Relations in Quebec during the Interwar period," in Alan Davies, ed., *Anti-Semitism in Canada: History and Interpretation* (Waterloo 1992), 135-67

3. *L'Actualité*, 15 juin 1991; René Lévesque, *Memoirs* (Toronto 1986), 74; Lionel Groulx, *Chemins de l'Avenir* (Montréal 1940) and *Mes Mémoires* (Montréal 1974), 235-50

4. Esther Delisle in *La Presse*, 10 January, 1992.

5. Hélène Pelletier-Baillargeon et Jean-Marc Léger to *La Presse*, 27 December 1991.

6. Ernest Renan, *Œuvres complètes*, I (Paris 1947), 892

AUTHOR'S NOTE

THIS BOOK COULD NEVER have been written without the support of many people and organisations. I want to first thank my thesis director, professor Jacques Zylberberg, for having given his complete support to this project whose subject, only a few years ago, could have been seen as heterodox. I consider myself privileged to have been able to benefit, over a number of years, from his wise counsel and openness of mind, qualities by whose presence we recognize the true intellectual and researcher.

I also thank all those who made possible my stay at the Hebrew University of Jerusalem: Professor Yehudah Bauer, president of the International Center for the Study of Anti-Semitism; Schmuel Almog, director of the Center, for the grants I received during three years, as well as for the numerous workshops he organised which helped me to better understand the many roads of analysis of anti-Semitism; professors Arye Sachar and Daniel Ben-Nathan, of the Canadian studies program of Hebrew University, for their kindness and for their financial support; Hebrew University and the United Israel Appeal of Canada for having accorded me the Pulver Bursary; and finally, the Friends of the Hebrew University of Jerusalem for their financial aid.

I want to give special thanks to Professor Zeev Sternhell, of the Department of Political Science of the Hebrew University of Jerusalem, who took an interest in my work, and who had the generosity to invite me to one of the annual workshops of the Institute of Advanced Studies of the Hebrew University.

I also warmly thank the Laval University Foundation, which, by means of the bursaries it granted me, allowed me to finish my doctoral studies.

Words are hardly sufficient to express my gratitude to old friends, all who helped me so many ways in this endeavour, as they have always done since our paths first crossed: firstly, Pierrette Pageau, whose support never ever waned, and also Céline

Villeneuve, Suzanne Auclair, Ann Lamontagne, Diane Béchade, Suzanne Harnois, Michel Lambert. Finally I want to express all my gratitude to my godmother, Yvette R. Gagnon, whose benevolence has protected me since my childhood.

Esther Delisle,
Quebec City, January 1993.

1

A SKELETON IN THE ATTIC?

"YOU MUST BE A JEW!"
"Or an enemy of Quebec!"

TRAITOR, OR A JEW. My word! The province of Quebec is probably one of the last places in the western world in which the hysterical outcry by a considerable part of the local élite makes it possible to open a book with this kind of quote. In fact, the reactions to my doctoral thesis for Laval University on which this book is based, and that are so revealing of the current intellectual climate in Quebec, practically fall into the realm of caricature.

Let's get the question of my ethnicity out of the way first. Many people with whom I discussed my research, people whose reactions covered the whole spectrum from the overtly hostile to the tentatively encouraging, asked me if I was Jewish. Always ill at ease, they managed to skirt the subject by taking inventive comic detours and using code-word euphemisms. My family genealogy was a favourite topic: Was my grandfather by any chance an important man in a Polish ghetto before the winds of chance deposited him at the foot of St. Lawrence Boulevard in Montreal, or behind Kensington Market in Toronto? Hope springs eternal, as they say! Another graceless *leitmotif* surrounded my first name, which as everyone knows…:

" Esther…isn't that a *Jewish* name?"

"Really?" I replied.

"Oh yes, I think so, I think so…

"Well (I added), what of it? What do you really mean?

Another variant:

"Are you a true French Canadian?" The question here implicitly concerned my religion.

The truth of the matter is entirely different. In point of fact, neither university research nor the gropings of intellectual curiosity dance to the tune of ethnic determinism. Do we assume that anthropologists who study Native peoples necessarily have aboriginal family connections? Does any serious thinker postulate that a doctor chooses to specialize in cardiology or oncology because of his or her ethnic origins? The famous sociologist Max Weber castigated in these words the pretensions of those who would use ethnic and racial analysis to explain individual scientific interest, and society at large: "I personally find myself in a somewhat uncomfortable situation, from that point of view, inasmuch as I feel I am a cross-section of many races, or at least many ethnic groups...Part of me is French, another part German, and as a Frenchman I most certainly have a Celtic tinge to my blood..."

It should be clear that the underlying motivations which explain any particular individual's interest in a subject or a discipline are almost infinitely variable: specifically, they add nothing to our understanding of his work. I personally became interested in anti-Semitism and extremist right-wing nationalism in Quebec because the totalitarian utopian ideologies which emerged in the 20th century after a lengthy period of gestation fascinate me. And even the most cursory glance at the shelves of any research library would confirm that this interest of mine is shared by a considerable number of persons, who belong—is it really necessary to add?—to many nationalities, many religions, and many age groups. But to only two genders!

Hidden beneath the skirts of these questions about my ethnic origins was the conviction that only a Jew could be *that* interested in anti-Semitism. It was highly improbable that a *real Québécoise* would develop an interest in this subject. Of course, this conclusion is postulated on the proposition that a person of the Jewish faith is not *"Québécois,"* belonging instead to a vaguely-defined constellation of "cultural communities"; we don't know exactly of what these beasts are made, but their existence has become undeniable in Quebec, and is constantly reaffirmed by an army of clerics and bureaucrats.

Pure laine, which literally means "pure wool," is a common expression in Quebec. It designates certain French-speaking Catholics who, rightfully or wrongfully, it doesn't matter much, claim to have many generations of ancestors in the province. In 1981 a new category, called "cultural communities," was coined and quickly institutionalized by the establishment of the Ministry of Cultural Communities and Immigration of the Government of Quebec, that same year. This shower of denominations old and new is really a house of mirrors in which the reflections of one group never quite meet those of the other: old-stock Quebecker versus immigrant, Québécois versus ethnic minorities, etc. What is interesting in the case of the concept of Cultural Communities, is that unlike the previously-used denomination of *ethnic minority*, their difference is no longer founded on language *per se*.

Even more interesting is the fact that this tendency became stronger after Bill 101, the so-called Charter of the French language, was passed into law by the Quebec National Assembly in 1977. This law was the key piece of legislation introduced by the new Parti Québécois government, which had been voted into office on 15 November, 1976. This political formation, led by René Lévesque, a well-known former journalist and Minister in the Liberal government of Jean Lesage, had as its chief reason for existence the transformation of the Province of Quebec into a sovereign state, while still maintaining an economic association with the rest of Canada.

But if the government decreed the fundamental importance of the French language to the definition of the Québec nation, it simultaneously denied this in its own definition of cultural communities.

The French Language Charter reaffirmed French as the official language of the Province, obliged the immense majority of immigrants to send their children to French schools, decreed French to be the language in the workplace and imposed strict rules on public signs. But at the same time the Minister of Cultural Communities, in a document entitled "Quebecers Each and Every One" clearly established the fact that the French language is no longer the distinctive hallmark of the Nation. Officially included among these Cultural Communities are people of

Italian, Jewish, German, Greek, and Vietnamese origin, among others, including by the way even *French* immigrants, which means that the descendants of the early French settlers who are generally deemed to have formed the "Nation," are also now just one more of the "Cultural Communities." Leaving aside for the moment the evident ideological-technocratic absurdity here, it is obvious that what this was all really about was the attempt to take measures to assimilate new immigrants into the francophone majority without destroying their presence as defined minorities whose very existence testifies to and confirms the presence of the majority. This labyrinthine saga brings us straight back to the myth of origins, more about that later.

But when does one cease to belong to a "cultural community" and actually become *"Québécois"*? Just how many generations have to be counted, and what characteristics must be acquired, before the club takes in some new members? Nobody really knows, or even pretends to know, which only demonstrates the shallowness of the whole concept. One day I happened to enquire of a Jewish friend how long he had lived in Quebec. It turned out that his family had been here for six generations! Even though I am somewhat hesitantly counted in among those lucky members of the blurred and elusive category of *"pure laine,"* I certainly can't match his pedigree. In fact, I recently learned, much to my amusement, that my great-grandmother was an American. This subtle branching of my family tree could have easily escaped my knowledge, had it not been for two of my aunts wondering one day in my presence, if they still had a photo of "Lésée." There followed a lengthy exchange about this (to me) mysterious person, and so I asked who she was. "Why Esther," replied my aunts in unison, "we are talking about our grandmother Elizabeth!" So I discovered that my American ancestress, then newly-married to my great-grandfather, arriving in the little village in the region south of the city of Quebec known as the Beauce, asked her neighbours to call her Lizzie. And "Lizzie" quickly became "Lésée," a much easier sound to pronounce in French. Her cousin Arthur who accompanied her became "Ate," a faithful rendition of the New Englander's way of saying "Art," and it is with this unusual name that his memory survives in the stories told around the family dinner table.

The myth of the origins of the French Canadian nation is probably the most important legacy of the body of work by Lionel Groulx. This myth shores up the belief shared by large numbers of Quebeckers that the majority of the French-speaking population of Quebec descends in an unwavering straight line from the original French colonists, who were obviously both Catholic and francophone.

Groulx in fact made almost desperate attempts to establish the Catholic and French nature of the first colonists of New France. "Ethnic, social, religious, moral homogeneity; homogeneity and intrinsic values, everything was in place for the development of an élite," Groulx writes in *La Naissance d'une Nation*.* "This predestined phalanx," to use Groulx's own words, came from all the regions of France although the Normans are dominant, not in numbers but in the decisive influence they exercised as first arrivals. Groulx concluded in *Notre Maître le passé*,** that from 1680 onwards, the essential characteristics of the young race are forever set. New France would be Norman, or nothing.

Groulx insists on affirming the supremacy of the Norman influence because he wanted at all costs to minimize the contributions of those groups who didn't fit his mould, who didn't speak French at all, for example, like the Bretons, or the lukewarm Christians from La Rochelle. According to Groulx, either the English prisoners of war, like the Germans, the Swiss, and the Portuguese, did not establish themselves in New France at all, or else were only present in numbers he qualifies as "specks of dust"; the same thing applies to the black and Amerindian slaves. But the vehemence with which Groulx applies himself in attempting to show that these people did not establish themselves in the colony suggests that he knew, in fact, that the opposite was more than likely closer to the truth.

* The Birth of a Nation.
** The Past is our Master.

The historian Marcel Trudel, one of the foremost experts on New France, states that more than 1,500 black slaves lived in New France; Marcel Fournier, in his book *Les Européens au Canada des origines à 1765** identifies more than 1,500 immigrants who, from the origins of the colony until 1765, arrived from 24 countries other than France. There were in fact a lot of skeletons that Groulx needed to keep out of sight.

In addition to all of this, in point of fact, most of the settlers from France didn't even speak French! French was an idiom which was not spoken by the majority of those living in France, as Eugen Weber reminds us in *Peasants into Frenchmen. The Modernization of Rural France, 1870-1914*. French was the language of the king, its use limited to public affairs. In the Pyrenees Treaty (1659), Louis XIV assures his new subjects of their right to use "the language of their choice, be it French or Spanish, Flemish or whatever."

Making France "French" was a difficult task for the state. The middle class in the cities, the lawyers, the nobles and the clergy were for obvious reasons among the first to add the French language to their local dialect, but the rest of the population was either uninterested by this linguistic nicety or actively opposed to the hegemony promoted by Paris. French would thus coexist with a number of dialects for more than two centuries. Often, French was reserved for the schools: at home and in the streets, life went on in patois. In 1858, for example, the Virgin Mary "miraculously" appeared to Bernadette Soubirous at Lourdes and spoke to her not only in French but also in the dialect of the Pyrenees. Another case in point: the grandfather of the writer and statesman André Malraux was a shipowner from Dunkirk. He died in 1909 unable to speak anything but Flemish. Eugen Weber, in reporting these facts, concludes that as late as the Third Republic, almost half of the population did not know French. The uncontested supremacy of French throughout the hexagon would not become a reality until the end of World War I. It is only logical to suppose that in New France, as in the mother country, French was first and foremost the language of

* Europeans in Canada from the beginnings until 1765.

the administration and of the clerical élites. Groulx himself recognizes this, albeit in an oblique way:

> From France came a mix of emigrations; but on Canadian soil, the nature of the colony's needs dispersed them, and through marriage, the different types quickly melded into a single, common type. The facts of colonial life obliged everyone, to be understood, to only speak the common tongue and to keep of their various dialects, only the universal forms and expressions. But the common language was French, the language of the Church, of the Administration, of our schools.[2]

In any case, the use of French eventually did become predominant among the waves of immigrants who from the start, settled in Quebec. Germans, Scots, Irish, Dutch, Spanish, Portuguese and Slavs are all among the 1,500 immigrants from 24 countries other than France noted by Marcel Fournier. After 1765, recalls Marcel Trudel in an interview which appeared in Le Devoir on 24 February, 1992, there was a wave of mixed marriages between anglophones and francophones—what Groulx terms a "betrayal of the blood"—then, there was the massive arrival of German mercenaries who came to the rescue of England fighting off the rebels from the thirteen American colonies: 2,400 of them settled in Canada, and of these more than 1,300 in Quebec. In a book he wrote about this group, Jean-Pierre Wilhelmy tells about a curious exchange of customs between these newly-arrived soldiers and their future colonial spouses:

> In fact, about half of these soldiers were Protestants when they arrived here, and although it may appear curious to us now, it seems clear that their young French-Canadian brides, blinded by love, and despite the hold the Catholic Church had over them, momentarily forgot their religious duties and married without church approval into the religion of their future husbands.[3]

Following this transgression however, the guilty parties, perhaps for practical reasons, returned to Catholicism, bringing with them their new families:

> ...it is noteworthy, perhaps because of the limited number of Protestant churches at this time, that birth certificates issued to children of such marriages show that a significant number of these "canadiennes" returned to their former religion, bringing with them their husbands and other family members.[4]

In return, the accommodating husbands often Frenchify their given and family names. During the 19th century, as Marcel

Trudel recalls in the same interview, the Irish arrived *en masse*, followed in the next century by the Hungarians, the Greeks, the Asians, and the Caribbean islanders. An American anthropologist writes that it was commonplace for young men from the Beauce to go and work for higher pay in Maine[5], which would explain how my great-grandfather met his American wife.

Marcel Trudel concludes: "Very rare are those Québécois who one could today describe with the racist connotation of "pure laine," i.e. who can draw a family tree in which their ancestors were always and only French, from France." To which I add, *who didn't necessarily speak french!*

If Canon Groulx had only sought to lessen the influence and the numbers of those groups who muddied his pristine image of New France, if he had only resuscitated a few heroes from the ranks—Dollard des Ormeaux among the now most famous—, had he but invented so-called traditions—such as the pilgrimages to Carillon and Long-Sault—or promoted national symbols—like the fleur-de-lis flag—, then his name could simply be added to the long list of intellectuals engaged in the creation and propagation of the myths and symbols which legitimate the modern nation-state.

But this is not the case. Right from the beginning of his myth of our origins, Groulx slides into one of the themes which will ultimately feed his Fascism: the purity of race. Not only does he deny any racial mixing between the French-speaking population of New France and black slaves—"this inferior element hardly mixed with our people"—, he writes in *La naissance d'une race*,* he applies this same approach to the Amerindian population. Voluntarily overlooking the fact that human reproduction can take place without the benediction of the Roman Catholic Church,—and here was an activity the French fur traders took vigourous advantage of—Groulx tries to reassure his readers, asserting that during two whole centuries only 94 marriages occurred between French and Amerindian partners. Once this "fact" is in place, he gives the *coup de grace* to the descendants

* The Birth of a Race.

of these sparse unions: "Moreover, these métis left among us no descendants, their children being all deceased before the end of the eighteenth century. That is the final, unassailable word of science on this affair: we are gloriously avenged."[6] Groulx also writes: "Oh, I suppose that the dishonour is not so great to have brought the sacrament, through the mixing of blood, to the soul of the ancient indigenous races...We can be proud enough to have in our veins the blood of France and this blood only."[7] For the sake of a twisted sense of pride and with unforgiving rancour, Groulx wipes out the existence of the métis with a stroke of the pen.

The purity of race in Groulx's thought is a part of the European intellectual current which developed at the end of the last century, and which confuses sociological fact with biological fact, the latter being often used to explain the former. Within this large current flow many political eddies, but the movement which mesmerized Groulx was extremist right-wing nationalism, with a Fascist tinge. Paris was then the intellectual magnet of the whole of the European extremist right and Groulx, like so many other ideologues of a continent spinning in a violent reaction against liberalism, became drawn to the likes of Charles Maurras and l'Action française, Maurice Barrès and Gustave LeBon.

From these last two Groulx acquires and defends a thesis brutal in its simplicity: socio-psychological characteristics are transmitted through the blood, and union between people of different "races" engenders firstly, the degeneration of the individual, and ultimately, on a larger scale, the degeneration of the "race" itself.

Gustave LeBon, prophet of the militant French Right, author of Lois psychologiques de l'évolution des peuples,* one of the biggest best-sellers of the late 19th century, of which Groulx kept a copy "full of approving notes"[8] in his personal library, is amply quoted in Groulx's novel L'appel de la race**, in itself an acme of racism.

---

*   The Psychological Laws of the Evolution of Peoples.
** The Iron Wedge.

To mix two peoples is to change at one and the same time their
physical as well as their mental constitution...The characteristics
become weak and disassociated right from the beginning. Long
hereditary accumulations are required to define them. The initial
effect of racial mixing is to destroy the soul of each one, and here I
mean the ensemble of common ideas and sentiments which are
the strength of a people and without which there can be neither
nation, nor homeland...This is why all the peoples who have arrived at a high degree of civilisation have always avoided mixing
with foreigners.[9]

This quote is just as revealing in another respect: whether he
uses the terms nation, race, ethnicity or culture, Groulx always
goes back to the idea of the biological transmission of psycho-
sociological characteristics. In the references to the soul one dis-
cerns the hold of religious frames of reference on racism.
However, the various Christian denominations always allowed
for the rite of conversion, while racist ideology, erecting the barrier of the blood, irrevocably excludes the Other.

In *L'appel de la race*, Groulx imparts the following thoughts to
the hero, a man with the presumptuously conspicuous French-
Canadian name of de Jules de Lantagnac:

Spontaneously, he remembered the words of Barrès: 'The blood of
the race remains the same through the centuries!' And the unhappy father surprised himself frequently ruminating on this painful
reflection: 'So it's all true, the cerebral disorder, the psychological
disorder that comes from mixing races.'[10]

This sad "conclusion" at which he arrives comes from observing his *own* children from his marriage to an English-
Canadian Protestant.

"Thirty years after the publication of his book *L'esclavage au
Canada français*,* wrote the journalist Clément Trudel, in the
same article (Le Devoir, 24 February 1992) Marcel Trudel
remains amazed that people are surprised to hear about a
phenomenon [race mixing] which doesn't quite fit into the
frame of the founding myths of a colony "pure of race" (the historian François-Xavier Garneau) where lived "a white and French

---

* Slavery in French Canada.

population, nothing at all like elsewhere in America where there was a mixed population, semi-indigenous...only one type was possible here, it was a colony of the white race" (Lionel Groulx, in volume one of his *Histoire du Canada*).*

It is somewhat curious that the myth of Catholic, French and francophone ancestors carries so much weight among Quebec intellectuals because in France, for example, no sensible person—and no serious intellectual—any longer gives credence to the myth of "our ancestors the Gauls." The Gauls, moreover, would not become the "ancestors" of the French nation until the July Revolution which confirmed the victory of the bourgeoisie over the nobility. The bourgeoisie laid claim to a Gallic ascendance in order to legitimate its right to govern, just as the nobility had founded its own similar pretensions upon its Frankish origins: it is a good example of the fact the myths of origin often have a political flavour.

The symbolic figure which dominates the myth of origins is the Hero, issuing from a pure and physically strong race. Groulx's description in this case is in fact quite troubling. In describing this race as "having an excellent physical quality"[11] he uses the language of the horse-trader, writing, for example, that only "units of irreproachable choice"[12] were allowed into the country, hardly surprising when we are told that the "Church and the State kept out suspect merchandise."[13] There would be no place in New France for "rubbish."[14] The fate of any physical or moral detritus who managed to sneak into New France is quickly settled by Groulx, now quite at ease in the role of Holy Father, holding the right of life and death over them all: "None of this riff-raff put down roots in Canada. And so we go on!"[15]

In this fictional New France, the Hero shares the scene with another symbolic figure, in the shadows for the moment, but who, in the description Groulx will make of contemporary Quebec, will eventually totally eclipse the Hero: he is the Traitor, this French Canadian enamoured with individualism who from degeneration through compromise will literally cease to be a part of humanity!

---

* History of Canada.

Even as he is busy painting a bucolic picture of a rural, agricultural and idyllic New France, a wonderland of chaste morals, where crime is absent, he describes in the very same breath an entirely opposite situation. In *La naissance d'une race*, he ascribes to the individualism of the colonists the folly of dispersion which leads to an exodus back to France and which sees fully half of the colony's husbands become trappers and fur-traders. "It did come to pass." writes Groulx, annoyed.

> The life of the trapper became a kind of profession, with easily un-derstood consequences for the mores of the young Canadian generation, for the working of the land and for the evangelisation of the natives scandalized by these fur-traders who pushed them into the arms of alcohol.[16]

So much for the lack of mingling between Europeans and Amerindians!

Since they were described by Groulx, the Hero and the Traitor have never completely left the ideological scene in Quebec, although they have been fortunately confined, most of the time, to the tool-box of a few diehards of a particular bent of nationalism. Himself now enthroned in the pantheon of Heros of the Nation, Lionel Groulx has become a cult figure among a tiny cohort of devotees. The mystification invented by this group is founded upon an abso-lute equation in their minds between Groulx and Quebec. He repre-sents for them the complete incarnation of the Nation. As a corollary, anyone who dares to criticize Groulx, even if only by means of quoting the master's own words, is really attacking the Nation and thus is a Traitor.

It fell to Jean Éthier-Blais to pen most succinctly and with the most clarity the equation Groulx=Quebec, as well as to vilify the treachery of those who don't share his own interpretation of matters.

> So now they bring up the so-called anti-Semitism of Abbé Groulx. His anti-Semitic words, they say! But he found them right in his breviary. This was no unusual phenomenon in Quebec...Everyone who knew him knew he was deeply anti-Hitler, against the con-centration camps. But the enemies of Quebec needed a scarecrow.[17]

I have to admit that I don't know if I should feel pride, or rather embarrassment, at being shanghaied from the humble ranks of doctoral students to shore up the platoons of those offi-

cially-declared enemies of the Nation. Who only have one idea
in mind, if we are to believe Éthier-Blais, and that is to destroy
Quebec. Nothing less.

> If they succeed in beating Groulx, in destroying the Myth, then
> Quebec is finished. They want to wipe it out, like they razed the
> French college of Sudbury...forgetting to place him in another era,
> when language was used differently. Groulx was much more harsh
> in his descriptions of the Québécois themselves than he was with
> regard to the Jews. Are we then to suppose that he was anti-
> Québecois?[18]

In other words, Groulx has himself now acquired the status of
the officially-recognized Myth. But what about reality?

The language and the times of Groulx are indeed those of the
rise of extremist right-wing nationalism, Fascism and national
socialism. Letting his pen meander inside this spectre, he here
and there borrows a number of themes, a stylized vocabulary,
and various quirks of language.

To cite but one example, when he pronounces the ejection of
the French Canadian from humanity, he is in reality just taking
his cues from l'Action française of Paris which over the years excluded, first from the Nation and eventually from humanity,
those French who supported the Republic, as well as other internal enemies. Which meant almost everyone, when all was said
and done. But while l'Action française was in favour of the
repression, even the execution of traitors, Groulx, for his part,
only sees salvation in the political and national re-education of
the French Canadians. Perhaps here he recovers a little
humanity...

Or take the theme of "The soil and the dead" which is at the
centre of the work of Maurice Barrès. Groulx picks it up and
uses it, on occasion, to stigmatise his own people: "Our people,
who know nothing of the fatherland, who are incapable of feelings for it, for its soil and its dead,...can nonetheless become
hysterically passionate about the myth of the Party and for the
puppets of political struggle."[19]

Back to the present. My supposed goal of destroying Quebec
was the paroxysm of the attacks elicited by the news of my doctoral research. Few actually went to that outrageous extreme;
several came close. A certain Stéphane Stapinsky accused me, in

Le Devoir on 22 January 1992, of being an intellectual Vychinsky (a reference to the infamous and sinister "show trials" prosecutor of Joseph Stalin's U.S.S.R.) who took on Groulx in order to better attack Quebec nationalism. The same refrain was picked up in a minor key by those who cloak their contemporary activities under the Canon's approving cassock.

After having "established" once and for all that Groulx *is* Quebec, his apologists then declared that the same goes for them, adding to the voluntary confusion in their minds between themselves and the nation. Showering excommunication with a generosity which would have pleased the Canon himself, they dutifully apply the lessons of the master. For now it is neither language, nor religion that defines the French Canadian. Oh, no! It is *ideology*. The right kind, of course. "We all know that speaking a second-rate French with which one can more or less make oneself understood is perfectly compatible with the soul of a turncoat."[20] And speaking French presupposes a French spirit, and a French soul, as Groulx makes abundantly clear in *Orientations*. A school, he solemnly warns, that teaches a language but not the pride to speak it is a school of treason:

> In the same way, the heart of the matter is not just to keep French in our schools, but more importantly to beware of the ideologies, the ends, the final interests of which the school is the instrument...There once was a time when Gaelic and Breton were spoken, but when however there was little or no conviction of the honour or opportunity to remain Breton or Irish. You must see that when one has reached that point, the teaching of the mother tongue in school has little importance, and the schools are very close to the path of treason.[21]

Upon learning that the number of people who speak and write a better French is on the rise, Groulx's reaction is to regret that "the number of those who have *lost* the spirit of the French language is growing even more."[22] Groulx is manifestly not the spokesman of French and Catholic identity of the time: he doesn't define this identity precisely because it is for him undefinable. It's an *essence*, as are all the symbolic categories of racism. Groulx could not imagine a more adequate reason to even exclude from the ranks of the Nation, when the time came in his delirium, all of the French Canadians themselves, and to cast aside any immigrant who wished to learn French. This essence, inheritor of the soul as conceived of in Christian theology,— but without recourse to baptism—would find its lay equivalent in the mastery of the French language. It became a means of declaring irreversible exclusion, with no right of appeal.

Interwoven with the myth of origin, the ideological definition of the French Canadian/Québécois has still not yet lost its appeal. For some, everything must be judged by the benchmark of ethnicity. There are those who believe that some subjects of research are more "Jewish" than "Québécois." To a journalist who informed me that the writer Mordecai Richler was hardly representative of his community, I asked if I was representative of mine or if she herself could have that pretension. Others, more pernicious, thought that Richler was, on the contrary, so *able* a spokesman for the anglophones and/or the Jews of the province that they demanded that the leaders of the two groups publicly disassociate themselves from his 1992 book *Oh! Canada Oh! Quebec. Requiem for a divided country.*

Some brought the controversy over the work of Lionel Groulx straight into the field of ethnic relations, going far beyond the scope of my research. And expressed the pious wish to establish a "real dialogue with the cultural communities," a task made more difficult, if we are to believe the above-quoted Stapinsky, by work like mine. The blackmail was not very subtle: if you want us to talk to you, show us your interest first, be "accommodating," dissociate yourselves from *these* kinds of enterprises. And never undertake them yourselves!

If I may make myself very clear on at least this one point, my research represents no one except myself. No one but me is responsible for it. But it is addressed to any interested parties. Full stop.

A diluted version of the ethnic obsession and of the idea of collective responsibility that goes along with it, reacting to my thesis, has quite correctly recalled that the French Canadians of the nineteen thirties were far from being the only ones to exhibit anti-Semitic behaviour. On the contrary, as has been emphasized in the English and French Quebec newspapers, English Canadians were just as guilty. McGill University required higher admission grades for Jewish students and in addition imposed quotas on them; private clubs refused them as members, they were not allowed to become full members of the Stock Exchange, and so on and so forth.

But the fact is that *nowhere* in my thesis is there any mention of *French Canadian* anti-Semitism. My thesis is only about the anti-Semitism of Lionel Groulx, of l'Action nationale, of the Jeune-Canada political movement and of Le Devoir from 1929 to 1939: there is no question at all of confusing them with the entire French-Canadian population of the time. This methodological precaution is ignored by those writers who, in their haste to absolve Groulx and his henchmen of anti-Semitism, promote them to the rank of voices of an oppressed people, obsessed by the need for national survival, and who, seeking a scapegoat, fall into the trap of anti-Semitism. But *all* the people did not exhibit this kind of racism. The historical context, about which much has been written and which I have been accused of ignoring, does in no way explain the delirium of hate cultivated by this small group. Even the miseries of the Depression did not gain them a mass following.

The industrialisation and move to urbanisation of the Province of Quebec was pretty well accomplished by the 1920s. Montreal, with its population of 618,506 was then the largest city in Canada. During the following decade, the thirties, a major realignment of political forces took place in the province. The Liberal Party, which had governed for 39 years, was defeated in 1936 by a new political formation, the *Union Nationale*, which brought together the conservative party and a movement of dissident Liberals. These dissidents who called their movement the Liberal National Action Group, attacked what they called Big Money, and staked out a position as the fearless knights of political and economic corporatism. Maurice Duplessis, *"le chef"* as his admirers liked to call him, quickly dispensed with these Liberal dissidents who were too radical for his liking, and under his guiding light the Union Nationale governed Quebec from 1936 to 1939, then from 1944 to 1960. Despite the many changes that took place during this period, Groulx and his ideological allies, still impermeable to reality, kept on playing out the same worn-out theme, over and over again: capitalism, democracy and modernity were propelling the Nation to its ruin.

But, even had I concluded that Quebec during those years was a society crippled by anti-Semitism, so what? What could be more infantile than to point a finger at our neighbours and cry, "Him too!" and underline what everyone knows, that in Europe, there was also anti-Semitism. Well, of course there was! I never declared Quebec to be a unique case on the surface of the earth!

Groulx, l'Action nationale, Jeune-Canada and Le Devoir represented a *minority* ideological current in French Canada during the 1930s.

Lionel Groulx was a priest who taught history at the University of Montreal from 1915 to 1949. Born on January 13, 1878 in Vaudreuil, a small town just west of Montreal. He died on 23 May 1967 in Montreal. In 1946, Groulx founded the *Institut d'histoire de l'Amérique française,* * which quickly began to issue its own review (1947); Groulx himself wrote some thirty historical works. The Jeune-Canada movement drew most of its membership from the student body of the University of Montreal. This movement remained somewhat informal until its demise around 1938, when its members were no longer as young or as ardent. The most interesting individual to emerge from this movement is André Laurendeau, who, after a stay in Europe in the mid-thirties began to question the Fascist and anti-Semitic outbursts which peppered his earlier prose. As of 1937 he became the editor-in-chief of l'Action nationale, but his self-doubts did not stop him from allowing the anti-Semitic and Fascist mud-slinging to continue in the magazine. In 1947, Laurendeau joined Le Devoir, becoming editor-in-chief in 1958. Finally, twenty-three years later, he publicly excused himself for the shameless anti-Semitism of the Jeune-Canada movement of which he had been a part. Notably, Laurendeau was the only one of the group, including those from l'Action nationale and Le Devoir, to make this kind of gesture. And yet, in the years following, he refused to recognize the racism of the mentor of his group, the mentor of the nationalist movement of the thirties: Lionel Groulx. Furthermore, he accused the English-language press, who went to town over the racism of the "distinguished ecclesiastic," of misunderstanding French-Canadian sensitivities. This kind of shilly-shallying and hemming and

* The Institute of French American History.

hawing, coming from Laurendeau who was in fact considerably more forthright that the others, is an excellent illustration of just how hard it is to look openly upon the hideous face of this kind of nationalism from the thirties.

L'Action nationale was a review that wrote for a well-informed, educated readership. Its precursor was *l'Action française*, which was run by Lionel Groulx from 1920 to 1927. A close ideological cousin of the French political movement of the same name (led by the extremist ideologue Charles Maurras), it changed its own name to l'Action *Canadienne*-française after Maurras incurred the Vatican's ire in 1927. But this mutation did not bring longevity with it and L'Action Canadienne-Française quickly ceased publication. Then, like the Phoenix, it rose from its ashes in 1933, reincarnated as l'Action Nationale.

Le Devoir was founded in January 1910, as a newspaper with a mission, i.e. the defense of a Catholic and nationalist doctrine. Its founder, the parliamentarian and nationalist firebrand Henri Bourassa, left the paper in 1932, and was promptly replaced by Georges Pelletier. There wasn't even a whisper of thanks given to Bourassa for a lifetime of services rendered, although in truth, Bourassa's religious faith had grown over the years even as his nationalist ardour waned, and this had alienated him from both the readers and journalists of the paper. Despite its lacklustre performance in the circulation department, and the varying political orientations given it by successive editors-in-chief, Le Devoir has always presented itself as the voice of the collective conscience of French Canadians (in the pre-1960 terminology) or the Québécois, in the terminology in vogue since that date.

In any case, there is something grotesque and ironic about this small group of intellectuals, well-informed and educated, spewing their endless and hate-filled madness upon the imaginary Jew—for the anti-semite's "Jew" is *always* a symbolic construct—and seeking desperately to convince the "ignorant" masses that this delirium is real, while all the while, the very same masses just don't seem to get it.

One example among many: Le Devoir unsuccessfully attempted to warn people against the large-circulation daily La Presse, that well-known Quebec branch of the International

Jewish Conspiracy. For, as recalled an editor of Le Devoir: "La Presse had, in the past, a Jewish editor-in-chief: if that was all we find fault with!"[23] The next day's edition brought the second course: "M. Helbronner (the Jew in question) is deceased, but 40% of La Presse [sic], in advertising, remains in the hands of the Jews. And isn't the editorial page 100% pro-Jewish?"[24]

Jules Helbronner was very *definitely* editor-in-chief of La Presse at the turn of the century. A French Jew, born in Paris in 1844 and established in Montreal in 1874, he became famous for his weekly articles on the conditions of the working class which he signed with the symbolic pseudonym Jean-Baptiste Gagnepetit. Published in La Presse from 1884 to 1894, these chronicles, in which Helbronner denounced, among other things, child labour and the wretched conditions for adult workers in the factories, gained him a wide following among a reading public shaken by the rapid industrialisation of Montreal. He sat on the Royal Commission of enquiry into relations between capital and labour created in 1886 by the MacDonald government. His biting comments on the corruption of the municipal administration and his condemnation of the poor sanitation and housing in working-class neighbourhoods got the attention of social classes who had only recently come into contact with the realities of urban life. According to the official historian of La Presse, Cyrille Felteau, the articles, chronicles and editorials of Jules Helbronner made him "one of the most influential journalists of his time, not only in Quebec, but throughout Canada."[25]

Montrealers of that time did not choose to chastise La Presse for having hired a Jewish journalist, nor for having promoted him to the post of editor-in-chief. An obvious case of myopia or lack of intelligence which Le Devoir, that trenchant beacon of French-Canadian consciousness, underscores with rage. La Presse, recalls a Le Devoir editorial, signed with a pseudonym, has prostituted itself to the Jews:

> La Presse is always there to give us the watchwords on Saint-Jean-Baptiste's day! The rest of the year it is the open door, the passage that leads to the Jewish house of commerce, the streetwalker-in-chief of Israel. But never mind, it publishes magnificent articles on the day we oppose our little lamb to their golden calf.[26]

Le Devoir sees the Jewish stranglehold on the press extending to other newspapers as well. Does not *Le Soleil* (Quebec city's major daily) suffer the insidious censorship of Jewish advertising?, complains Pamphile (yet another pseudonym):[27] "Jerusalem doesn't want Quebeckers to know who rules two of its three French papers. The occult powers conspire to help each other."[28] If the large-circulation dailies pay scant attention to Le Devoir, it must obviously be the doing of international Jewry, whose dangerous plenipotentiary in Quebec, we are amazed to discover, is none other than the seemingly innocuous little paper-boy, holding court on the street corner:

> The Jew went to the right school. With universal experience, he is essentially cosmopolitan, the natural vehicle of internationalism in all things. He knows how his cousin from Frankfurt or Warsaw, a newspaper-boy like himself, went about boycotting the papers that didn't please him or his race: he also knows how his uncle Jacob of Vienna, who made a fortune in the clothing business, controlled the newspapers that accepted his paid prose.[29]

Tragically "blinded" to the terrible scourge of the International Paperboy Conspiracy, the people of Quebec just go on blithely reading the major newspapers of the province. Whereas Le Devoir during the thirties had a readership of hardly more than 15 000, on average. It sometimes teetered on the brink of financial ruin and launched many a desperate subscription campaign.[30] Its readers came from among the clergy, the university community, civil servants and from the liberal professions.[31] During the same decade, Groulx, then at the height of his powers, could only attract a small (but very outspoken) minority of intellectuals, young people and militant nationalists.[32] And yet, his influence on nationalist thought of the time was very real. Any group, any publication that considered itself nationalist sought his seal of approval, so that he became, in those circles, the authority of reference.

It is also interesting to note that in 1934, the interns at five French Montreal hospitals, outraged at the hiring of a Jewish colleague, went out on strike to get him fired. Samuel Rabinovitch, the intern in question, the head of his graduating class, was a part of the handful of Jewish students admitted to the Université de Montréal, where, as we learn from Le Devoir in 1933, "...the maximum is required from foreign students and particularly from Jewish students. And so, in the Faculty of Medicine last year, out of 160 Jewish candidates, only 7 were admitted."[33] Rabinovitch, who had stuck to his guns until that point, finally decided to give up and resigned when the entire medical staff of the hospitals threatened to join the strike.

The American sociologist Everett Hughes mentions that some Montreal students apparently attacked news stands and book stores run by Jews, accusing them of distributing Communist literature and "American obscenity."[34] Le Devoir ran headlines such as: *"The father of yellow journalism was the Jew Pulitzer"*[35] over articles which began: "The father of yellow journalism is Pulitzer, a Hungarian Jew who came to the United States. Calling newspapers 'yellow tracts', is in fact calling them Jewish tracts. It would be hard to say anything more insulting about them. But who knows?"[36] This kind of talk was hardly aimed at calming the waters of inter-ethnic relations...

As far as I have been able to determine, no similar incidents took place among the masses. Even among the élite, not everyone agreed with Groulx, l'Action nationale, the Jeune-Canada movement and Le Devoir: *Le Canada*, published by Olivar Asselin and *l'Autorité* and *Le Jour*, published by Jean-Charles Harvey, would stand up forthrightly against anti-Semitism.[37] La Presse had no truck with this anti-Semitic madness, but *l'Action catholique*, on the other hand, propounded it with an uncommon ardour.[38]

So they were small in numbers. It would, however, be a mistake to believe that these people were insignificant, for this would be a way of denying that a violently anti-democratic and anti-Semitic current of thought existed in Quebec outside of Adrien Arcand's Fascist party. The retrospective importance now given to Groulx and Le Devoir, the former consecrated as Quebec's "national historian," a man whose œuvre is the quintessence of the national consciousness, the latter represented as the tireless defender of the rights of French Canada, possibly explains the controversy brought up by my research and the malaise it provoked.

But others before me have also noticed the racism of Canon Groulx: "We conclude that the historian of French Canada had racist attitudes, if only by his opposition to mixed marriages. That is the main thrust of his first novel,"[39] writes Jean-Pierre Gaboury. Talking about l'Action nationale, Jeune-Canada and Le Devoir, André-J. Bé-langer writes: "l'Action nationale and Jeune-Canada are united in ferociously attacking the Jewish community living in Quebec. Like Le Devoir, they go at it with a vengeance."[40]

Even *before the depression*, during the twenties, Groulx and the *Action française* movement that he led denounced urbanisa-tion, to which they imputed the declining birth rate and the spread of immorality.[41] Action française attacks the popular press, the theatre and the cinema, which being "in the hands of foreigners," impart only foreign morality,[42] and give the name "Americanisation" to this constellation of dangers behind which lurks the Jew: "Whether visibly occupying positions that were the prerogative of French-Canadians or invisibly manipulating the sordid scenes of the cinema and the press, the Jew was an unwelcome figure for Action française."[43]

Le Devoir, which was the ideological ally of Groulx during this decade as well as the next, reproduced many articles of *l'Action française* of Paris[44] and freely opened its pages to the most famous—and vicious—of French anti-semites, Edouard Drumont,[45] author of "The Jewish France," one of nineteenth-century France's best-selling books. Earlier on, in 1910-1911, Joseph Denais, the director of Drumont's *Libre parole,** became the Paris correspondent for Le Devoir.[46]

According to Michael K. Oliver, there is no doubt that anti-Semitism formed an important aspect of nationalism during the twenties and thirties.[47]

When l'Action française rejects many aspects of daily life of a modern and industrialised society, it also rejects the ideas of democracy and parliamentarianism.[48] Jean-Pierre Gaboury brings up the attraction Groulx felt for Fascism: "...he wanted to move his people backwards, from the Liberal State to the Fascist State in which he felt existed a community of outlook with the authoritarian and feudalist New France. That was the con-clusion to which he was led by an anti-liberalism dictated by purely moral criteria."[49] And he adds: "French Canada, even though it was little attached to democracy, refused to alienate it-

* Free Speech.

self from individual freedoms, and the reforms Groulx fought for did not come to pass."[50] Groulx's movement was thus a failure.

The particular perspective of this book differs from that of other authors who have written about nationalism and/or anti-Semitism of the twenties and thirties, in that anti-Semitism is its *primary* focus. The theoretical framework was developed from classical and contemporary studies of racism and anti-Semitism which support and confirm the thesis that the objects of racism are symbolic constructs. They have no existence outside of the phantasms and deliria of those who create and support them. From this standpoint it is clearly useless to pick to pieces the historical "context" frequently invoked by my critics, inasmuch as it brings nothing to the understanding of the delirium, nor gives us any key with which to penetrate it. The reality of the "International Jewish Conspiracy," for example, only existed inside the heads of people like Lionel Groulx, and groups like l'Action nationale, Jeune-Canada and Le Devoir. We are not at all in the presence here of a kind of warped ecumenical dialogue between two equally homogeneous and unified groups, i.e. the "French Canadians" and the "Jews." The editors of Le Devoir—who by the way don't represent the whole of French Canadians—are not involved in a "dialogue" with the Jews: what they are really doing instead is spitting in the face of "the Jew"—a symbolic object. As Pierre Sorlin wrote about the anti-Semitism of the French paper *La Croix*:*

> It [their anti-Semitism] is particular in that it is completely independent of Jews. The editors of this paper don't know any Israelites, and don't even need to know any: what they need is a scarecrow, who can contain in itself everything they fear, and not any particular individual to whom one could impute any particular crime.[51]

The anti-semite's Jew is a construct unfettered by reality. For this reason, it is absurd, and a waste of time, really, to try and track it down in the real world. Michel Herszlikowicz writes in *Philosophie de l'antisémitisme*: "They would have us discover the so-called *real* Jew, i.e. the one no one can empirically

---

*   The Cross.

know."[52] André Laurendeau supplies a striking example of the veracity of this assertion when he writes: "The Jews, who can be, and often are, in fact, just ordinary citizens, nonetheless symbolize a dangerous and fantastic chimera, a Messianism which we must at all costs wipe out."[53]

This Jew has a different corporal *essence*. But combing the *Jewish* community in order to understand anti-Semitism is an absurd and gross error of perspective. For it is precisely not here that the understanding of anti-Semitism is to be found. Besides which, this topsy-turvy approach is pernicious, for it suggests that flesh-and-blood Jews have some real link to—or worse, a responsibility for—the crimes imputed to the terrifying figure of the Jew as described by the anti-semite.

Anti-Semitism did not originate in a vacuum. Anti-judaism mutated into anti-Semitism when the adherents of a despised *religion* became the members of an inferior *race*, explains Léon Poliakov, "...as if the Jewish badge of the middle ages or the *schtreiml* of old were now somehow engraved in the flesh, as if Western consciousness somehow required the assurance of a distinctive characteristic which became, once the *visible* signs which identified the Jews disappeared, an *invisible essence*."[54]

Anti-Semitism was a part of the ideological arsenal of extremist right-wing nationalism and of the ideologies radically contesting liberal values. Many authors suggest that in these ideologies, the Jew is not comprehensible except in relation to the Nation/Race, of which he serves as a negative underpinning. In other words, by symbolising the antithesis of the nation, he permits the national and racial identity to define and affirm itself. But Colette Capitan-Peter's analysis of the ideology of l'-Action française[55] shows us that this binary equation is not airtight: the nation does in fact betray the ideal, and so can no longer embody absolute good in the face of absolute evil. The paired symbolic constructs are similar, diametrical opposites of liberal society. The principal difference between the Traitor and the Jew emerges in the utopian project: the Traitor, re-educated, can now belong, but the Jew is forever excluded. Old Man is dead, and cedes his place to the New.

In the eyes of Lionel Groulx, l'Action nationale, Jeune-Canada and Le Devoir, the evils of capitalism, democracy, parliamentarianism and modernity form an evil totality whose chief devils are the Traitor and the Jew. Capitalism, "this abominable power of gold unbridled by principle,"[56] is in cahoots with democracy to exploit the people. Worse, capitalism, via democracy, is busy daily inoculating "the virulent germ of the worst social cankers"[57] into the body of the nation. The vocabulary of decomposition, purulence, sickness and death, a powerful echo of the Nazi's imaginary world, is used to describe contemporary society. A plague of microbes, fevers and poisons assails the nation. We have before us a "fatal, invasive illness, one that no *cordon sanitaire* can artificially arrest."[58]

Because, says Groulx:

> "A nation destroys itself, by its own hand; it commits suicide, through moral decay and voluntary abdication which are the fruits of a doctrine of cowardice and dissolution. What matters is to remain healthy as a nation."[59]

It is the French Canadians themselves who will hasten their own demise, by wallowing in vice. The nobility and the bourgeoisie commit treason after the conquest, allowing their blood to mix with that of the victor; the politicians abandon the interests of the nation in order to promote their own personal and party interests; the Liberal Party of Quebec, a bootlicking oligarchy of the financial powers, has become, by 1936, "what cancer specialists call 'the giant cell,'" "a canker on the State."[60] The people are "eaten away to the bone by all the diseases of the parliamentary system," these people have become treasonous. A storm of anathema and excommunication falls upon just about everyone: farmers, teachers, intellectuals, workers, who all ignore their lessons of devotion to the nation.

> Whole classes have divorced their actions from patriotic service: our 'professionals' seal themselves off in their professions; our business men, our merchants hardly recognize the responsibilities of capital; our workers treat with the foreigner; our farmers cross the borders as if the fatherland was no longer there at all.[61]

The most trivial gesture becomes treasonous in Groulx's mind. Some French Canadians prefer hockey games, golf or the Rotary Club, others make cosmopolitan small-talk, and commit who knows what other sins...until we arrive at the ultimate judgement: *there are no French Canadians*. Since there is no humanity possible without belonging to a nation, race, or ethnic group, the French Canadians no longer belong to the human race. Worse, they even insult it to its face; wherever he looks, Groulx is haunted by:

> ...only those kinds of French Canadians that we see too much of: inconsistent people, with no dignity, no pride, who appear to belong to no race, no country, a mockery of men who are an insult to mankind and an insult to Catholic upbringing.[62]

These denunciations of capitalism, democracy, parliamentarianism and modernity lead to the same kinds of conclusions by other writers. The economic dictatorship of a small group of foreigners, writes Hermas Bastien in l'Action nationale, is transforming French Canadians into physical and moral trash which encumber the leper-ridden neighbourhoods. Democracy, which divides the people and foments civil war, is termed "party politics" or "political partisanship," and qualified as a "hideous sore which we wear on our foreheads and which rots our entire body"[63] by a member of Jeune-Canada. Democracy has led the nation astray into "moral decadence and political inertia,"[64] writes an editor of Le Devoir.

Even if they all don't go so far as to throw the entire nation out of the ranks of humanity, they all *do* denounce the treason of their own kind. In the mass grave of mediocrity where the French Canadians rot, writes Guy Frégault in l'Action nationale, flutter the politicians, stars of the parliamentary circus, "marionettes controlled by the hidden hands of the forces of our distress," writes Roger Duhamel in the September 1938 edition of l'Action nationale. And the people, intoxicated by "political partisanship," blinded by individualism, see only the dancing lights.

Capitalism, often denounced using the epithet of the "trusts," is completely manipulated by the Other: the American, the English Canadian, the Syrian, the Jew. They are all-powerful, puppeteers who make the people, the politicians and the press all dance to their tune. But in short order the Other takes on the face of the Jew. André Laurendeau, a member of the Jeune-Canada movement, warns in the pages of Le Devoir:

> The actions of the trust, i.e. foreign capital, are felt everywhere. The trust is master in Ottawa, and master in Quebec. The hour is too late for equivocation. It is time to make them fear the indignation, the rage of a people that awakens from its deep lethargy....one day, we will do to the trusts here what they did to the Jews in Germany. We'll give them the boot. And if they don't get up safe and

sound on the other side of the forty-fifth parallel, well, just too bad.[65]

Anatole Vanier, writing in l'Action nationale, is excited, in September 1933, by the awakening of the New Germany which is sprouting seeds everywhere the Jews are considered as invaders. "And where, one might ask, are they judged differently?," he asks.

The Traitor is not very far away, personified by this French-Canadian people with no national conscience, that enrich Jewish cinema and finance. The latitude given to the Jew to act as he wishes has only multiplied the number of traitors, declares Lambert Closse: "It must be admitted, we have always treated them [the Jews] as negligible and inoffensive quantities: that is why we have so many traitors in our midst."[66] More about Mr. Lambert Closse later on.

The delirious currents which carry the Traitor and the Jew into the same vortex of hatred are by now clearly unleashed. The violence, the vulgarity, the vile nature of the statements about Jews constitute a veritable gutter ideology that leaves the reader flabbergasted. Le Devoir, for example, employs the following terms, and the list is not exhaustive: aliens, circumcised, criminals, mentally ill, trash of nations, Tartars infected with Semitism, malodorous,—they smell of garlic, live in lice-ridden ghettos, have greasy hair and pot bellies, big crooked noses, and they are dirty. Filthy, even.

> The city of Nuremberg was obliged to decree obligatory baths for the Israelites, but then having discovered they actually began to *like* to wash, because everything changes, even the most marked racial mores, the civil authorities there today order the police: Get rid of the bath, they like it![67]

I am shocked that it has been affirmed that Le Devoir never used offensive language or insulting adjectives with regard to the Jews, that the Jewish community's leaders French was too weak for them to be able to fully understand what was written in Le Devoir, and that the subtle ethical preoccupations of this paper, coupled with its lofty contents, put it out of the reach of the poor immigrant Montreal Jews.[68] But when the leaders of the Canadian Jewish Congress denounce the anti-Semitism of Le Devoir, it is, on the contrary, because they understand perfectly *well* what is being printed on its pages. Or, more to the point, on its *front* page. Out of the 1007 Le Devoir articles researched for this book, 800 concern Jews and almost all appear on the front page. The anti-Semitism of Le Devoir is neither discrete, nor ashamed of itself; it is in clear view, for all to see. Only the Buy-at-Home campaign and the controversy it stirs up with H.M. Caiserman, secretary-general of the Canadian Jewish Congress in 1935, are relegated to the inside of the paper; even then, several editorials on the matter signed by Omer Héroux are given prime coverage.

The articles on the Buy-at-Home campaign are interesting, among other ways, in that they reiterate a gross prejudice, which later on will serve as an explanation of the attitude of this nationalist current towards Jews. Since the Jews and the anglophones, as it is with every ethnic group in any case, buy exclusively from their own kind, it's about time that the French Canadians, an unhappy exception to this rule, do the same. Some take up a learned discourse on the supposed admiration of Groulx and his associates for the admirable solidarity of the Jews. But phrases like: "I would be hardly surprised to learn that the Jews had invented this policy of Buying-at-Home....For in Berlin, Paris, London or Montreal, one finds hundreds of thousands of Jewish merchants who earn a living and even become rich thanks to the local population, never the contrary,"[69] should have "awakened" them to the fictional and racist solidarity of the Jews to this province.

The supposed and unshakeable solidarity attributed to the Jews and other ethnic groups for their own kind, never proven of course, is but another facet of racism. It is the obverse side of disdain. The Jews become a group with a daunting solidarity, pushed on by a collective will that never falters. This Jew only exists in relationship with the Traitor, the French Canadian *incapable* of solidarity. As we read in one of the Jeune-Canada tracts: "How can the uncontrollable individualism of the French Canadian resist this kind of collective might?"[70]

A stranger to all nations, unassimilable virus to the national and religious body of French Canada, agent by which capitalism and democracy are transmitted, fermenter of Communism, the Jew that Groulx, l'Action nationale, Jeune-Canada and Le Devoir designate for the vindictiveness of the masses is never as terrible or as terrifying as the menace he symbolizes.

And these same groups do not hesitate to make use of the most infamous forgery of our century, the *Protocols of the Elders of Zion* (in fact written in 19th century Russia by a *provocateur* of the Tsar's secret police), to convince the distracted masses of the existence of a world Jewish conspiracy. I have in my library a book entitled *La réponse de la race. Le catéchisme national des Canadiens français,* * signed under the pseudonym of Lambert Closse. Dedicated to Abbé Groulx, it is prefaced by Arthur Laurendeau, a mainstay of l'Action nationale. It contains a number of articles by Georges Pelletier, who was editor of Le Devoir from 1932 and by Fadette, who wrote the women's column in the same paper, as well as by Esdras Minville and Father Papin Archambault, other well-known collaborators of l'-Action nationale, without forgetting, of course, Lionel Groulx himself. The imprimatur of Cardinal J.M. Rodrigue Villeneuve, Archbishop of Quebec, dated May 8, 1936, figures at the very beginning of the book, next to an illustration of Jesus Christ pointing at his resplendent heart. But significantly, there is no mention at all of the publisher of this national catechism.[71]

This book takes the classic question-and-answer form of a catechism:

> 257. How must we consider a child who does not love its mother?
>
> It is a monster.
> 258. And he who doesn't love his nation?
>
> A national monster.
> 259. What is the nation for the French Canadian?
>
> A mother.[72]

The last part of the book, aimed at "our enemies" (pp. 506-539) and signed by the pseudonymous Lambert Closse, reproduces many passages of the infamous Protocols of the Elders of Zion, including the 22 "resolutions" by means of which the Jews intend to dominate the world. For example:

---

* The Response of the Race. The French Canadians' national catechism.

1. Corrupt the younger generation through subversive teachings.
2. Destroy family life.
3. Dominate people through their vices.
17. Grant universal suffrage, so that the destiny of nations is placed in the hands of incompetents.
19. Abolish all forms of constitution and substitute in their place the absolute despotism of the Bolsheviks.
22. Prepare the agony of Nations; exhaust humanity through suffering, anguish and want, because HUNGER CREATES SLAVES.
8. Poison the mind with worthless theories; ruin the nervous system by constant noise and weaken the body through the inoculation of various sicknesses.

Talking about sickness, we learn that:

Since they apparently haven't succeeded with 'Protocol' n° 2, 'destroy the life of the family through the preaching of liberalism', they chose to pull out all the stops. The police have seized bacilli, microbes, the germs of venereal diseases in Jewish laboratories, with which sanitary napkins were to be infected. Is that criminal enough?[73]

The perfidy of the Jews is a constant astonishment even though we already "know" the Talmudic commandment that allows:

7. The Jew is not obliged to respect Christian women"[74]

Freemasonry serves as another cover for the evil designs of the Jews. Lambert Closse calls it "judeo-masonry" and accuses it of having infiltrated the *Institut canadien* during the nineteenth century[75] Free-masonry having a usefully-broad back, Closse also blames it for the Rotary Clubs,[76] "where everything imaginable goes on, even Catholic priests, now fanatic Rotarians, calling themselves by new and intimate secret names and exchanging vows which are apparently more important to them than their baptismal promises or their vows of the priesthood."[77] Imagine!

But who hides behind the pseudonym of Lambert Closse? The compendium of Quebec pseudonyms written by Bernard Vinet indicates that Abbé Jean-Baptiste Beaupré used this name.[78] That is true. This obscure priest wrote two inoffensive parish monographs, using the identity of Closse, a contemporary of Dollard des Ormeaux. But I do not believe him to be the author of *La réponse de la race*. This priest had no contacts among the ultra-nationalist élite of the time and it would be strange, to say the least, for him to have accomplished this quantum leap from parish pamphleteer to editor of a collective national catechism of some 539 pages. I believe the real author to be none other than Lionel Groulx himself, even though I cannot yet prove it. This book is most mysterious. Among the bibliographies of the works of the prolific Canon and those accompanying the studies of thirties' nationalism only one mentions *La réponse de la race* without, however, naming Groulx as the author. In the end, it doesn't matter much because this is a collective work, and all those who share in its writing have a shared responsibility for its contents. Lionel Groulx used so many pseudonyms that it's hard to believe he could always recall which went where. I have identified thirteen to date, and the list is not exhaustive. Jacques Brassier, André Marois, Alonié de Lestres, Lionel Montal, David La Fronde, Aymerillot, Nicolas Tillemont, XXX, Un renard qui tient à sa queue*, Guillaume Un Tel**, Marc André, Jean Tillemont, L. Adolphe.

Two editors of Le Devoir also make ample use of pseudonyms. It's worthwhile mentioning them because their signatures crop up time and time again:

Paul Anger: Louis Dupire
Pierre Kiroul: Georges Pelletier
Jean Labrye: Georges Pelletier
Le Grincheux: Louis Dupire
Nemo: Louis Dupire
Nessus: Louis Dupire
Pamphile: Georges Pelletier
Paul Poirier: Georges Pelletier.

---

* A fox that holds dear his tail.
** William Nobody (A reference to William Tell, *Guillaume Tell* in French).

To come back to the fictional and terrifying symbolic figure of the Jew, Le Devoir believes that there exists something called "Judeo-American Finance with Bolshevik sympathies,"[79] with whose support "the Jews rule in Russia just as in Hollywood."[80] Communist and at the same time capitalist, democrat and simultaneous dictator, the Jew has only one real ambition:

> The Israelites aspire—as everyone knows—to the happy day when their race will dominate the world. They are from no people, but from every land; everywhere, through the power of money, they control politics until the day when in a violent reaction, the people free themselves and cast them aside.[81]

International financial institutions and the press, governments of every political shade all fall under the Jewish grasp. Hitler will have a tough time in the open war he declares on the Jew, sighs Paul Anger in Le Devoir:

> When Hitler attacks the Jew, he attacks the most formidable power of deceit in the world: because the Jews not only control the newspapers in all the important cities in the world, but also many press agencies which are like the arteries of information.[82]

The cinema, fashion and publicity are also the doing of the Jews. Jazz suffers the double sin of being both Negroid *and* Semitic: "...it is a Negro invention. Later on, it was modified by American composers, notably the Jew [Irving] Berlin. So it is a Negro-Semitic cocktail. I don't care for that kind of cuisine, personally."[83] This tiresome madness never seems to exhaust those who spout it. Navigating with ease through this labyrinth drawn by hatred, defying both reason and logic, they show the self-assurance of those who owe nothing to reality or truth. The Jewish Hydra has wrapped itself around the Province of Quebec as it has the rest of the planet. Quebec is sagging under the yoke of a Jewish commercial dictatorship because of what Groulx calls "Jewish internationalism." This internationalism, l'Action nationale recalls one day, comes neither from the Jewish religion nor the Jewish nationality, but in fact from the Jewish "spirit." In other words, a disembodied Jew, with no connection to real Jews! And here we have a perfect example of what anti-Semitism truly is.

The Jew is also the symbol of a disgraceful democracy. The two Montreal electoral ridings represented in the provincial parliament by Jewish members, Saint-Laurent by Josef Cohen and Saint-Louis by Peter Bercovitch, become "Jewish electoral strongholds," the embodiment of "party politics," of democracy usurping the interests of the nation. It is useful to learn, however, by reading Le Devoir of December 14 1935, that these Jewish electoral fiefdoms, representing the flowering of divisive party politics, are in reality inhabited by a majority of good French-Canadian and Christian electors! Apparently indifferent to the International Jewish Conspiracy, blind and deaf to the imminent danger, a majority of "pure laine" Quebeckers elects two deputies from the enemy camp...

The Jew is also the City, i.e. Montreal, where he ruins whole neighbourhoods and crowds the tramways. As it was in the case of the Traitor, the most trivial acts are here seen as crimes.

But even his "integration," to use a now popular expression, becomes a liability. Whatever he tries, he is castigated. Aaron Hart, *Seigneur* and citizen emeritus of Three-Rivers, is described in the following way by André Laurendeau:

> This little Jew, whose oblique looks, rolling of the head and verbose gestures we can well imagine, was a commercial genius. Not satisfied with impoverishing the cream of Three Rivers society, he sometimes even gained their respect. The Ursuline Sisters, for example, never speak disrespectfully of the good Mr. Hart. Meanwhile, endless equations reverberate in his brain, he has the spider's planning, flair, and deliberation,—then suddenly, the brilliant manoeuvre, like the adversary who, certain of having exhausted his enemy, and having surrounded him, brusquely administers the fatal blow.[86]

Now we are at last at the heart of the matter, where it really hurts. "Men fear their own likeness, that is the source of racism," writes Jean-Pierre Dupuy.[85] The caricature of the Jew with his big nose and crooked fingers, his smells and his dishonesty, his criminality and vice, comes precisely from the fear stemming from his invisibility. The Jew is an alien who stretches his perfidy to the point of looking like everyone else. An icy wind of panic blows through the editorial room of Le Devoir at the idea that Jewish citizens might speak French and Francisize their names. "If Mr. Horowitz wants to change his name, he could at least have the decency to take a name from his own ethnic group, and not try to usurp a name carried proudly for so many generations by French Canadians," writes

Omer Héroux in Le Devoir of 18 October, 1937. The actor
Gratien Gélinas, in l'Action nationale of May 1935, is indignant
that the mastering of the French language by the Jews might
deceive a naive public, proud to be addressed in the language of
Dollard des Ormeaux.

It is not the arbitrarily decreed "difference," that irritates
these people so much as its very absence. The difference must
be maintained at all cost. If the Jews speak French and abandon
the name Goldenberg for Godbout, how on earth will we recognize them? What was the aim of the yellow star, really, if not to
identify those who were no different from anybody else? The
European anti-semites always berated the democracies for
having abolished all visible signs of identification of the Jews.

A profound nihilism emerges from this discourse on the
Traitor and the Jew. Both figures inhabit a universe of miasma
and decay. Groulx opposes to this putrefying world a utopian
project of absolute purity inspired by the Fascist Millennium.
"The feeble minds that believe in democracy even as they don't
believe in the Church or in Christ, only feel horror for Fascism,
whatever its form. However, it is undeniable that some peoples
are happy to have found, through this political form, the most
magnificent renaissance."[86] In 1935, Esdras Minville, in the
name of l'Action nationale, gives admirative chapter and verse
on German national-socialism, which he holds up as a model
for his movement. Once the Jew has been excluded, deported,
parked in ghettos, deprived of political rights, exclaims Groulx,
the Traitor passed through the rollers of re-education, French
Canadians can again become, if they so desire, supermen and
even Gods.[87]

This book is a condensed version of my doctoral thesis in
political science entitled "Antisémitisme et nationalisme
d'extrême droite dans la province de Québec 1929-1939."
Readers interested in going through the complete demonstration
should refer to the original, in the library of Laval University. If
this new version still includes a great number of quotations, I
beg the reader's indulgence: I felt unable to render in my own
words the powerful hatred they express. It does make for repeti-
tive reading, but what is this madness if not endless repetition?

The thematic order could have been different: I have tried as best I could to find a tenuous logic in the course of presenting what is really a tautological insanity.

The works by Lionel Groulx, published or reprinted from 1929 to 1939, the *Tracts* and the *Cahiers des Jeune-Canada*, the issues of l'Action nationale appearing from January 1933 to January 1940, and all the issues of Le Devoir from 1929 to 1939 were read in their entirety. The first two sources were used in toto, while for analytical purposes, 234 articles of l'Action nationale and 1007 articles of Le Devoir were retained. The methodology used for this work was content analysis.

Notes

1. Quoted in: Léon Poliakov: *Bréviaire de la haine.*, Bruxelles, Éditions Complexe, 1986, p. XXII-XXIII.

2. Lionel Groulx: *Notre maître le passé.*, Ottawa, Éditions internationales Alain Stanké, 1977, tome 2, pp. 276-277, ("Québec" 10/10 series).

3. Jean-Pierre Wilhelmy: *Les mercenaires allemands au Québec du XVIII siècle et leur apport à la population.*, Belœil, Maison des mots, 1984, pp. 196-197.

4. *Ibid.*, p. 197.

5. Richard Handler: *Nationalism and the Politics of Culture in Quebec*, Madison, University of Wisconsin Press, 1988, p. 69.

6. Lionel Groulx: *La naissance d'une race.*, Montréal, Bibliothèque de l'Action française, 1919, p. 26.

7. Lionel Groulx: *op. cit.*, p. 258.

8. Jean-Pierre Gaboury: *Le nationalisme de Lionel Groulx. Aspects idéologiques.*, Ottawa, Éditions de l'Université d'Ottawa, 1970, p. 106.

9, Gustave LeBon: *Lois psychologiques de l'évolution des peuples.*, pp. 60-61. Quoted in: Alonié de Lestres: *L'appel de la race.*, Montréal, Fides,1976, p. 131.

10. Alonié de Lestres: *L'appel de la race.*, Montréal, Fides,1976, p. 130.

11. Lionel Groulx: *La naissance d'une race*, p. 42.

12. *Ibid.*, pp. 56-57.

13. *Ibid.*, pp. 55-56.

14. *Ibid.*, p. 63.

15. *Ibid.*, p. 55.

16. *Ibid.*, p. 197.

17. Jean Éthier-Blais: "Regard sur une époque révolue," *Le Devoir,* 28 March 1992, p. D1.

18. *Ibid.*

19. Lionel Groulx, "Notre destin français." *l'Action nationale*, p. 134.

20. Lionel Groulx: *Orientations.*, Montréal, Les Éditions du Zodiaque,1935, p. 204.

21. *Ibid.*, p. 203.

22. *Ibid.*, p. 256.

23. Pamphile: Carnet d'un grincheux, *Le Devoir*, 2 February 1934, p. 1.

24. Pamphile: Carnet d'un grincheux, *Le Devoir*, 3 February 1934, p. 1.

25. Cyrille Felteau: *Histoire de La Presse.*, Tome 1: *Le livre du peuple*, 1884-1916, Montréal, Les Éditions La Presse, p. 191.

26. Paul Anger: "Ainsi parlait Abraham..." *Le Devoir*, 4 August 1934, p. 1.

27. Pamphile: Carnet d'un grincheux, *Le Devoir*, 16 January 1934, p. 1.

28. Le Grincheux: Carnet d'un grincheux, *Le Devoir*, 28 May 1936, p. 1.

29. Paul Anger: "Faites-vous ceci?" *Le Devoir*, 12 April 1933, p. 1.

30. Pierre-Philippe Gingras: *Le Devoir.*, Montréal, Libre Expression, 1985, p. 101.

31. *Ibid.*, p. 112.

32. Guy Frégault: *Lionel Groulx tel qu'en lui-même,.* Montréal, Leméac, 1978, p. 25.

33. "Les étudiants étrangers à l'Université," *Le Devoir*, 9 September 1933, p. 3.

34. Everett C. Hughes: *Rencontre de deux mondes.*, Montréal, Boréal Express, 1972, pp. .376-377.

35. *Le Devoir*, 26 January 1934, p. 1.

36. Pamphile: Carnet d'un grincheux, *Le Devoir*, 20 January 1934, p. 1.

37. Jacques Langlais et David Rome: *Juifs et Québécois français. 200 ans d'histoire commune.*, Montréal, Fides, 1976, Coll. "Rencontre des cultures," p. 172.

38. Richard Jones: *L'idéologie de l'Action catholique (1917-1939)*, Québec, Presses Universitaires de Laval, 1974.

39. Jean-Pierre Gaboury: *op. cit.*, p. 31.

40. André-J. Bélanger: *L'apolitisme des idéologies québécoises. Le grand tournant 1934-1936.*, Québec, Presses de l'Université Laval, 1974, p. 263.

41. Gérald-Adélard Fortin: *An Analysis of the Ideology of a French-Canadian Nationalist Magazine: 1917-1954. A Contribution to the Sociology of Knowledge.*, Ph.D. Thesis, Cornell University, June 1956, p. 52; Susan (Mann) Robertson: *L'Action française. L'Appel à la race.* Doctoral thesis, February 1970, Université Laval, pp. 127-128; Mason Wade: *Les Canadiens français de 1760 à nos jours.*, Ottawa, Cercle du livre de France, 1963, tome 2, p. 313.

42. Susan Robertson: *op. cit.*, p. 286.

43. *Ibid.*, p. 305; Victor Teboul: *Antisémitisme: mythes et images du Juif au Québec.*, dans: Voix et images du pays., Montréal, Presses de l'Université du Québec, 1980, no.4., p. 106.

44. Susan Robertson: *op. cit.*,p.52.

45. *Ibid.*, p. 50.

46. Pierre-Philippe Gingras: *Le Devoir*, Montréal, Libre Expression, 1985, p. 82.

47. Michael Kelway Oliver: *The Social and Political Ideas of French Canadian Nationalists 1920-1945.* Ph.D. Thesis, September 1956, McGill University, p. 282; Gérald A. Fortin parle de xénophobie: Gérald A. Fortin: *op. cit.*,p.189.

48. "*Behind the general attitude to politics was a moral distaste for democracy. Abbé Groulx admitted that part of his disdain for democracy had originated in his reading of Charles Maurras. Even when perusing Maurras':"L'avenir de l'intelligence" in the late 1920's. Groulx noted his argument to a quotation from*

Auguste Comte: "...I always maintained that the sovereignty of the people comes from an oppressive mystification and that equality is an unjust falsehood." Susan Robertson: *op. cit.,* p. 310-311; Jean-Pierre Gaboury: *op. cit.,* p. 141, p. 143.

49. Jean-Pierre Gaboury: *op. cit.,* p. 151.

50. *Ibid.*

51. Pierre Sorlin: *La Croix et les Jews.,* Paris, Grasset, 1967, p. 217.

52. Michel Herszlikowicz: *Philosophie de l'antisémitisme,* Paris, Presses Universitaires de France, 1985, p. 17.

53. André Laurendeau: *Partisannerie politique:* dans: Les Jeune-Canada: *Politiciens et Juifs.,* p. 62.

54. Léon Poliakov: *Histoire de l'antisémitisme.,* Paris, Calmann-Lévy, 1981, Coll. "Pluriel," tome 2, p. 63.

55. Colette Capitan-Peter: *Charles Maurras et l'idéologie d'Action française.,*Paris, Éditions du Seuil, 1972, coll. "Esprit".

56. Lionel Groulx: *Directives,* p.20.

57. *Ibid.,* pp. 233-234.

58. *Ibid.,* p. 100.

59. Lionel Groulx: *Orientations,* p.23.

60. André Marois (pseudonym of Lionel Groulx): "Réforme d'un parti ou réforme d'une politique.," *Le Devoir,* 20 September 1932, p. 1; Lionel Groulx: *Notre maître le passé.,* tome 1, p. 237.

61. Lionel Groulx: *Notre maître le passé.,* tome 1, p. 10.

62. Lionel Groulx: *Directives.,* pp. 173-174.

63. Thuribe Belzile; *Nos déficiences, conséquences, remèdes.* Tract Jeune-Canada, no.4, Montréal, May 1935, p. 20.

64. Paul Anger: "Les Jeune-Canada," *Le Devoir,* 14 November 1933, p. 1.

65. André Laurendeau; "Le trust, danger social et national," *Le Devoir,* 14 November 1933, p. 2.

66. Lambert Closse: *op. cit.,* p. 515.

67. Paul Anger: "Quand Israël se baigne," *Le Devoir,* 8 August 1933, p. 1.

68. Pierre Anctil: *Le Devoir, les Jews et l'immigration. De Bourassa à Laurendeau.,* Québec, Institut québécois de recherche sur la culture, 1988, p. 73, p. 98 et p. 24.

69. Clarence Hogue: "Politique de suicide," *Le Devoir,* 6 July 1935, p. 8.

70. René Monette: *Commerce juif et commerce canadien-français.,* dans: Les Jeune-Canada, *Politiciens et Juifs.,* p. 47.

71. Lambert Closse: *La réponse de la race.,* 1936.

72. *Ibid.,* p. 265.

73. *Ibid.,* p. 527.

74. *Ibid.,* p. 509.

75. *Ibid.,* pp. 528-532.

76. *Ibid.,* pp. 535-537.

77. *Ibid.,* pp. 535-536.

78. Bernard Vinet: *Pseudonymes québécois.,* Québec, Éditions Garneau, 1974, p. 51.

79. Paul Poirier: "Un surhomme," *Le Devoir*, 22 April 1935, p. 1.

80. Paul Anger: "Si vis pacem...," *Le Devoir*, 31 January 1935, p. 1.

81. André Laurendeau: *Partisannerie politique*, op. cit., p. 62.

82. Paul Anger: "Mme Blaschke," *Le Devoir*, 16 May 1933, p. 1.

83. Paul Anger: "Le jazz, c'est le jaunisme musical," *Le Devoir*, 7 February 1930, p. 1; Le jazz est une musique de nègre: Paul Anger: "Le musicien," *Le Devoir*, 20 October 1932, p. 1.

84. André Laurendeau: "Histoire d'un petit juif," *l'Action nationale*, (March 1939), p. 271.

85. Jean-Pierre Dupuy: *Rôle de la différenciation dans les structures sociales.*, quoted in: Pierre-André Taguieff: *La force du préjugé. Essai sur le racisme et ses doubles*. Paris, Éditions La Découverte, 1988, p. 163.

86. André Marois (pseudonym of Lionel Groulx): "Pour vivre," *l'Action nationale* (May 1937), p. 311.

87. Lionel Groulx: *Orientations*, p. 113.

2

NATIONALISM, RACISM AND ANTI-SEMITISM

"Whether it stems from ancient christian rumours, modern scientific speculation or the political climate of the years 1917-1923, the West laid the groundwork for the rise to power of a racist state. In the light of the universal horror provoked by the crimes of Hitler, this responsibility has been hidden, or at least understated."[1]

LIONEL GROULX IS NOT the kindly but wayward country historian who some have called innocuous. His ideology, and that of the movement he inspired, are part of the set of intellectual and political changes that shook Europe and tore it asunder from the end of the 19th century to the middle of the 20th century. Out of this crucible, certain terms emerge, others take on new meanings, and a number of new myths, symbols and traditions take shape and put down roots.

The eruption of the term "anti-Semitism" into the European political vocabulary points to the first fissure in a world view that had been previously dominated by Christian theology. It appears around 1880, when anti-Jewish propaganda campaigns are begun in Germany and France,[2] and it was in the 19th century that the category of "race" appeared, when the "Jews" suddenly became "Semites," a different race. Colette Guillaumin writes of this:

> From the 19th century on, everything changes, race becomes a priority intellectual and perceptive category. The term race itself leaves the more restricted sense of lineage and takes on the meaning of a human group. It previously was a term of social class, an expression which one would have hardly thought to apply to people whose obscurity and rank would never merit such prestige. But above all, we find at this time the birth of specific concepts relating to what we now consider race.[3]

Out of this flowering of specific terms:

"Semitic" is the first-born, relatively early on, from about 1836: it designated the group of Semitic languages; for the moment, it has no racial connotation. "Semite" is the second, appearing from about 1845 and designates "racial" qualities. "Semitism" marks the next step, being the word of the "racialization" of a race, the entry into the intellectual universe of a particular trait supposedly characteristic of a race [1862]. Finally the word which pushes the concept on to the end-point of an approach which makes race a "closed" concept, "anti-Semitism" enters into the language around 1889.[4]

Proceeding from Jews to Semites, the use of the concept of race redrew mankind with borders that were as fragmented as they were impermeable. The Semite is seen as possessed of immutable characteristics, engraved inside his person, which no rite, religious or otherwise can ever erase. A perceptual change of this magnitude was obviously not accomplished in only a few decades. Already, the Enlightenment had classified and divided mankind using morphological criteria, as we see from the works of Buffon and Linneus, works which mirrored the exploration of Africa and the discovery of America. The 18th century also affirmed the predominance of national genealogy over the universal genealogy which linked all men to Adam. In the wake of the French Revolution (1789-1815), new myths imposed themselves in the majority of European countries— among them, and fundamental, was the myth of origins—, new symbols (the flag, the sacred flame, the national anthem) which affirmed the existence of nations and by this fact shored up the still-frail legitimacy of the Nation-State. One ceased being the child of Man and became the child of one's race, nation or ethnic group.

But it is not until the 19th century that this break with theological thought is consummated. The fall of Adam marks the fall of Sacred theology which had previously accounted for humankind's diversity. Now, the variety of mottled shapes, colours, languages, all so diverse, becomes a fact of Nature to be dissected by Science, after having been for so long the object of erudite theologians' treatises.[5] A decisive bridge has now been crossed, since the essentialist determinism postulated by racism finds its starting point in this internal "logic" of human heterogeneity.[6] As Colette Guillaumin writes: "The feeling that there was a difference of essence arises as soon as the question of the existence of the Other is posited as a function of humanity and no longer in terms of divine dependence."[7] The soul is seen as an essence engraved in the body, undefined, undefinable, permanent and irreversible.

From now on, the concept of race supplants both Divine Will and the idea of progress, so dear to the Enlightenment, in that it becomes the touchstone which explains universal history. All events great and small can now be understood by the existence of races and by their hereditary sociological, and psychological characteristics. The past is now understandable even as the future is predictable. In other words, race become for some the basis of a new cosmogony.[8]

Arthur de Gobineau, in his book *Essai sur l'inégalité des races humaines* *(1855) offers the first in a long series of these racial cosmogonies in addition to gathering together many ideas which were widespread at the time. But the rupture with Christian theology was perhaps not as complete as de Gobineau would have wished. He proposes the idea, common at the time, that humanity is divided into three races: white, yellow, and black, which he places in exactly that order. In doing this, "...he restates the ancient biblical genealogy while giving it a new signification."[9] His most important contribution, "is to have postulated that race is more important than universal history.... His distinction between superior and inferior races is sufficient for him to explain the course of history, in which Aryans enjoy a predominant position."[10] He also believed that the disappearance of great empires could be explained by the racial mixing of their populations and that it was only a question of time before Europe would suffer the same fate.[11] His thought is also revealing in that it "represents in exemplary fashion the confusion between sociological and biological fact which marks the 19th and 20th centuries."[12]

Even though de Gobineau defends the existence of races endowed with different and incompatible blood—hence the peril represented by miscegenation—while taking a page from biblical genealogy is hardly surprising, because in the world of ideas, the "tabula rasa" phenomenon, i.e. the ambition of making a clean break with the past, remains elusive. There may be in fact a break on one front, but usually accompanied by a reinterpretation of ideas, legends and myths gleaned from the past.

---

*   Essay on the inequality of human races.

De Gobineau having shown the way, there would follow a number of successors, embroidering numerous variations on the same theme. So much so that by the end of the 19th century, the concept of "race" is widely accepted in European intellectual circles.[13]

Following in the wake of the celebrated Count, who by the way was not a real Count at all, Lionel Groulx interweaves his racial cosmogony with biblical references. God presides over the birth of races, he writes: "Of all the events which retain the attention of God, none is more precious than the birth of races and of peoples, these vast spiritual organisations so much a part of Divine plans."[14] The diversity of races also obeys a Divine Plan,[15] and if the races fight among themselves, it's because they wear the stigma of original sin: "Let's dispense with foolish optimism. As long as humanity bears the mark of original sin, the struggles between races will remain inevitable."[16] Providence had wished the deportation of the Acadians, as well as the conquest of 1760,[17] and the thousand perils which shook New France prior to the defeat of the French army on the Plains of Abraham.[18] The valiant colony would not have suffered in vain its baptism by fire, since Providence exacted this tribute in order that "a new human type could begin to exist: yes, we may say it, a superior race comes to life."[19] We can hear in this the dull echo of the division of humanity into superior and inferior races, the cornerstone of all racial cosmogonies. Even better than a superior race, Groulx goes on, in a daring tone and with renewed optimism: the French Canadians are a *chosen* race: "God put on our foreheads the mark of the chosen."[20]

If God created and desired races, writes Groulx, become historian-botanist for argument's sake, they grow and develop according to the laws of the physical universe:

> The philosophers and psychologists all admit that the national environment possesses a kind of generating power. It creates a human variety, just as the soil and the climate create biological varieties. It engraves in us psychological predispositions, predestines us towards ways of feeling, thinking and acting, and fashions the collective originality of a people.[21]

When Groulx writes that race represents "a collection of physical facts," but that it also encompasses "amalgams of psychic and social facts,"[22] he states, with an unusual (for him) economy of words, the confusion between sociological and biological fact which has haunted western thought until the present.

Culture, nation, race: the terminology used is of little importance, as the idea of a biological transmission of psychological and sociological characteristics is constantly reaffirmed:

> We can observe at the same time that this *cultural milieu* acts upon us, for the most part, without our knowing it. By simply being of a particular *nation*, we are born with certain psychological predispositions; a certain determinism already influences us. Through our birth, by the blood that flows in our veins, by the heredity with which our being is endowed, *we are predestined to certain ways of thinking and acting.*[23]

Groulx is here a true representative of his time, since from the 19th century on, the terms race and nation tend to overlap. The nation is understood as a natural division of the human race, desired by God, and whose purity its citizens must protect.[24] The different nationalisms which arise right after the Napoleonic wars and the study of linguistics will link even more tightly the idea of nationalism to that of the subdivision of Europe into distinct races.[25]

The concepts of "nation" and of "race" become related due to the fact that they are both based on the same principle of exclusion[26]— no race/nation can exist without its negative counterpart. Many authors, Jacques Zylberberg recalls, have come to similar conclusions:

> From Simmel to Coser, from Poliakov to Girard, from Guillaumin to Delumeau, from Weber to Faye, numerous works have shown that the construction and integration of civil societies passes through the construction of a chauvinist or sectarian "we," united against the fear of the Other, who is presented as an internal or external menace to social order.[27]

In addition, the concepts of Nation and Race call upon a myth of origins in order to legitimate their existence, and further, their political claims, whether it be as a state or an empire.[28]

The emancipation of the Jews i.e. the abolition of the juridical, legal and political restrictions inherited from the Middle Ages and the Ancien Régime, happened just when the Nation State became the fundamental political unit in Europe.[29] From that time on, the place of Jews in society was no longer a matter of theological prescription but instead, of ideological criteria, and their inclusion in the nation was to always be, at best, uncertain and transitory.[30]

The exclusion of certain groups from the nation also appears in semantics: in Germany, for example, before 1871, the concept of the nation designated those who were for national unity and excluded those feudal powers who were opposed to it. After Bismarck defeated the forces of liberalism, the term "nation" was to become ever more exclusive: social-democrats were thus excluded, as well as the Alsatian and Polish linguistic minorities, religious minorities like the German Catholics, whose connections with the Church of Rome were distrusted, and of course, the Jews.[31]

Coming back to Lionel Groulx and his racial cosmogony, he endows the blood-line with such power that miscegenation is to be the cause of serious mental disorders in the children of these unfortunate unions. The hero of Groulx's novel *L'appel de la race*, Jules de Lantagnac, in the throws of an overwhelming "regain of the instinct of race"[32] (meaning a return to his French-Canadian and Catholic origins which he had renounced when he married Maud Fletcher, a Protestant Anglo-saxon), expresses this strange obsession:

> And now he discovered in two of his students, his own children, a kind of morbid vagueness, a kind of mental disorder, an incoherence of the intellectual personality, an inability to follow a clear reasoning to its logical conclusion, to focus a series of impressions, slightly complex ideas turning around a central pole. It was as if they were possessed of two souls, two spirits struggling for predominance, rising and falling in turn. Strangely enough, this mental dualism showed itself above all in William and in Nellie, the children who presented the morphology of the Fletchers. Whereas Wolfred and Virginia showed almost exclusively the traits of the French race.[33]

The vulgarity of the plot and the characters would make the reading of this book laughable, were it not for the knowledge of the tragedies this kind of nonsense encouraged. The Anglo-Saxons, and the "anglicized" Irish," those traitors who sold out body and soul to the enemy, are cast as having a bilious complexion, low foreheads, and menacing look; they are self-satisfied fools, while the French Canadians have clear skin, high brows, a noble bearing, and a frank countenance.

What is true for individuals is true *a fortiori* of nations/races/ethnic groups, states Father Fabien, who is the spiritual/racial mentor of one de Lantagnac, more than ever fascinated by the blood and Holy water: doesn't the French Canadian nobility owe its decline "to the blood-mixing it so easily, even eagerly accepted and sought? It is certain that a psychologist would take keen interest in observing their descendants," who, dizzy with panic, abandon themselves to dishonour and ruination.[34] The betrayal of the blood is in fact the first act of the Traitor after the conquest, as we will see in chapter 4. Maintaining the purity of the line is the first commandment in Groulx's racial cosmogony, a faithful echo of the writings of his mentors Barrès and LeBon, those high priests of the theory of the integrity of the bloodline through the ages and the downfall of mixed-blood peoples.

For once he has traced the philosophical outlines of his theory of race, Groulx leaves de Gobineau and embraces an extremist right-wing nationalism tinged with Fascism. To the theme of the blood-line now is added that of the soil and the dead, which are at the core of the work of Maurice Barrès. This theme, close to German nationalistic romanticism recalls the Hitlerian slogan promoted by Walter Darré: *"Blut und Boden,"* the blood and the soil.[35] Groulx brings all three themes together in one trinity. After the blood-line, here are the soil and the dead:

> We are bound, inescapably bound to a part of the physical universe....From the soil to ourselves flows a determinism, not absolute, but considerable. As it is with the past, with history, the soil is our master. We are the sons of our land, as we are the sons of our race, of our time....The land of our dead forefathers becomes, in its own way, an immense page of history.[36]

The whole of the heredities we receive from our ancestors, explains Groulx in *Directives*, "all of this dictates, often without our knowing it, most of our reflexes and our acts. We have, how shall I say, in our spines, the apathy or the pluck of our forefathers."[37] The combined determinism of the bloodline, the soil and the dead seems quasi-absolute. The individual doesn't really exist, neither does the free will to which centuries of humanist tradition had subscribed. Groulx, like Barrès and other tenors of extremist right-wing nationalism and Fascism, are involved in the crisis of civilization that shook Europe during more than a half-century. To a man, they reject, not only bourgeois society and liberal democracy, "but an entire civilization founded on the belief in progress, the rationality of the individual and the postulate according to which the final aim of all social organization in the well-being of the individual."[38]

Even history is subordinate to the iron will of the ancestors: history's role is to make certain that "the living continue to be governed by the dead."[39] History, he repeats, quoting Charles Maurras, counters the threat of a past reduced to nothingness: "It is through history," as Charles Maurras would say, that we feel inside ourselves that "no living being, no precise reality has the same value as the force and the latent power of the collective will of our ancestors, and that it is their impetus, their imperious guidance that propel us towards our future."[40] In thus saying, Groulx legitimates his ineluctable political project, while protecting himself against the nihilism counter-point which supports his ideology. The history of the French-Canadian people must obey an "ascendant curve," aiming towards an "ever-growing, more complete national autonomy, towards the completion of its political personality," Groulx affirms, adding: "Either this line has a specific direction, or it has none at all."[41] "I refuse to believe that we have lived three hundred years in vain,"[42] reiterates an anguished André Laurendeau.

"The past is nothing if not truth and if we cannot ask of it, like a seed hibernating in the earth, to give us a vital force that propels us towards the future"[43] If the past counts for nothing, then each generation only exists by and for itself, and the ancestors are definitively dead and gone. This is the case for the present generation of French Canadians, Groulx deplores: "The majority of our poor people alas! knows only the age in which it lives, the forty or fifty years of its existence. It doesn't see itself as 'one moment of an immortal chain,' but an isolated moment, a broken link."[44]

Against the ever-menacing destruction, against the past reduced to an incomprehensible succession of generations isolated each from the others, Lionel Groulx erects a people/nation/race "moment of an immortal chain," a depositary of the blood and the soul of the ancient ones, leaning on a history through which it will always remain "consubstantial to its past, to its ancestors, to the genius of its race."[45] Against inevitable death, Groulx invokes "a perpetual intention which is tradition"[46] and "the preservation and transmission of life by history."[47]

Groulx's nihilism is not limited to a past heavy with absurdity and chaos. Humanity is only possible, he repeats, in the belonging to a nation/race/ethnic group. "He [Father Delos] would say further: "in order to be a complete man, one must first belong to a particular ethnic and national group, have been subject to its influence through its culture."[48] Whence the importance of being born and raised in a healthy environment, one that is truly national, capable of forming real men. "Does ours possess these virtues?" the doubtful Canon asks himself, and goes on with his questioning:

> Is it healthy, and vital? Can it fashion us efficiently according to our inborn selves? The German culture infallibly makes one German, the French milieu makes one French; the Italian culture makes one Italian. Is it within the power of French Canadians, with no other effort on the part of those of our nationality, to be born in their own place, of their own race and country?[49]

Could it be possible that certain groups, one hesitates now to call them "human," deprived of a healthy and vital environment, will remain outside of history and thus humanity? To state the condition is to already predict its transgression. In the manner of the post-Kantian German philosopher Fichte who designates to the state the mission of making those who inhabit its territory into veritable human beings through its culture,[50] Groulx designates both the nation and the state to accomplish this task. In both cases, strong mystical vectors orient their conception of the State. This is no longer the former Liberal State, preoccupied with problems of bread, butter, roads and railways, but a social organisation nourished by a "national mystique," a fabric of "the convergence of supreme truths" susceptible of producing the "supreme collective impulses" whereby the blood and traditions would out-shout the forces of destruction.[51] A French state established outside of the Canadian federation, or more autonomy within it, the wavering of Groulx here matters little inasmuch as it is always a question of "polarising" the life of the nation around "a mystique, a national credo."[52]

From this perspective, writes Élie Kedourie: "Politics is a method of realizing this superhuman vision, of assuaging this metaphysical thirst."[53] From these aspirations to a metaphysical destiny, he goes on, flows "the nihilist frenzy of Nazism."[54] Groulx doesn't only dream of a Fascist dictatorship: in his desperate search for a mystique which could breath grandeur into a dying people, "who had only heeded the call of appeals to its stomach,"[55] he looks favourably on the example of the Soviet Union; the "extraordinary and mysterious" staying power of this regime—abominable in many respects—is attributed to "the revolutionary mystique with which a whole army of teachers has intoxicated the Russian youth."[56]

The forces of death that must be beaten back by this State endowed with supernatural powers are those of liberalism. Capitalism, democracy and modernity have set upon French Canada just as they have taken aim at France. Once again, Groulx's ideology does not stem exclusively from the French-Canadian soil. The extremist right-wing movements of France, beacon and inspiration of the nationalist and anti-democratic European right, hold this triad responsible for the decadence and the social disintegration haunting their country.[57] In the mind of Charles Maurras, for example, there is no doubt that, since the French Revolution, "the country has only slid towards chaos, defeat, and invasion, as the nation was handed over to its external and internal enemies."[58] In the writings of Barrès, and of Édouard Drumont—the most famous and one of the most prolific French anti-Semites—and again, in the works of Maurras, we see an obsession with decadence, death, and imminent catastrophe.[59]

National socialism shares this eschatological vision of the future. Hitler believed the German people to be in danger of extermination, surrounded as it was by rapacious enemies whose victory would be its death knell. The threat of a Bolshevist revolution within Germany's borders, and the presence of France, the secular enemy, on the outside, are looked upon as mortal dangers. This death was not necessarily taken in the physical sense: the Germans risked becoming an uprooted and soulless people. Nothing represents more clearly for Hitler, in 1928, the dependence and the alienation of modern Germany than the fleets of American cars which invade the market in alarming fashion.[60]

For Groulx himself, "a North America where all the demographic, geographical, political and economic powers...conspire against us" occupies the horizon of his nightmares, so that, in a century or two, "our original soul, half-destroyed, would leave us with the dubious and fugitive traits of half-breeds or those races on the verge of disappearing?"[61]

These kinds of apocalyptic fears are so widespread that they affect French intellectuals as level-headed as Taine, Renan, Durkheim and Zola, who see in the crisis shaking French society a prelude to the final collapse.[62]

For the avowed adversaries of liberal democracy, the Jew is at once the cause and the symbol of the scourges affecting their respective countries. They denounce in turn the Jewish Republic, Jewish finance, Jewish capitalism, and Jewish socialism. The enemy is the Jew: an inferior race, a supranational force, invisible and terrible, whose triumph bears witness to the decadence of Europe.

Learned minds had well prepared the way for this delirium of hate: "At the end of the 19th century, recalls Léon Poliakov, international science had promoted to the rank of axiom the idea of the division of mankind into the Aryan and Semitic races."[63] The Semite, also called the Jew, is no longer the object of scorn and discrimination based on religion. Anti-Judaism justified the fall from grace of the Jews by the Divine curse which fell upon them, by their status of witnesses to the Truth of Christianity—much as a canker whose revolting features which would bear witness to the beauty of Christianity, as the illustrious Pascal wrote—and by the certitude that this downfall would bring them to convert to the Christian faith. Anti-Semitism now invoked science and nature to justify its hostility. It offered no recourse, no escape: no religious conversion was possible. The mark will remain indelible, fastened to the very core of an undefined, undefinable essence. However, the influence of the former can be seen in the latter. As Jean-Paul Sartre wrote:

> This principal is magical: one the one hand, is an essence, a substantive form, and the Jew, no matter how much he tries, cannot change it....on the other hand, since it must be possible to hate the Jew, as one cannot hate an earth-quake or a cutting of phylloxera, this is seen as a virtue and defined in terms of freedom.

> "The freedom is restricted to the domain of Evil. There is only one other entity which is both free and condemned to Evil, and that is Satan.[64]

In the same way, certain authors have remarked, anti-Semites and ideologues in their struggle against liberalism present contemporary reality as a vast metaphysical battle-field where Good and Evil are locked in combat.[65]

Assimilated with Evil, the Jew shares with this latter another property: invisibility. In France as in Germany, the Jewish citizen who openly manifests the signs of his religious faith, such as the sideburns and the caftan, is far less frightening than the one who looks no different than anyone else, who pushes his insolence to the point of imitating, in his appearance and style of life, his Christian fellow-citizens. It is assimilation that the anti-Semites are concerned about, and not the Jew's voluntary separation from society. For example, Nessus, writing in Le Devoir, expresses this way his fears about the behaviour of young ladies from good upper-class French-Canadian families: in their world, he deplores, there exists no more "differences between an English Canadian girl, a Jewess or a French-Canadian. They are all a part of the same world, where cocktail parties mould essentially different souls and brains into similar shapes."[66]

The studies on anti-Semitism in general, and in particular on anti-Semitism in Germany, Austria and France from the end of the 19th to the middle of the present century, agree on one point: the anti-Semite's Jew is only defined metaphorically, deriving from of the formers' universe of phantasms. The Jewish internationalism castigated by Groulx, the world, provincial and local Jewish hydra, which l'Action nationale, Jeune-Canada and Le Devoir attack relentlessly, all these evils only exist on the writers' copy-paper. They are the symbols of the evil totality incarnated by capitalism, democracy and modernity.

The studies on anti-Semitism in Germany, Austria and France concur on another point: anti-Semitism is, in most cases, an integral part of the ideologies which contest liberalism. Extremist right-wing nationalism, Fascism and Nazism all display a virulent anti-Semitism. Anti-Semitism is in fact consubstantial to these ideologies. In waving the Jewish scare-crow, the champions of these ideologies hope to mobilize the masses against a particular political regime and the economic system associated with it; moreover, national unity would be reinforced in the struggle against a common enemy. Political and ideological conflicts as well as social confrontations are put aside as long as it takes to lay low the omnipotent Jew. The latter takes on all the functions of the scape-goat: his existence explains everything that is wrong with the present state of affairs. In fact, anti-Semitism is so vital to the struggle against liberalism that Charles Maurras writes, with unusual ingenuity, that it is nothing less than a "methodological imperative":

> It all appears to be impossible, or terribly difficult, were it not for this providential anti-Semitism. Through it, everything works out, settles down and becomes easier. If one wasn't an anti-Semite because of patriotism, one would turn into one by the simple requirements of opportunism.[67]

The cardinal function of anti-Semitism, maintain many authors, is to supply the negative pole which is indispensable to the definition of the nation/race. From the French extremist right to German National socialism, the procedure used is the same: "In only being able to define itself by opposition, as Maurras has explained, nationalism found in racism and anti-Semitism a way to define all that it was not."[68] The Jew of Nazi ideology was the fictional negative image of the Aryan, the one that the theoretician of anti-Semitism called the "Gegenrasse," the counter-race, whose vocation was to make Germanic splendour all the more evident.[69]

But the nation itself is only this virginal fiction in the vision of utopia, because it is mirrored by another fictional figure: the Traitor, i.e. he who adheres to the values and principles of liberalism, or who simply sees his interest it. L'Action française, under the guidance of Charles Maurras, tracks down and ousts, over the course of time, such a number of these traitors—brandished as the "internal enemies"—that they will come to constitute the quasi-totality of the nation.[70] More often than not, states Colette Capitan-Peter, l'Action française brands "the abnormality, the monstrous nature of these beings by excluding them from the human race."[71] National restoration requires the repression or even the execution of traitors.

Betrayal consists, essentially, in embracing the republican regime. The condemnation of democracy and parliamentarianism by l'Action française is of such violence as to recall Hitler's *Mein Kampf*:

> There is also an entire vocabulary more normally used to designate sickness or contagion that takes upon itself the signification of the

horror inspired by the democratic system.... Democracy is an insidious poison, a leper, a contaminated world full of bacilli; it attacks the vitality of the race or the nation.[72]

It is also well known that Hitler rails against those Germans who are "infected" by humanist and democratic ideas.[73] The internal enemy is the first to be interned in concentration camps which spread rapidly in Germany in the years leading up to World War II. From the camps' inception in the spring of 1933 until 1939, one million German citizens suspected of being hostile to the Nazi regime were imprisoned.

The figures in Groulx's racial cosmogony are the Hero, the Traitor, the Other and the Jew, the latter three being associated with contemporary liberalism. The Hero, pure of race and who blossoms in the paradise lost which is New France, remains confined to that epoque. The Other make intermittent appearances: his existence in New France is denied, but stoutly reaffirmed in the post-conquest period, when in the person of the British victor he is the agent of the blood betrayal. Germs and poisons, the first ferment of decomposition, infiltrate the vanquished colony. The Other returns just long enough to affirm the alienating and exogenous character of capitalism, democracy and modernity. Once this is done, he cedes his place to the Traitor and the Jew. If Groulx and his fanatical disciples l'Action nationale and the Jeune-Canada describe the surrounding decay even before attributing it to the joint action of the Jew and the Traitor, Le Devoir, for its part, describes this decomposition via the acts of the Jew here in this province and in the world.

The narrative which accompanies these four symbolic constructions can be stated as follows: a legendary past, of absolute purity, which was followed by the present decay, which is itself a prelude to the next act: the apocalypse. Redemption is never more than glimpsed, a distant, unattainable hope until the Traitor is re-educated and the Jew excluded, events which will mark a rediscovered purity. The past is the antithesis of the present, as the Jew and the Traitor, symbols of the present, are antithetic to the utopian dream.

All of these figures are symbolic constructs deriving from racism. They obviously have no real existence. What intellectual history teaches us about extremist right-wing nationalism and Fascism, and what the classic and more recent analyses of racism endlessly repeat, is that the symbolic constructs of racism seized on by various ideologies come from the realm of phantasm and see everything through the filter of the racist phantasmic universe, creating the characters they need and writing their own scenario. Physical characteristics become here "that which signifies the radical difference,"[74] this difference being one of essence, as permanent as it is irreversible.

Whether the differences are real or imaginary is of little importance, since they all come back to a difference of essence. There is a current trend in social sciences which sees racism as the rejection of a difference. This "explanation," facile and short-sighted, ignores the fact that the need or even the necessity of distinguishing precedes the recognition/creation of these differences. It also endorses, perhaps unconsciously, one of the most constant elements of racism: the existence of individual members of a group considered to be a race is completely dependant upon the existence of the group. A black-skinned person is only seen as a tracing of the Black. A person of the Jewish religion is seen as the personification of the Jew. Besides which, explaining racism by the concept of difference, ignores the fact that people are as much attracted to what is new and different as by what is familiar. Their reactions are not inevitably those of rejection. Finally, this kind of reasoning doesn't explain why attention is focused on certain differences and not others when the time comes to demarcate the members of one group from those who are to be excluded. The racist retains those differences he decides to use for his own ends. Thus, to take an extreme example, strictly political reasons incited Hitler to recognize the Japanese as honourary Aryans.

"It is clear that the racist reconstructs his victim according to his own needs" writes Albert Memmi. "This mythical reconstruction serves as a mediation, an alibi specific to the oppression he wishes to exercise or that he is already exercising."[75] The mythical constructs of the Traitor and the Jew are in effect the alibis of Canon Groulx's utopian dream. The re-education of the Traitor, a Fascist dictatorship and the expulsion of the Jew appear to be required to purify a world fallen into decay through their pernicious actions. These mythical constructs are also infinitely useful in that they are undefinable terms. "Jewish internationalism," "the Jewish spirit," distinct from the Jewish people and religion, allow Groulx and his cohorts to attack anyone they define as a Jew. An analogous fate awaits the "Jewified," those corrupted by "the Jewish spirit," such as La Presse and the Montreal Star who "live in fear of displeasing the large advertisers who are all Jews."[76]

Even when Groulx attempts to demonstrate the existence of a French Canadian nation, it becomes rapidly clear that it too is undefinable. Its existence is first affirmed in a tone that tolerates no rejoinders: "Thus, warns Groulx, whether or not this displeases the contemptuous and the pig-headed, we are a nationality."[77] That is to say: "...a human group enjoying a common origin, language, and faith; who possess among other things a common heritage of memories, glory, aspirations, legal and cultural institutions...."[78] The voice of the blood makes itself heard, if only to demarcate French Canadians from other peoples of less breadth who live in North America: "Unlike many others, we did not arrive here yesterday. In the form of a physical and moral alluvion we bear in our veins the blood of the great Europeans who brought us Christian civilization."[79]

However, the situation is not quite as clear as appearances would suggest. Groulx has some reservations; in his definition of French Canada, language is seen in terms of a *trompe-l'œil*: "For though we may conceive of it as a vehicle of culture or a creator of culture, the fact is that the French language, elevated to the dignity of this role, presupposes a French spirit, a French soul."[80] For this simple reason: "One can easily imagine an official bilingualism perfectly well-established and respected in Ottawa, without us being French Canadians any more."[81]

Neither language, nor place of birth, nor French-Canadian parents suffice to "make" the true French Canadian; "and here again, to be totally of one's race, being born of french-speaking parents somewhere in Quebec is not enough...." It needs more and better, Groulx goes on, a "forming of the soul that, need we say, a quick study of a elementary-school textbook on geography or national history can hardly bring, but which requires the slow, active and profound infiltration of the spirit by all the powers of the environment, the soil, and the past."[82] The impregnation of the spirit by the all-powerful forces of the blood, the soil and the dead will sort out the wheat from the chaff. Of course, this dramatically increases the risk of decimating the ranks of the nation.

Entirely pre-determined by the blood, the soil and the dead, his "innate qualities" and "hereditary culture," the French Canadian is at the same time a creature moved only by his volition. "If it is true that we are born French, says Groulx, here contradicting himself, it is nonetheless true, that because of historical and geographic facts..., we cannot remain French without effort and struggle. Instinctive Frenchmen or Frenchman by habit, cannot here remain moribund Frenchmen. There is only one viable species, and that is the Frenchman by choice."[83] This breach in Groulx's racial determinism corresponds partly to his desire for French State. As determined as they are, he reasons, the French Canadians must demand this state, even if, in the image of the French Canadian himself, one will not know exactly of what it consists. The year 1867 having marked the political resurrection of French Canada,[84] declares the Canon who, however, does not hesitate to brand the federalists of the previous century as traitors, there only remains to demand the application of a dearly-won right. This French state, which is "since 1867, a positive constitutional right,"[85] will only see the light of day when "our clouded and idiotic colonized brains"[86] will have been persuaded of its necessity and its legitimacy. The appeals to will-power and to constitutional law belong to the part of Groulx's work which looks toward the legitimisation of a French-Canadian Nation-State to which also belongs the creation of the Hero, the invention of traditions, and the promotion of the fleur-de-lis as national flag. This sketching of the classical idea for the legitimisation of the Nation State will remain a sketch because Groulx, resolutely anti-liberal, is unable to formulate it on the model of an ideology he rejects. The Nation and constitutional law give way to the symbolic constructs of the Traitor and the Jew, to nihilism and a millenarian Fascism. His racism and his Fascism force him to very quickly deviate from the classical discourse on the legitimisation of the Nation State.

"We observe that racism often gains sway when a group steeped in its own importance perceives its position to be threatened: in periods of crisis, war or latent revolt."[87] Groulx, l'Action nationale, Jeune-Canada and Le Devoir depict themselves as the exclusive representatives of the French-Canadian nation, and the crisis they face resides in what they perceive as the refusal of the population to obey their decrees. French Canadians will continue to abound in the cities, they will persist in enjoying jazz, in going to hockey games, in reading La Presse and even in neglecting the practice of religion in favour of...the cinema. On Sundays, for example, throngs of film-lovers stay away from the road to Church and crowd into the dark halls where the magic of the silver screen awaits them. For more than twenty years, laments Léo Pelland in the pages of l'Action nationale, Catholics "crowd in, despite being forbidden by the bishops and the legislators." With lucid desperation he adds: "What can the public authorities do when an entire people shows such disregard for the warnings of the Bishops and the civic leaders? It is hardly possible to fine or imprison people by the hundreds!"[88] How true!...But it *is* possible to accuse them of treason and to simultaneously lapidate the Jew, the architect of the Seventh Art.

If the history of extremist right-wing nationalism in Quebec is one of failure, the reasons are perhaps similar to those which explain its defeat in France and England. In these countries, the hold of the bourgeoisie on the political system was sufficiently strong that it was able to check Fascistic nationalism.[89] In Germany, by way of contrast, the political structure of the country remained that of a pre-industrial society, well after the country had already become a leading economic power on the continent. The conservative and clerical forces had not lost, at this turning of the century, their predominance in the state and in society as a whole. Liberalism's victory had not been decisive, and the German bourgeoisie, weakened and fallen back upon itself, turned to Hitler to defeat the Communist forces.

Another reason, perhaps even more important, has to do with the delirium which is an intrinsic part of extremist right-wing nationalism. The French Canadians did not recognize themselves in their accursed double any more than they recognized the Other and the Jew as their implacable enemies. They refused to see in their own reality—as harsh as it was—the putrefied universe painted by Lionel Groulx, l'Action nationale, Jeune-Canada and Le Devoir. They turned a deaf ear to the idea of a Fascist dictatorship, preferring rather than a dictatorial saviour of the nation, a potentate of merely provincial stature: Maurice Duplessis. A lop-sided democracy, after all, was better than no democracy at all.

Notes

1. Léon Poliakov: *Le bréviaire de la haine.*, Bruxelles, Les Éditions complexes, 1986, p. XXIV.

2. "Anti-Semitism is a term coined in 1879 by the German agitator Wilhelm Marr to designate the current anti-Jewish campaigns in Europe. It soon came to designate all forms of hostility manifested toward the Jews throughout history." Encyclopedia Judaica, vol.3, p. 87;

"It appears around 1880 in Germany, at the time when anti-Jewish propaganda campaigns were begun. Two or three years later, we again find this new terminology in most European languages: political and social developments require the adoption of an original formula. But what is new here, is the function given it." Zeev Sternhell: *La droite révolutionnaire. Les origines françaises du fascisme 1885-1914.* Paris, Éditions du Seuil, 1978, p. 177. (Coll. "Histoire"); Jacob Katz: *From Prejudice to Destruction. Anti-Semitism 1700-1933,* Cambridge, Mass., Harvard University Press, 1980, p. 261.

3. Colette Guillaumin: *Idéologie raciste: Genèse et langage actuel.*,Paris, Mouton, 1972, p.19.

4. *Ibid,.*p.19;

"By granting the notion of race a central role, the immutable character of the Jewish mentality is implicitly predicated. The act of baptism could, accordingly, make no difference whatsoever. Dühring was not the only one who took this stand. It was inherent in the very term "Anti-Semitism." Jacob Katz: *Ibid.*, p. 269.

5. For a description of this process consult:

Michael Banton: *Race Relations,* London, Sydney, Toronto, Tavistock Publications, 1967, p. 14; Christian Delacampagne, Patrick Girard; Léon Poliakov: *Le racisme,* Paris, Seghers, Coll. "Point de départ,"1976,pp. 79-80; Colette Guillaumin: *op. cit.*, p. 19; François Lovsky: *L'antisémitisme chrétien,* Paris, Cerf, 1970, p. 44; George L. Mosse: *Toward the Final Solution, A History of European Racism.*, New York, Harper and Row, 1978, pp. 1-2 et p. 17; Léon Poliakov: *Le mythe aryen, essai sur les sources du racisme et des nationalismes,* Paris, Calmann-Lévy, 1971., p. 140; Léon Poliakov: *Racisme et antisémitisme. Bilan provisoire de nos discussions et essai de description,* cited in Pierre Guiral, Emile Temime: *L'idée de race dans la pensée politique française contemporaine.*, Paris, Éditions du Centre national de la recherche scientifique, 1977, p. 26; Louis L. Snyder: *The Idea of Racialism.*, Princeton, D. Van Nostrand and Company Inc., 1962, p. 140.

6. Colette Guillaumin: *op. cit.*, p. 16.

7. *Ibid.*

8. "The romantic movement then developed a double rejection: rejection of the Judeo-Christian God and rejection of the goddess of Reason or the Pantheon of the Enlightenment. A new cosmogony seemed indispensable. Race could hence take the place of Divine Providence or of the idea of progress and serve as a system to explain universal history." , Christian Delacampagne, Patrick Girard, Léon Poliakov; *op. cit.*, p. 72; A like analysis may be found in: Louis L. Snyder: *op. cit.*, p. 41.

9. Christian Delacampagne, Patrick Girard, Léon Poliakov: *op. cit.*, p. 74; Patrick Girard; Léon Poliakov; "The new anthropology was perhaps not quite as detached as it would have like from Christian anthropology. Its division of mankind into three major races was in fact an echo of the myth of Noah's three sons." In addition, "The terminology it employed is identical to that of the Bible: Blacks and Jews are called Chamites and Semites. Europeans don't receive the logical designation of 'Japhetites', but that of 'Aryans' because the term came from the same root as 'honour' (Ehre). At the end of all this, race was promoted to the rank of great motor of human destiny, taking the place of Providence.," Léon Poliakov: *Histoire de l'antisémitisme*, Paris, Calmann-Lévy, 1981, volume 1, p. 169 et p. 171. (Coll."Pluriel").

10. Christian Delacampagne; Patrick Girard; Léon Poliakov: *op. cit.*, p. 75; . A like approach is to be found in: George Simpson Eaton: *Racial and Cultural Minorities: An Analysis of Prejudice and Discrimination.*, New York, Harper and Brothers, 1953., p. 105; Milton J. Yinger; George L. Mosse: *op. cit.*, pp. 52-54.

11. Christian Delacampagne, Patrick Girard, Léon Poliakov: *ibid..*, p.75; George L. Mosse: *op. cit.*, p. 54 et 58; Léon Poliakov: *Le mythe aryen,*p.243; *Louis L. Snyder: op. cit.*, pp. 46-47; Zeev Sternhell: *Le déterminisme physiologique et racial à la base du nationalisme de Jules Soury.* dans: *L'idée de race dans la pensée politique française contemporaine*, p. 124.

12. Colette Guillaumin: *op. cit.*, p. 24. She adds that we find this confusion in nearly all sociologists, historians and essayists of this period, such as Spencer, Fustel de Coulanges, Taine, Renan, to only mention a few. For more on Taine and the idea of race: François Léger: *L'idée de race chez Taine, dans:L'idée de race dans la pensée politique française*, pp. 89-99.

13. Christian Delacampagne, Patrick Girard; Léon Poliakov: *op. cit.*, p. 80; Lydia Flem: *Le racisme.*, Paris, M.A. Éditions, Coll. "Le monde de..." no.5, 1985, p. 153; Léon Poliakov: *op. cit.*, p. 209 et p. 215; "Thus scholars feeling the need for racial classification count, depending on which one you check, from 2 to 35 races." Louis L. Snyder: *op. cit.*, p. 11.

"That Taine had never heard l'*Essai sur l'inégalité des races humaines* is a piece of exceedingly revealing information. It leads us to the conclusion that an intellectual current using the racial explanation of history did indeed exist in France, independent of de Gobineau. In fact, the Restoration had seen rise to the surface a whole generation of historians whose theories already accorded a considerable weight to the idea of race." Zeev Sternhell: *La droite révolutionnaire*, p. 156.

14. Lionel Groulx: *La naissance d'une race.*, Montréal, Bibliothèque de l'Action française, 1919, p. 110.

15. Lionel Groulx: *Orientations.*, Montréal, Les Éditions du Zodiaque, 1935, p. 293.

16. Lionel Groulx: *L'enseignement français au Canada.* Volume 2: *Les minorités.*, Montréal, Librairie Granger Frères Ltée, 1933, p. 254.

17. Lionel Groulx: *Notre maître le passé.*, Montréal, Éditions internationales Alain Stanké, 1977, volume 1, p. 160, (Coll. Québec 10/10).

18. Lionel Groulx: *La naissance d'une race.*, p. 165.

19. Lionel Groulx: *Ibid.*, pp. 180-181.

20. *Orientations*, p. 31.

21. Lionel Groulx: "Notre enquête. Une politique nationale. Notre destin français.," *Action nationale*, March 1937, pp. 132-133.

22. Lionel Groulx: *La naissance d'une race.*, p. 74.

23. Lionel Groulx: *Directives.*, pp. 133-134. Author's italics.

24. Élie Kedourie: *Nationalism.*, New York, Frederick A. Praeger, Praeger University Series, 1961, p. 58.

25. Christian Delacampagne, Patrick Girard, Léon Poliakov: *L'invention du racisme. Antiquité et moyen-âge.*, Paris, Fayard, 1983, p. 284; Christian Delacampagne: *op. cit.*, p. 71; Lydia Flem: *op. cit.*, p.26; George L. Mosse: *op. cit.*, pp. 33-34, p. 45, p. 52 et p. 94; Louis L. Snyder: *op. cit.*, p. 33; Émile Temime: *Races, Nationalités et Régionalismes*, cited in:Émile Temime, Pierre Guiral (présenté par): *L'idée de race dans la pensée politique française*, p.275; This is how Jacques Zylberberg resumes this phenomenon: "The ideological discourse creates a series of slippages and alteration of the real substrata of a symbolic system which structures a political project which is supported by a quasi-religious cosmovision: a) The group is given attributes which are spatially and temporally invariable. The distanced group becomes a primitive, homogeneous ensemble, an ethnicity characterized by a religious, linguistic and ethno-biological identity. The spatially-distant identity is also projected temporally: historical identity is confirmed by myths of origin: b) these myths of origin are obviously associated with heroic myths: the ethno-cultural entity requires its founders, its martyrs, its heretics" Jacques Zylberberg: "Fragments d'un discours critique sur le nationalisme.," *Anthropologie et Société*, vol. 2, no.1, pp. 186-187.

26. George L. Mosse: *op. cit.*, pp. 33-34 et p. 39; Léon Poliakov: *op. cit.*, p. 195; Louis L. Snyder: *op. cit.*, p. 33.

27. Jacques Zylberberg: *La régulation étatique des minorités religieuses*, Dans: Pierre Guillaume, Jean-Michel Lacroix, Réjean Pelletier, Jacques Zylberberg: *Minorités et État*, Bordeaux, Presses Universitaires de Bordeaux, Presses de l'Université Laval, 1986, p.118.

28. Léon Poliakov: *ibid.*, p. 40 et p. 141; Élie Kedourie: op. cit., p. 58.

29. In France: on 27 September 1791 the legal emancipation of all Jewish citizens is decreed. In the Low Countries: it arrives in the wake of the Napoleonic conquest, on 2 September 1796. Italy: It also happens after the invasion of the French army, in February 1798. The decree is then abolished, and afterwards reestablished on the reunification of the country, more precisely on 15 December 1870.In Germany: on 14 April 1871, immediately following reunification; in Austria: on 20 and 27 December 1867; in Hungary: 20 and 27 December 1867. In England: it becomes total in 1871. Source: *Encyclopedia Judaica*, vol 6, p. 700-701; "From the 1780's onward, the old social and political patterns were in a process of desintegration. The state based on late feudal estate and guilds or corporations gave way to one of independent citizens under direct jurisdiction. In this state there was no place for the familiar type of Jewish community structures like a corporation, albeit the lowliest of corporations. The Jews confronted the

state and its institutions as individuals; it was essential to confer citizens status upon them if they were not to be removed from the state" Jacob Katz: op.cit., p. 8

30. "No concept that might have replaced the nationalist principle, and so might have secured the inclusion of the Jews in the community ever appeared on the scene." Jacob Katz: op. cit., p. 289; "As generous as the criteria of admissibility could ever be for nationality, there will always exist the inclusion of some and the exclusion of others." Lydia Flem: op. cit., p. 134.

31. Paul W. Massing: *Rehearsal for Destruction. A Study of Political Anti-Semitism in Imperial Germany.*, New York, Howard Fertig, p. 138; Élie Kedourie: *op. cit.*, p. 13-15.

32. Lionel Groulx: *L'Appel de la race.*, Montréal, Fides, 1976, p. 128.

33. *Ibid.*, p. 130.

34. *Ibid.*, pp. 130-131.

35. Pierre Milza: *Les fascismes.*, Paris, Imprimerie nationale, 1985, Coll. Notre siècle, p. 47.

36. Lionel Groulx: *Directives.*,Saint-Hyacinthe, Éditions Alertes, 1937, pp. 155-156.

37. *Ibid.*, pp. 190-191.

38. Zeev Sternhell: *op. cit.*, p. 22.

39. Lionel Groulx: *Notre maître le passé.*, volume 1, p. 20.

40. Lionel Groulx: *Notre doctrine.*, dans: *Soirées de l'Action française.*, Montréal, Éditions de l'Action canadienne-française, 1939, p. 11.

41. Lionel Groulx: *Directives.*, p. 108.

42. André Laurendeau: "Qui sauvera Québec?," dans: Les Jeune-Canada: *Qui sauvera Québec?*, p. 59.

43. Lionel Groulx: *op. cit.*, p. 190.

44. Lionel Groulx: *Notre maître le passé.*, volume 1, p. 21.

45. Lionel Groulx: *op. cit.*, pp. 192-193.

46. *Ibid.*, p.146.

47. *Ibid.*

48. *Ibid.*, p. 133.

49. *Ibid.*, p. 134.

50. Élie Kedourie: *op. cit.*, p. 38.

51. Lionel Groulx: *Directives.*, p.82 et p. 130.

52. Lionel Groulx: *Avenir de notre bourgeoisie*, p. 120.

53. Élie Kedourie: *op. cit.*, p.85.

54. *Ibid.*, p. 87.

55. Jacques Brassier (pseudonym of Lionel Groulx): "Pour qu'on vive," *Action nationale*, (November 1934), p. 205.

56. Jacques Brassier (pseudonym of Lionel Groulx): "Pour qu'on vive," *Action nationale*, pp. 204-205.

57. Éva G. Reichmann: *Hostages of Civilisation. The Social Sources of National-Socialist Anti-Semitism.*,Westport, Conn., 1949 / 1970, p. 161; Zeev Sternhell: *La droite révolutionnaire*, p. 197.

58. Colette Capitan-Peter: *Charles Maurras et l'idéologie d'Action française*, Paris, Seuil, 1972, p. 84. She also remarks that: "L'Action française was living in the midst of an apocalypse." *Ibid.*, p. 83.

59. Stephen Wilson: *Ideology and experience. Anti-Semitism in France at the time of the Dreyfus affair.*, Rutherford, Madison, Teaneck/Fairleigh Dickenson University Press, London, and Toronto Associated Press, 1982., p. 355; Léon Poliakov: *Histoire de l'antisémitisme*, volume 1, p. 273.

60. Ernst Nolte: *Three Faces of Fascism.*, New York, Chicago, San Francisco, Holt, Rinehart and Winston, 1965, pp. 402-403.

61. Lionel Groulx: *Orientations.*, pp. 16-17; *Ibid.*, pp. 52-53; Lionel Groulx: *Directives*, p. 104.

62. Stephen Wilson: *op. cit.*, p. 428; Michel Winock: *Édouard Drumont et Cie. Antisémitisme et fascisme en France. Paris, Seuil, 1982.*, p. 8; Zeev Sternhell: *op. cit.*, p. 197.

63. Léon Poliakov: *op. cit.*, p. 215.

64. Jean-Paul Sartre: *Réflexions sur la question juive.*, Paris, Gallimard, 1954, Coll. "Idées," pp. 45-46.

65. *Ibid.*, pp. 46-47; Zeev Sternhell: *Maurice Barrès et le nationalisme français.*, Paris, Fondation nationale de science politique, 1976, p. 316.

66. Nessus: "Henri VII et les femmes," Le Devoir, 30 November 1933, p. 1.

67. Charles Maurras: Action française, 28.3.1911, cited in: Colette Capitan-Peter:*op. cit.*,p.75.

68. Colette Capitan-Peter: *ibid.*, pp. 75-76.

69. Christian Delacampagne: *op. cit.*, p. 142; Patrick Girard; Léon Poliakov; Adolf Leschnitzer: *The Magic Background of Modern Anti-Semitism. An Analysis of the German-Jewish Relationship.*, N.Y., International Univ. Press, 1956, p. 96 et p. 136.

70. Colette Capitan-Peter: *op. cit.*, p. 60.

71. *Ibid.*, pp. 68-69.

72. *Ibid.*, p. 166.

73. Ernst Nolte: *op. cit.*, pp. 416-417.

74. Colette Guillaumin: *ibid.*, p.67.

75. Albert Memmi: *Le racisme.*, Paris, Gallimard, Coll. "Idées," 1982, pp. 98-99.

76. Paul Anger: "Naïveté des grands canards," Le Devoir, 28 August 1935, p. 1; Georges Pelletier: "Les Juifs d'Allemagne font déraisonner le Star," Le Devoir, 26 November 1938, p. 1.

77. Lionel Groulx: *Directives.*, p. 132; *Ibid.*, p. 127.

78. *Ibid.*, pp. 129-130; Lionel Groulx: *Orientations.*, p. 277.

79. *Orientations*, p. 278; *Ibid.*, pp. 148-149; Lionel Groulx: *Notre mystique nationale.*, pp. 2-3.

80. Lionel Groulx: *Orientations.*, p.206.

81. *Ibid.*, p. 203.

82. Lionel Groulx: *L'enseignement français au Canada*, t.2, p. 258.

83. Lionel Groulx: *Directives.*, p.93.

84. Lionel Groulx: *Ibid.*,pp. 61-62; Lionel Groulx: *Orientations.*, p. 245.

85. Lionel Groulx: *op. cit.*, p. 108; *Ibid.*, p.50, p. 52, pp. 166-167; Lionel Groulx: *L'enseignement français au Canada.*, t. 1, p. 246.

86. Lionel Groulx: *Directives.*, p. 108.

87. Christian Delacampagne, Patrick Girard, Léon Poliakov: *Le racisme.*, Paris, Seghers, Coll. "Point de départ,"1976, p. 127.

88. Léo Pelland: "Pour une politique nationale," *Action nationale*, (April 1937), pp. 204-205.

89. This is notably the case for France about which Zeev Sternhell writes: "This is why we can write the history of the radical and populist right in presenting it as a failure." Zeev Sternhell: *La droite révolutionnaire*, p. 31. This was because: "In England and in France, a national ideology had been developed by the middle classes which regarded themselves as the backbone of the modern state". Paul W. Massing: *op.cit.*, 1967, p. 80.

3

PARADISE LOST

The phantasmic world of racism is like a fairy tale, with its immutable sequences constantly repeated throughout the narrative. Once upon a time, there was only good, then the Hero was overtaken by misfortune, but he triumphed and happiness was restored to its rightful place. Good was victorious over evil and the villains paid for their crimes. Lionel Groulx used precisely these terms to describe the history of French Canada. In the beginning was the Hero. Then came the Conquest, which brought great unhappiness and permitted the Traitor, the Other, and the poison of liberalism to triumph. Finally, the Traitor was re-educated, the Jew excluded forever, and the kingdom restored. The Hero was resuscitated, and went on to become a superman and a god.

THUS, ONCE UPON A TIME there was a pure, strong, beautiful, and prolific race that lived in a kingdom with no evil. In New France, described by Groulx as "perhaps the masterpiece of all colonial enterprise,"[1] lived a people homogeneous from all points of view: "Ethnic, social, religious, moral homogeneity; homogeneity and intrinsic value, with nothing lacking to construct the nucleus of an élite."[2] This "chosen phalanx"[3] came from all regions of France,[4] although those from Normandy dominated not just in numbers, but also in the decisive influence that they exercised as the first arrivals.[5]

Groulx used horse-trading language to describe the first inhabitants of the colony-kingdom. Almost entirely agricultural and rural,[6] this population was in excellent physical condition, for it had been scrupulously selected:[7]

The recruiters wanted these colonists strong and healthy...No cripples, no impotent; if some managed to slip in, an order by the Sovereign Council dictated, from the start, the return to France of this rubbish.[8]

The suspect merchandise to whom the colony was mercilessly closed included not only the unfortunates afflicted with physical defects. The Huguenots were forbidden entry to the country in 1628, as were "jailbirds"[9] and other "precocious trash," in order to preserve religious homogeneity and moral purity.[10] Prostitutes suffered the same fate, which distinguished New France from the Antilles, a refuge for Europe's damned.[11] The generalized practice in the seventeenth and eighteenth centuries was thus to "send the riff-raff back to France."[12]

In spite of all efforts made to make New France a homogeneous, healthy, and morally irreproachable colony, Groulx is obliged to admit that there were some stains—tiny ones!—on the immaculate canvas he is attempting to paint. Girls with suspect morals, delinquents, and criminals all landed on the shores of the St. Lawrence, but, happily, without serious consequences for the chaste colony: "But we maintain, supported by the facts of history, that they were always a negligible minority, lost in the masses."[13] He adds a further precaution: "All attempts at colonization with convicts, prior to those of M. de Champlain, had led to a total failure. None of this trash put down roots in Canada. And so we go on."[14] These criminals, with no descendants, stopped all of their nefarious activities, thanks to the prodigal example of the vast, virtuous majority.[15]

Groulx erased another shadow from the painting: the métis. They did not put down roots in New France either, in spite of repeated efforts by the mother country to encourage their establishment. Indeed, Samuel de Champlain, Richelieu, Colbert, and Louis XIV unendingly encouraged the "mixing of the races" between aboriginals and the French. Samuel de Champlain said this to the Algonkins in so many words: "Our boys will marry your girls and we will make a single people," while Richelieu and Colbert, "feeding the same utopia," Groulx writes, endowed baptized aboriginals with the legal status of colonist or metropolitan. "As well, Louis XIV constantly exhorted the Intendants to ensure that the races merged."[16]

"It didn't happen," proclaimed Groulx, architect and anxious guardian of the myth of the pure race. What he called "the *francization* of the savages" was termed a "brilliant failure," resulting from the lack of cohabitation between the two races.[17] The Indians, even those educated by the Ursulines and by Marguerite Bourgeoys, refused "to marry with the civilized."[18]

Groulx hammers one of the last nails into the "calumny" of interbreeding[19] with the help of statistics. In *Notre maître le passé*, he returns to the proof that he had expounded in *La naissance d'une race*: an archivist had examined more than two million records lying dormant in old registers and found only 94 marriages between French and aboriginals (why is it never the other way round?). He also proved—but we are not told just where this little proof is written down—that "these métis have left no descendants among us, as their families were extinguished at the end of the eighteenth century."[20]

Black and aboriginal slaves arriving in New France around 1690, all of whom had the face of the Other, suffered the fate reserved by Groulx for undesirables: they landed "only in very small numbers" and, "needless to say, this inferior element mixed almost not at all with our population."[21] Germans, Bretons, Portuguese, and Swiss did not settle in New France or did so in numbers termed "specks of dust."[22] Very few English prisoners of war were allowed to stay, and these were hand-picked.[23]

Satisfied with his efforts to establish the purity of this new race in North America, the Canon continued his description. They were strong,[24] prolific,[25] and beautiful, and the evidence did not end with "the beauty and robustness of their shape."[26] Thus, even ugliness, as well as physical, moral, and religious deficiencies, was absent from the kingdom. So true is this that Groulx writes:

> We have here the origins of our race and the influences that moulded its soul. Those who came after 1700, and even after 1680, found the young race in full formation. Its general characteristics would still be modified under the action of the milieu and of history; in their essential lines they were fixed forever.[27]

All later waves of immigration would thus be carbon copies of the original pure, virtuous, strong, and beautiful race. This élite race would inevitably create a perfect social state.[28] "It was a good time, when nothing was locked with a key, neither houses, nor chests, nor cellars. Good-for-nothings, if they were discovered, were pitilessly banished."[29] Chastity reigned supreme,[30] and social classes worked in harmony for the prosperity of the colony.[31]

However, one element was missing from this little feudal society to provide it with full, complete perfection: the death of individualism, which would sanctify the supremacy of the nation. "Patriotic sentiment was by no means alien to our forefathers, but their very strong and very intrusive family spirit was willingly developed in an exclusively parochial spirit...Social feeling remained more or less tarnished by individualism."[32]

Groulx has suddenly introduced the soiled underside of the pristine icon image that he had so meticulously drawn up to this point. Overly strong individualism, coupled with the weakness of nationalism, constituted the prelude to the figure of the Traitor that would appear only after the conquest.

It then seemed that the almost entirely agricultural and rural population of New France, lovingly created by Groulx, was stricken by a "true mania for dispersal [which extended] to Louisiana, Santo Domingo, and the Antilles. At least three hundred men left the colony."[33] "In Quebec, the Council had to take severe measures to prevent an exodus to France."[34]

Trapping and fur-trading accentuated the mania for dispersal. Around 1680, there were already between five and eight hundred trappers, representing half of the married men in the colony.[35] Among the reasons leading a large number of settlers to go into the woods, the search for new revenues was matched in importance by "the charm of wanderlust, the lure of easy profits, a life full of the unexpected and adventure, a life of unrestrained liberty, and too often of libertinage,"[36] made possible by this blissful remoteness.

The danger was such that vigorous action was required to convince the recalcitrant men to stay close to the hearth:

And the laws, the repression, the punishments accumulated. They tried everything: flogging, imprisonment, and even obligatory marriage to restrain and immobilize these vagrants. In 1672, repression went truly beyond reason and it was forbidden, on penalty of death, to tarry in the woods without permission for more than twenty-four hours. These useless harsh sentences did nothing to stem the tide. What could be done to reach the delinquents? "The country is so open," Frontenac wrote, "and it is so difficult to know exactly when they leave, or when they will return through their secret correspondences with the settlers and even with the principal merchants."[37]

"For more than half a century, there was uncontrollable scattering of the population,"[38] Groulx comments laconically.

Behind the lightly sketched face of the Traitor is hidden that of the Other, through whom misfortune comes. The antagonism between the commerce dominated by the Other—in this case, the fur merchants—and the agriculture identified with the nation appeared at the very beginnings of the colony and never left the stage:

> Thus, it remains that, since the beginnings of the foundation, a powerful, irreducible antagonism was plunged in between commerce and culture, between the interests of a group of strangers and exploiters and the very existence of the colony. This pernicious antagonism was to dominate part of our history: it is at the beginning and the end of almost all of our miseries.[39]

It is interesting to note that before the conquest that signalled the victory of the Other, he was already being assigned the role of the despoiler and exploiter.

Sedentary and nomadic, virtuous and libertine, New France seems to have almost succumbed under the weight of irreconcilable contradictions. "Time was pressing to save the small communities from the peril of individualism, followed by scattering."[40] Now, a veritable *deus ex machina* entered the scene to free New France from the claws of the Traitor and the Other. The Leader, of a temporal stature superior to that of all of his contemporaries, is also, first and foremost, a supernatural figure:

> The same Providence, always attentive, has chosen to this end a candidate for sainthood, this Montmorency de Laval, a man of noble race, great spirit, and greater character, with the dominant qualities of a leader. His election in itself is already surrounded with a providential significance. It is a victory over Gallicanism.[41]

Groulx emphasizes that by according preference to immigrants from Normandy to those from La Rochelle and the neighbouring islands, "it assured the nascent people with religious homogeneity, the moral purity that is its primary nobility."[42] The value of François Montmorency de Laval was not limited to preserving the religious homogeneity of the colony; he overcame the "peril of decay" brought on by alcohol abuse, by confronting various intendants on the commerce in spirits. This gesture consecrated him as saviour of the race.[43]

The saviours of the nation followed and resembled each other. "Every day, and especially under grave circumstances, conscious of his role as leader, Maisonneuve always wanted to act most perfectly, to elevate his acts to the greatest supernatural dimensions."[44] In the 1930s, he whom Groulx implores to appear, is invested with the extraordinary power to guide his nation on the road to resurrection:

Happy Austria, to have found its leader and, with him, the road to resurrection! How we too need a National Front and a man who, like the young and captivating chancellor of Austria, would dare to say these moving words: "I want to reconstruct my country on the basis of the *Quadragesimo Anno* encyclical.[45]

The passing centuries had apparently changed nothing: be it 1690, 1919, or 1934, the tragedy that hit French Canada was identical. Thus, in 1919, Groulx addresses this ode to Dollard des Ormeaux:

Call us with your virile charm, with your heroic tone. We would lift to you hands trembling like palms, ardent with the ambition to serve...And for the defence of French, and for the defence of Catholicism, if you command, O Dollard, O intoxicating and magnetic leader, we will follow you to the supreme holocaust.[46]

Since, Groulx writes, "The story begins again, the soul of New France is continuously assaulted, we know, under which conditions, the same sacrifices, the same redemptive actions will be possible."[47] We do know how: it will be through a Fascist dictatorship.

Notes

1. Lionel Groulx: *Notre maître le passé*, tome 2, p. 256; Lionel Groulx: *Notre mystique nationale*, speech given at the Windsor Hotel in Montreal on the occasion of a dinner celebrating St. Jean-Baptiste Day, June 23, 1939, brochure, p. 3.

2. Lionel Groulx: *La naissance d'une race*, p. 19.

3. *Ibid.*, p. 69.

4. *Ibid.*, p. 27.

5. *Ibid.*, p.30.

6. *Ibid.*, p. 257.

7. "Can we establish that this peasant population is of excellent physical quality, in short, an élite? Nothing to argue about here, concerning in the first place physical traits: the selection was scrupulous." *Ibid.*, p. 42.

8. Lionel Groulx: *Notre maître le passé*, tome 2, p. 257; Lionel Groulx: *La naissance d'une race*, p. 43.

9. Lionel Groulx: *Notre maître le passé*, tome 2, p. 258 et tome 1, p. 272; Lionel Groulx: *La naissance d'une race*, p. 115.

10. Lionel Groulx: *Notre maître le passé*, tome 1, p. 275.

11. Lionel Groulx: *Notre maître le passé*, tome 2, p. 260.

12. Lionel Groulx: *La naissance d'une race*, p. 63.

13. *Ibid.*, p. 54.

14. *Ibid.*, p. 55; Lionel Groulx: *Notre maître le passé*, tome 1, pp. 271-272.

15. Lionel Groulx: *La naissance d'une race*, p. 69.

16. *Ibid.*, p. 24.

17. *Ibid.*, p. 25.

18. *Ibid.*, pp. 25-26.

19. *Ibid.*,

20. *Ibid.*, p. 26.

21. *Ibid.*, p.22.

22. *Ibid.*, p.29.

23. *Ibid.*, pp. 21-22.

24. *Ibid.*, p. 82.

25. *Ibid.*, p. 85.

26. *Ibid.*, p. 246.

27. *Ibid.*, pp. 35-36; *Ibid.*, pp. 269-270; The same goes for the Acadian race: Lionel Groulx: *Notre maître le passé*, tome 1, p. 158.

28. Lionel Groulx:*La naissance d'une race* p. 260.

29. Lionel Groulx: *Notre maître le passé*, tome 1, p. 33.

30. Lionel Groulx: *op. cit.*, p. 285.

31. Lionel Groulx: *Notre maître le passé*, tome 2, p. 269.

32. Lionel Groulx: *La naissance d'une race*, p. 292.

33. *Ibid.*, p. 221.

34. *Ibid.*, p. 204.

35. *Ibid.*, p. 195.

36. *Ibid.*, pp. 190-191. The war against the Iroquois also resulted in "...men letting themselves revel in the passion for arms. This caused great misfortunes for the cause of peace and for the colony. Canada would soon be full of adventurers and short of farmers." *Ibid.*, p. 192.

37. *Ibid.*, pp. 195-196.

38. *Ibid.*, p. 194.

39. *Ibid.*, pp. 140-141.

40. Lionel Groulx: *Notre maître le passé*, tome 1, pp. 104-105.

41. Lionel Groulx: *op.cit.*, p. 127.

42. Lionel Groulx: *Ibid.*, p. 103.

43. *Ibid.*, p. 104.

44. Lionel Groulx: *Notre maître le passé*, tome 1, p. 27. The same goes for Dollard des Ormeaux. *Ibid.*, pp. 53-54.

45. Jacques Brassier (pseudonym of Lionel Groulx): "Pour qu'on vive.," *Action nationale*, (January 1934), pp. 53-54.

46. Excerpt from the speech: "Si Dollard revenait," given at the Monument national hall on 31 January, 1919. Quoted in: Guy Frégault: *Lionel Groulx tel qu'en lui-même.*, Montréal, Leméac, 1978, p. 137.

47. Lionel Groulx: *Notre maître le passé*, tome 1, p. 58."Today, as in the past, we must keep a taste for perilous tasks; against the new barbarians, we must be prepared for the supreme sacrifice in the defense of the French fact; Let us hope that these memories will free us more often from the nightmare and from the raucous materialism of the bustling city...." *Ibid.*, p. 25.

4

THE TRAITOR

And the lawyer, who had studied literature, remembered that, even in the time of Eschylus, treason was called "the most foul of diseases."[1]

An epidemic of treason swept across conquered New France. The individualism and materialism that had previously been held in check by the Leader blossomed freely. Groulx introduces the evil totality, which is the subject of the following chapter, by assimilating the Traitor to democracy, capitalism, and modernity, and by pronouncing his reckless fall from humanity. It is here that the nihilism and the delirium of extremist right-wing nationalism find their characteristic power of expression. But before unreservedly embracing the evil totality, the Traitor wantonly commits the treason of the blood.

INDEED, THE CONQUEST, then the arrival of numerous Loyalist immigrants, demolished the ethnic and religious homogeneity of New France.[2] The contamination began with the classes at the summit of the social pyramid—the seigneurs and the bourgeoisie—who, without decency or shame, hob-nobbed with the occupiers. They did not hesitate to share "the courtly charms" of their salons with army officers and lonely British civil servants.[3] Very soon, the children of the two enemy classes were attending the same schools; the Ursuline convent in Quebec, for example, lowered its guard to the point of receiving a large number of Anglo-Protestant students within its walls.[4] And vice versa: "French-Canadian children were found, at this time, in all the Anglo-Protestant schools in Quebec and Montreal, and sometimes in quite considerable numbers."[5] The consequences of this cheerful minuet were not long in coming: "In any case, very early, difference of religion ceased to seem an affair of consequence, an insuperable barrier to those wishing to marry."[6]

It was thus through the Traitor that the mixing of blood first began. Obeying only the call of his own pleasure, he irremediably sullied the purity of his race. Whether it was the treason of "the old nobility of New France, who managed to dishonour themselves in the abdication of blood"[7] or that committed by the twentieth-century French-Canadian bourgeoisie, where "mixed marriages are torn asunder with wrath...where betrayals take place with appalling rapidity,"[8] they all obey an inflexible determinism:

> Would one not conclude, the Father said, that it is a law of History, within all nationalities struggling for life, that the upper classes commit treason and kill themselves off as a group as much as they construct themselves? Placed in more direct, closer relations with the conqueror or the oppressor, you can see how they succumb in an ineluctable series of falls: self-interest leads them to practise assiduous social relations with the foreigner; then, in contact with the richest, they yield little by little to the temptations of vanity...And then, through pride, through absence of national faith, they accept marriage, the mixing of blood: this is their downfall and their end. [9]

No matter in which era or country, the bourgeoisie betrays, as "the too-well-known axiom that peoples, like fish, rot from the head"[10] has it, or one might believe "History [which] teaches...that once it has begun down the fatal slope, a class rarely climbs back up."[11]

The Traitor also opens the door to pluralism. "Impressed by the power of the new master and by some of his far-reaching pretensions, did our brave fathers not generously lean toward the acceptance of new ideas?"[12] Alas! Their generosity would be their ruin, for, Groulx notes, "our ancestors let themselves go, as they went through life, to a sufficiently disquieting tolerance. And since this practical liberalism is always inspired by a more or less conscious doctrinal liberalism, already we see some indefinable wavering in the faith of this generation."[13]

Indeed, while French-Canadian children attended Anglo-Protestant schools, their fathers were hatching even more sinister plans. A petition was presented to Lord Dorchester on 31 October 1791 in which some sixty signatories requested "the erection of a neutral university, free and open to all Christian denominations," where "languages and sciences will be taught to the exclusion of theology."[14] After Lord Durham's report was submitted, the lawyer Charles Mondelet recommended, "in the Canada Times of Montreal, a system of completely neutral schools" a startling example of "what the Irish call the enslaved mind, a servile state of mind sometimes customary among peoples long subjugated,"[15] which was spreading like wildfire among French Canadians. The proponents of the neutral school were to gain a momentary victory, as evidenced by "the laicizing trends that had inspired the school legislation of Lower Canada in these years."[16]

Along with practical and doctrinal liberalism came the popularity of light entertainment: "In Quebec, in 1789, a young Canadian, arrived from France, opened a theatre very popular among high society, in which stylish French comedies were performed."[17] In these distant times, the city already presented an ideal context for a growing relaxation of morals. Monseigneur Hubert informed Rome, in his 1794 report, that "the corruption of morals has wreaked terrible ravages in the cities over the last thirty years, particularly in Quebec and Montreal. According to reports by foreigners, it is not this advanced in many cities in Europe."[18] Modernity, and the city, the place *par excellence* for its expression, were as reprehensible in 1789 as in 1935.

"Around 1778," Groulx tells us, doctrinal liberalism was expressed, among other things, through a "pretty little Voltairist school [which] publicly frolicked around the *Gazette littéraire de Montréal*."[19] "As well," he continues, "books were not alone in spreading the poison of eighteenth-century French. The most undesirable of France's newspapers made their way into Canada."[20] As if this wasn't enough, "we must remember the voyages to the old country, which, for their part, contributed to the contamination."[21]

In this tainted environment, "the atmosphere from outside that no closed window kept from entering," the credibility of the church caught a fatal flu. "In Canadian high society of the time, the texts tell us how willingly a posture of incredulity was adopted and how the church's authority was diminished."[22]

To the Roman Catholic church, which it treated cavalierly, Canadian high society, under the spell of fumes of another poison originating in the mother country, opposed a penchant for democracy. "Like the French in 1848, they began to believe in the definitive triumph of democracy, in universal emancipation of the working classes, in all the grandiloquent, hollow chimeras."[23]

"The ravages of parliamentarianism," sanctioned by the Union of the Canadas, was not the least of democracy's failings: "Less than eight years under the parliamentary regime, aggravated by too much unprepared participation, brought us to this degree of moral abjection."[24] This moral decrepitude came from the unbridled liberalism professed by the French-Canadian parliamentarians. It did not occur to them to resort to reprisals against the minority, nor even to ostracism, but no, mourns Groulx: "Rather, they were inclined toward facile, extravagant liberalism, which, under the pretext of accommodating the rights of all, usually did not accommodate the rights of anyone."[25]

Another target of the traitor-hunting Canon is the democratic party, or red party, whose members supported the American Declaration of Independence and the *Déclaration des droits de l'homme*,[26] and for whom, "as for all ideologues of their type, political institutions will be 'pure' and effective, in the sense that they will draw their source more directly from the people and that the people will have a greater part to play in it."[27] Their presumptuousness went as far as advocating annexation to the United States, which they saw as the "supreme incarnation of modern democracy."[28]

It was an easy step from this frenzied liberalism to the 1867 Confederation, established while the French-Canadian race was in "a period of lethargy," haunted by a "morbid taste for rest." This same moral and ideological collapse was explained by "the rapid and fatal influence of a doctrine over a people, this doctrine which dissolved, and prevailed over, the most vigorous atavistic instincts."[29]

The supporters of federalism were traitors. "Being or not being a federalist signified, at the time, betraying or not betraying one's race."[30] Their victory meant that, from then on, the only passion that would move the population of the province of Quebec was that of partisan politics; French Canada became "drunk with politics," making it "the most profitable national industry" and the politician "the only leader."[31]

Groulx cannot find words cutting enough to castigate the politicians who embraced federalism, whether in 1867 or in 1935. They spent most of their time vaunting the merits of the *"bonne entente,"* which was "an abominable verbal hypocrisy, a banquet formula for lips running with scotch," defended by "the most foolish and ignoble of hangers-on, the show-offs who think they are geniuses because they have pot bellies."[32]

The francophone supporters of the *bonne entente* between French and English Canadians, "these opium charlatans," played at being "revolutionary agitators" by knowingly keeping their compatriots in a state of inferiority within the Canadian Confederation. For, threatens Groulx, "with such serious evils, the worst danger is to preach indefinite resignation."[33]

They accomplished their goals: by 1936, Groulx states, French Canadians constitute a "politically degenerate"[34] race. The proof is that the French-Canadian M.P.s in the federal parliament, "the fifty or so cowards and back-room boys invariably sent to Ottawa by Quebec," prisoners of "their idiotic party spirit" and incapable of standing up to English Canadians, are plunging the Canadian Confederation, more unerringly than their nationalist opponents could have done, into "the ignominious end that awaits it."[35]

These same "small party men" defend only "their individual welfare and the interests of their clan," invariably placing "the party above the national...without taking into account the terrible repercussions likely when one generation, less pacified by electoral narcotics, would no longer accept as a national destiny a progressive and definitive subjugation."[36]

Lionel Groulx, alias Jacques Brassier, has just defined the quintessence of the treason as it was practised in the political arena: to accord supremacy to individual or party interest, to the detriment of national interests.[37] "Not one true Catholic left," he fulminates, whom one can say is "capable of putting his faith above votes; one or two perhaps; [there is left] not a true French Canadian, not a man."[38] Neither Catholic, nor human, it seems...The Liberal Party of Quebec also runs afoul of the Canon's ire. He describes it as:

> ...an assembly rife with parasitic individualism, awakening appetites, cupidity of every type, especially of high finance, that insatiable oligarchy that prowls the alleyways of government, subjugating it to the point that government and oligarchy become one.[39]

Groulx has now introduced a new theme: political parties in a democracy, especially those in power, consort with the financial powers, to the point that they are fused together. The illegitimate components of liberalism reinforce each other; the political parties divide the country, valorize individualism, and pledge their allegiance to the financial powers.

Never tiring, Groulx uses an ever-finer sieve to separate the wheat from the chaff. Among the self-satisfied prigs "who deserve to be whipped"[40] are "a good number of our journalists and directors, themselves asleep and more or less embroiled in political partisanship."[41] They belong to the bourgeoisie, which was as traitorous in 1930 as it was after the conquest, repeating as if at will "the betrayals from above," this time by "dividing the members of parliament into two irreconcilable enemy camps,"[42] and convincing the people to do the same: "But no, we must keep our fists cocked against one another, for the parties to work."[43] In the themes of civil war generated by the political parties, in their valorization of personal interest to the detriment of that of the nation and the ensuing enfeeblement of the latter, one recognizes the warhorses of the Action française rising against democracy and parliamentarianism.

Wherever he was born, wherever he lived, the French Canadian, although he was a member "of a race perpetually betrayed by the politicians,"[44] could not help carrying his passion for politics with him like a curse:

> However, here is the phenomenon: the party holds him, from one end of Canada to the other. Wherever he emigrates, the French Canadian takes his clan with him, and since he is the product of a blue* or red** Quebec family, he will remain unfailingly blue or red, in Saskatchewan, Alberta, and even beyond the Rockies.[45]

Democratic alienation represents an even greater threat since French Canada shows "all the signs of nations who are heading for the final fall," that is, "incoherence, disintegration, abandonment to mediocrity, servitude, powerlessness to live collectively, the victory of individualism."[46] In this province, ravaged by a triumphant individualism, agitated by convulsions of agony, one solidarity alone is active, Groulx bitterly states, and it is that of its old demon. "In this misery, one community, one solidarity remains, never weakening: the solidarity of the political party, the most destructive form of individualism."[47]

---

*   Conservative
**   Liberal

"If a people is not overcome with suicidal folly," Groulx adds, "it should become fed up with undergoing this puerile game, this scourge every four or five years, every time the electoral circus returns."[48] Groulx turns threatening again, as he was previously toward *bonne-ententiste* French-Canadian politics and toward the politicians who were dividing the people. The revolution roars...

Continuing his attack on all aspects of liberalism, Groulx emphasizes yet another fault in democracy; citing a certain Vallery-Radot, he denounces the inability of this political regime to propose anything other than "a destiny with excessive drinking, eating, hygiene, charcoal, mechanics and all the mediocre desires inside of which our democracy wanted to enclose man's entire horizon."[49]

Sprawling in the middle of these mediocre needs and desires is the bourgeoisie, which "abdicates its leadership function, accords little or no importance to national concern, less, surely, than to its amusements and frivolity: 'parties' of all sorts, ski trips, golf parties."[50] Idle, knowing nothing of life but "the frivolity of the sporting life or social climbing,"[51] this bourgeoisie has made of its children "pomaded, painted whipper-snappers, invertebrate idlers who, one would say, are hit with ataraxia or arteriosclerosis when they turn twenty."[52]

Groulx lingers for a moment upon the treason committed by a specific group, businessmen: "Statistics, whose authenticity we don't deny, tell us that in Montreal—and do things happen so differently in Quebec?—out of 6,000 French-Canadian businessmen, about 600, or one tenth, do their income-tax return for the National Revenue Ministry in French."[53] "Great industrialists, great financiers" rejected the call of the "Buy-at-Home" campaign, they "who grow pale with fear, throw in your face the cry of laziness and stupidity: 'Don't mix patriotism and business!'"[54] They are "exploiters of their profession, machines for pocketing dollars," Groulx exclaims sorrowfully, who ignore ways to amuse themselves and lead their lives by confirming the originality of their race, and who, in a province that is four fifths French, "know only how to found branches or sub-branches of the Rotary Club, the Kiwanis, the Knights of Columbus, the Quebec Library Association, and I don't know what else!"[56] Groulx solemnly warns all these people what they can expect:

If you don't get hold of yourselves, you, anti-patriotic, anti-nationalist bourgeois, you will succeed in eliminating your own kind. An apostasy never happens all by itself. See where, save a few noble exceptions, our old aristocracy, that of the times of New France, has gone. Like it, by the next generation or the one after, you will no longer be French, nor will you be Catholics. You may kill yourselves, but we will not let you involve us in your suicide.[57]

This said, he turns his wrath towards the educators, who encourage the "pure perversion" that is interest in sport, particularly hockey.

Educators show more fervour for melees of brawlers and brutes than for study and the cultivation of souls, and it seems that they talk more often about hockey than about patriotism or the spiritual, read the sports pages more carefully than the pages of the classics; meagerly remunerated professors invoke the pretext of poverty for not buying books, but at night they drive 80 miles in automobiles to attend a hockey game, then, when they go to class the next day, instead of a history or literature lesson, they find nothing better to do, before adolescents with malleable spirits, than recount the feats in the stadium. We say, weighing our words well, that it is, on the part of the masters of the Latin spirit, pure perversion.[58]

The French-Canadian people—dimwitted as only they can be—rush to imitate them:

No, let's admit it: worse than the revolting regime is the perfect idiocy with which we tolerate it. Every week, and sometimes two, three times a week, there are ten or twenty thousand, at the hockey games in Montreal, yelling and shrieking as wildly as savages. Out of these twenty thousand, you will find no more than five hundred who would be capable of opening their mouth to end the tyranny of Ottawa.[59]

Groulx does not let this go easily; he returns to these teachers who "could not have raised three or four generations of children, young boys, young girls, without wondering from time to time which national ideal to guide them toward."[60] Then it was the turn of the intellectuals, all of them utterly absorbed with "minor verses and minor prose", who turned away from national problems in the name of a false artistic liberty of "anonymous personality" and "cosmopolitan soul."[61]

"Together, they are all responsible for our 'spiritual and national failure,'"[62] our "total absence of any pride, of the slightest patriotic concern,"[63] "for the degree of abjection or nihilism to which they have fallen from the national point of view,"[64] all of "the country people who persist in their stubbornness, petrifying themselves in their frantic individualism...traditional and apparently incorrigible individualism. [They] who easily catch fire before the blue or red rag,"[65] they who "with mummified spirits, are opposed to any change, to any effort, and who do not want not to be put in the position of having to be active and working,"[66] "the light, superficial spirits, with no horizons, unable to see what is going on, in their country, in North America, persuaded that they can live indefinitely, in isolation, in their goldfish bowl,"[67] "the defeatists for whom there is nothing to do but go to bed, because they are already dead, horrified of the living,"[68] "the doctrinaires for whom all nationalism is appalling, heretical,"[69] "the cohorts of voluntary slaves, those passionately in love with their chains."[70]

The French-Canadian person himself, his attitude and physical bearing, betrays his servility, his laziness, and his fear. He is characterized by "the flabby, soft pronunciation, the talk of just-about, the sentence half spoken and half swallowed," as well as by "the stooped back and the rounded shoulders," portraying "postures of weak people or slaves." Groulx thus enjoins the masters: "In the end, when one sees such passing on the street, the soft step, the dangling arms, the bowed back, the air of a beaten dog, one can say with infallibility: 'That's a French Canadian!'"[71]

They must do even more:

> For example, relieve our poor peasants and farmers of these humiliating attitudes that they show us, when they enter certain large stores in the west of Montreal, with their eyes spellbound with mystique, as if they were entering the door of a temple or a national sanctuary, and with the air of searching for a basin of holy water where they can cross themselves.[72]

The sheep quietly moved toward Anglophone pastures: was it not true that "a lower class, supposedly French, [was] in the process of Anglicizing, for the most part, the face of its country"?[73] That it suffered from a morbid penchant for Anglicization? And what is Anglicization? It is "a serious error to make a telephone call in English, to let oneself be spoken to in English by railway employees, to accept a receipt, a packing slip, an invoice written in English, as do the large businesses of the other race,"[75] and it is also: "To create ugliness, an ugly house, an ugly church; to throw up along the highways, signs, billboards in a strange or baroque language, it is like putting warts on the face of the country...it is to sin against our French community."[76]

To be French Canadian was not limited to speaking French, but required having a French soul, as Groulx has already explained. By virtue of this same reasoning, one could "Anglicize" the province without having anything to do with the use of the English language.

The people turned a deaf ear to the "re-Francization" campaign. "Another disquieting and humiliating symptom is the resistance by our people opposed to re-Francization, a resistance almost always opinionated, often surly, because the people do not understand."[77]

The people were relentless in their incomprehension. At the coronation of George VI, the French-Canadian balconies of Montreal were indiscriminately draped with American, Canadian, and British flags, especially the Union Jack, which had the place of honour. This cosmopolitanism of flags was extra proof "of the non-existence, the incoherence or anarchy of the patriotic ideology in our country."[78] If French Canadians' obtuse fondness for the Union Jack was a sign of treason, that which they demonstrated for the French flag was a sign of the purest stupidity: "To someone who suggests displaying the *fleurdelisé*, a clumsy, self-satisfied imbecile would have responded, according to the one who tells the story, 'We already have the tricolour. Do we need this other rag?' Yet more words to reveal the extent of our stupidity."[79]

Insult was added to injury when he confirmed that the French Canadians, in addition to ignoring their future national flag, simply rejected Saint-Jean-Baptiste Day: "Here, outside of two or three towns in our province, do you think that June 24th moves 10 per cent of French Canadians?"[80] Of course not...

French Canadians suffer "from an obliterated national feeling, in full dissolution,"[81] and Groulx explains elsewhere that "what is suffering dreadfully from anaemia is national feeling."[82]

The conclusion is inevitable: "The great misfortune of French Canadians, I must dare to say, is that there are no French Canadians."[83]

And since humanity is possible only through belonging to an ethnic group/nation/race, as Groulx has already explained, an inexorable logic is built up:

> But one sees, at the same time, what outrage erases our Catholicism, when we force people from the outside to ascribe to it, as to an education springing from it, inspired by its principles and its life, *so many droll beings, so many mockeries of men and women who leave our training.* Is it, in particular, our business only to form nationless people, if it is true, as Cardinal Mercier says, that "every true Christian must be a patriot"? And are they truly the products of a Catholic education, the authentic sons and daughters of Catholic faith, these grand young people of the Catholic faith, *these young men and women, only shadows of what they should be, who do not have the courage of their blood, or of their language, or of their culture, who apparently belong to no country or race and who, tomorrow, thanks to the daily betrayal of their civic or national duties, will bring to their province and their institutions only the disdain of the foreigner!*[84]

Worse than the shadows and the mockeries of men and women, there are still "French Canadians too much like those we see cluttering the streets: beings without consistency, without dignity, without pride, whom one would say are from no race, no country, mockeries of men who are an insult to mankind, and above all an insult to Catholic education."[85]

Nonexistent, the French Canadians are unworthy of humanity. The same nihilism will require, in time, a utopian counterpart if Groulx does not want to fall, forever, into destructive hopelessness.

Notes

1. Lionel Groulx: *L'Appel de la race*, p. 192.

2. "The Conquest, but above all the mass of loyalist immigrants, wrecks thrown across the border by the winds of American independence, broke the ethnic and religious homogeneity of French Canada." Lionel Groulx: *L'enseignement français au Canada.*, tome 1, p. 63; Lionel Groulx: *Notre maître le passé*, Montréal, Éditions internationales Alain Stanké, 1978, tome 3, p. 162. Coll. "Québec 10/10."

3. Lionel Groulx:*Notre maître le passé*, tome 2, p. 170.

4. "Already, and it's the first symptom of the inevitable penetrations, the schools, and especially the girls' boarding schools, like the Ladies of our Sacred Heart, the Congregation of our Holy Lady, the Ursulines of Quebec City open their doors to contingents of English-speaking or Protestant students from Lower and Upper Canada, the Gulf Colonies or even the U.S.A. How tempting to modify the study program to accommodate these foreigners, whose wealth and drive have ne-

ver ceased to impose themselves! Above all, once the abdication of these pompous houses where the daughters of the French-Canadian bourgeoisie are educated, is complete, it will be impossible to stop the tone and the content of a new kind of education from flowing all the way down to the small convents and the most modest of schools." Lionel Groulx: *L'enseignement français au Canada,*, tome 1, p. 257

5. Lionel Groulx: *Méditation patriotique,* in: *Soirées de l'Action française,* Montréal, Éditions de l'Action canadienne-française, 1939, p. 8.

6. Lionel Groulx: *Notre maître le passé,* tome 2, p. 170.

7. Lionel Groulx: *Notre maître le passé,* tome 1, p. 194; Lionel Groulx: *Méditation patriotique,* p. 8.

8. Lionel Groulx: *L'Appel de la race,* p. 160; *Ibid.,* pp. 130-131.

9. *Ibid.,* p. 159.

10. Lionel Groulx: *La bourgeoisie et le national,* p. 99.

11. *Ibid.,* pp. 117-118: "Let us not forget this phenomenon of the submission of the bourgeoisie, that every people under the yoke of cultural or political servitude had to suffer: the Irish prior to the Free State, the Poles before independence, the Alsatian-Lorrains [sic] after 1870, the Belgian Flemish before the awakening of Greater Flemish nationalism." *Ibid.,* pp. 99-100; The same axiom holds true in the case of ancient Gaul." Cf.: Lionel Groulx: *Orientations,* p.269.

12. Lionel Groulx: *Notre maître le passé,* tome 2, pp. 168-169; Lionel Groulx: *Nos positions,* p. 241.

13. Lionel Groulx: *Notre maître le passé,* tome 2, p. 171.

14. Lionel Groulx: *L'enseignement français au Canada,* tome 1, pp. 70-71."At the bottom of this petition we find almost sixty French-Canadian names, among the most notable of the colony, including the signature of Father Félix de Bérey, "general of the Récollets in this province," and that of Abbé Edmund Burke, director of the Seminary of Quebec, and last, but not least, that of Charles-François de Capse, of Quebec" *Ibid.*

15. Lionel Groulx: *L'enseignement français au Canada,* tome 1, p. 101.

16. *Ibid.*

17. *Notre maître le passé,* tome 2, pp. 175-176.

18. *Ibid.,* p. 176.

19. *Ibid.,* p. 172.

20. *Ibid.,* p. 175.

21. *Ibid.*

22. *Ibid.,* p. 182.

23. *Ibid.,* p. 193.

24. Lionel Groulx: *Notre maître le passé,* tome 1, p. 205.

25. Lionel Groulx: *L'enseignement français au Canada,* tome 1, p. 148; *Ibid.,* p. 224.

26. Lionel Groulx: *Notre maître le passé,* tome 2, p. 214.

27. *Ibid.,* p. 224.

28. *Ibid.,* p. 227.

29. Lionel Groulx: *L'Appel de la race,* pp. 97-98.

30. Lionel Groulx: *op. cit,* p. 240.

31. Lionel Groulx: *L'enseignement français au Canada*, tome 1, pp. 159-160.

32. André Marois (pseudonym of Lionel Groulx): "Pour qu'on vive.," *Action nationale*, (June 1935), p. 369.

33. Lionel Groulx: *Directives*, p.236.

34. "For in fact, if in 1936 it has become criminal, even revolutionary to demand what could have and what should have legitimately existed for the last 69 years [a French state within the Confederation], how are we to show in more overwhelming fashion that the federal system has made us into a politically degenerate race." *Ibid.*, p. 110.

35. Jacques Brassier (pseudonym of Lionel Groulx): "Pour qu'on vive," *Action nationale*, (November 1934), p. 244.

36. Jacques Brassier (pseudonym of Lionel Groulx): "Pour qu'on vive," *Action nationale*, (October 1934), pp. 153-154.

37. "Everywhere and always, he perceives the rule, the universal and total triumph, of personal interest, often even of the most sordid passions." Lionel Groulx: *L'Appel de la race*, p. 203; Lionel Groulx: *Notre maître le passé*, tome 1, p. 237; Jacques Brassier (pseudonym of Lionel Groulx): "Pour qu'on vive," *Action nationale*, (April 1933), pp. 244-245.

38. Jacques Brassier(pseudonym of Lionel Groulx): "Pour qu'on vivre [sic]," *Action nationale*, (October 1935), p.

39. André Marois (pseudonym of Lionel Groulx): "Réforme d'un parti ou réforme d'une politique," *Le Devoir*, 20 September 1932, p. 1.

40. Jacques Brassier (pseudonym of Lionel Groulx): "Pour qu'on vive.," *Action nationale* (April 1933), p. 142.

41. *Ibid.*

42. Lionel Groulx: *Ibid.*, p. 227.

43.*Ibid.*, p. 110."And all that for the pleasure of a few local bourgeois, election supervisors, who saw their interest in that kind of work."Lionel Groulx: *La bourgeoisie et le national.*, p. 107.

44. André Marois (pseudonym of Lionel Groulx): "Pour qu'on vive," *Action nationale*, (March 1935), p. 170.

45. He goes on:"Who has never met stolid Franco-Américains, who emigrated to the United States thirty or even forty years ago, who still become light-headed and wild about one party or another, whenever we hold our general elections." Lionel Groulx: *Orientations*, pp. 258-259; Lionel Groulx: *Directives*, pp. 221-222; The same goes for francophone minorities across Canada. Cf.: Lionel Groulx: *L'enseignement français au Canada*, tome 2, *Les écoles des minorités*, Montréal, Librairie Granger Frères, 1933, p. 253.

46. Lionel Groulx: *op. cit.*, p. 210. "...after more than sixty years,...the federal system has become, for our small people, a death certificate...." André Marois (pseudonyme de Lionel Groulx): "Pour qu'on vive," *Action nationale*, (March 1935), pp. 168-169.

47. *Ibid.*

48. Lionel Groulx: *Orientations*, p. 101.

49. Lionel Groulx: *Directives*, p. 26.

50. Lionel Groulx: *La bourgeoisie et le national*, p. 99; Lionel Groulx: "L'esprit estudiantin." *Action nationale*, (March 1934), p. 171.

51. Lionel Groulx: *Orientations*, p. 15.

52. *Ibid.*, p. 99.

53. *Ibid.*, p. 97.

54. *Ibid.*, p. 226. On the treason of businessmen, cf.: Lionel Groulx: *Directives*, p.78. Lionel Groulx: *Méditation patriotique*, p. 12

55. Lionel Groulx: "L'esprit estudiantin." *Action nationale*, (March 1934), p. 170.

56. *Ibid*, p. 171; Lionel Groulx: *Orientations*, p. 259.

57. Lionel Groulx: *La bourgeoisie et le nationale*, pp. 123-124.

58. Jacques Brassier(pseudonym of Lionel Groulx): "Pour qu'on vive.," *Action nationale*, (November 1934), pp. 245-246.

59. André Marois(pseudonym of Lionel Groulx): "Pour qu'on vive," *Action nationale* , (March 1935), p. 172.

60. Lionel Groulx: *Directives*, p. 77.

61. *Ibid.*, p. 76; Lionel Groulx: *Orientations*, pp. 271-272.

62. Jacques Brassier(Pseudonym of Lionel Groulx): "Pour qu'on vive." *Action nationale*, (December 1933), p. 262.

63. *Ibid.*

64. Jacques Brassier(Pseudonym of Lionel Groulx): "Pour qu'on vive.," *Action nationale*, (October 1935), p. 264. On patriotic nihilism cf.: Lionel Groulx: "Un signe des temps." *Le Devoir*, 30 November 1935, p. 1.

65. Jacques Brassier(pseudonym of Lionel Groulx): "Pour qu'on vive," *Action nationale*, (December 1933), p. 265-266.

66. Lionel Groulx: *Directives*, p. 95.

67. *Ibid.*, pp. 95-96.

68. *Ibid.*

69. *Ibid.*

70. Lionel Groulx: *L'Appel de la race*, p. 149; Alonié De Lestres (pseudonym of Lionel Groulx): *Au cap Blomidon*, Montréal, Granger Frères Limitée, p. 18.

71. Lionel Groulx: *Directives*, pp. 163-164.

72. *Ibid.*, pp. 80-81.

73. Lionel Groulx: " L'éducation nationale.," *Action nationale*, (January 1934), p. 11.

74. Lionel Groulx: Directives, p. 101.

75. Lionel Groulx: *Notre maître le passé*, tome 2, p. 293; "And now again, if you ask our poor people for what reason, for what over-riding interest it paints the French face of its country English, I can hear them reply, their eyes full of amazement, with the empty reflex of their soul: "What's the difference?," Lionel Groulx: *Orientations*, p. 228; *Ibid.*,pp. 97-98; Lionel Groulx: *Directives*, pp. 140-141, p. 207.

76. Lionel Groulx: *Directives.*, pp. 157-158.

77. Lionel Groulx: *Orientations.*, p. 252.

78. André Marois(pseudonym of Lionel Groulx): "Pour qu'on vive," *Action nationale*, (May 1937), p. 308.

79. *Ibid.*, p. 310.

80. Lionel Groulx: *Orientations*, p. 94.

81. *Ibid.*, p. 225.

82. *Ibid.*, p. 107; *Ibid.*, p. 265; Jacques Brassier (pseudonym of Lionel Groulx): "Pour qu'on vive," *Action nationale*, (March 1934), p. 178.

83. Lionel Groulx: *Orientations.*, p. 231; "What am I saying? A people, a nation? Us? Come on!...A grouping of social clubs, more lie it." Lionel Groulx: *Directives*, p. 205; *Ibid.*, p. 205.

84. Lionel Groulx: *Orientations*, p.153. (Author's italics).

85. Lionel Groulx: *Directives.*, pp. 173-174. (Author's italics).

5

THE EVIL TOTALITY

The evil totality is the subject of this chapter. It is presented according to the logical framework that more or less supports this delirious anathematization. Capitalism is evil in itself; it is evil also because it permits the Other, via his eternal accomplice, the Traitor, to exploit the nation and infect it with unnameable germs; democracy is evil because it is the tool of capitalism and the Other. Finally, modernity is evil because in it blossom all cankers and putrefaction.

HAVING SUBMITTED THAT contemporary society is "the expression of an anti-personalist, inhumane civilization," Groulx links it to the specific situation of French Canada, "where a tiny handful of the well-to-do" possess the economic wealth, dominate political life, and threaten the cultural existence of a population the vast majority of which is French.[1] In this society, "the vast majority of employers, held back by the outdated fads of economic liberalism, infect us daily with the virulent germ of the worst social cankers,"[2] among which are the failure of the middle class and the rural exodus.

Groulx quickly raises the ante. In the province of Quebec, he maintains in another text, economic domination is exercised with an acuity unmatched in the world. "In our country, the economic evil carries within itself an acuity, a seriousness that is not seen anywhere else...A population that is 80 per cent French Canadian thus sees its economic life dominated by a caste that has a different origin, language, and faith from the majority."[3] The economic domination exercised by this caste entails its political domination, thanks to the very nature of parliamentary democracy. "There is no point in looking scandalized: it is a truism in parliamentary democracy,"[4] he states, repeating that social cankers blossom in this double domination.

The delirious logical framework of the evil totality and the Other could thus be interpreted as follows: first of all, Groulx condemns capitalism, "that abominable power of gold dominated by no principle,"[5] "creator of an inhumane society" in which a small number exercise a dictatorship over the masses. Second, he confirms the uniqueness of French Canada in the world mosaic by the fact that this dictatorship was exercised by men of whom, for the moment, we know only that they differ from the rest of the population by "origin, language, faith." Third, the Canon links an illegitimate economic system to a disgraced ideology and political practice, by confirming that one inevitably flows from the other. Democracy thus appears as the obliging ally of the Other, while remaining the favoured vehicle of the Traitor.

Groulx returns to the collusion between democracy and capitalism, based this time on the words of the Portuguese dictator Salazar:

> And you know how, in every country in the world, they speak poorly, as time goes by, of the parliamentary regime. "In the parliamentary regime," someone said recently, "the State is not free, because it is manipulated more or less consciously by economic concentrations." And he who speaks thus is none other than Oliveira Salazar, the Portuguese dictator, the least noisy, but, in my view, the most dignified, the most constructive, the greatest of the contemporary dictators.[6]

Governments are not the only ones at fault, far from it. All French Canadians blindly contribute to their own economic servitude. If "all peoples, all ethnic groups, Anglo-Saxon, Jewish, instinctively practise economic solidarity," as nationalist wisdom would have it, "no people practises solidarity less than they [the French-Canadian people]," with the result that, "with their own hands, they are now willingly in the process of building an economic regime in this province in which they will be content to reserve for themselves the role of client and manipulated and very little else."[7] This mirror game of contradictions, in which the all-powerful Other necessarily reflects the total powerlessness of a people, is typical of racism.

Feeding on the failing national instinct of the French Canadians were the English, American, and cosmopolitan financiers and industrialists, who—the myth of origins requires—are descended directly from the conquerors of 1760. "The right of conquest, we think, cannot extend to the economic order. On the soil which was for three hundred years the property of their forefathers, the French Canadians retain, at least, a birthright."[8]

This birthright is trampled by democracy and by the politicians who foment the servitude of their own, "born in Canada and of French origin"—as the myth of origins again requires—by condemning them "to die of hunger or find their way to the woodlots or the suburbs of cities, then the poor devils have their money grabbed away, on the land of their country, and are replaced with a bad lot from overseas."[9]

His tone turns threatening: "No, but for a people, armed with a ballot, to tolerate indefinitely such a comedy of cynicism, must we not be stunned by the parliamentary regime and the petty politics through which it works?"[10]

Stunned, despoiled, exploited, the nation finds itself in a state of self-defence. Groulx contemplates on resorting to force:

> Now, it [the world of politics] must know it: we are at the point of danger that is called the case of self-defence. On the other hand, young men, remember that in no country in the world, and in particular in no parliamentary or democratic nation, has politics brought down the financial powers without powerful help, if not force.[11]

Finally, the last section of the treatise on the evil totality and on the Other is set forth thus: the majority of employers, "including the Other," infatuated with economic liberalism and its "outdated fads," would infect the nation with "the virulent germ of the worst social cankers." The Traitor and the Other are thus characterized by their proximity to—"if not their complete identification" with—liberalism, and the vocabulary attached to them evokes disease, infection, purulence.

The failure of the middle class constitutes the first social canker caused by the infection of liberalism. "Slow and underhanded preparation, gaudy, repulsive blossoming, that gnawed at us for almost a century," this evil "has advanced through our structure like a cancer," entailing the emigration of thousands of French Canadians, who have rapidly gained a taste for uprooting themselves, to the United States. "Once, necessity forced our people to uproot themselves; today, it is by sheer capriciousness."[12]

The tumble of the middle class to the lower echelons of society converges, it's not clear just how, with the development of a deplorable mentality among the popular masses,

> a sort of serene resignation to domesticity, to subordinate jobs, to perpetual proletarianism...From father to son, they will live in the same slums, they will be under the same bondage, with no ambition to better their lives, content to obey a master, especially if this master is a foreigner.[13]

The city, where "the cancer of unemployment"[14] blooms, and which is a "dangerous culture medium for subversive ideas,"[15] is the second canker. The city is the preferred precinct of the Other, whether it is Jews, Greeks, or Syrians,[16] immigrants from the lower depths of Europe who are only passing through, while the sons of the founders of the country, "uprooted, the bastardized version of the race,"[17] wallow in the suburbs.

The city is a cosmopolitan magma where the Other conceals himself behind strange disguises in order better to fool his innocent victim; "too often in the cities of Quebec, he [the French Canadian] has terrible difficulty distinguishing a French-Canadian place of business from a Jewish or English one"[18] since, while their compatriots adopt English names for their businesses, "the Jews 'blend in' through taking a French business name."[19]

By "city" is meant, "in particular," Montreal, "Montreal in the tow of Anglo-Canadian finance, Anglo-Canadian business, Anglo-Canadian public utilities, American movies, restaurants, and dubious and cosmopolitan theatre, music, and radio,"[20] Montreal, "perfect disguise for the most authentic American emporia,"[21] Montreal, "a monstrous city...because it is the reception station for Americanism...a city without character or soul, so completely is it dominated by everything that does not belong to us, or to our province, or even to our country," intones the Canon. He then throws out a desperate question:

> ...what do you see, in the architecture of these houses, in their interior design, in their furnishings, in all these little things that give our soul its atmosphere, a French style, what do you see that is specifically ours? In every sense of the word, such cities are man-eaters.[22]

It is as impossible to define Americanism—which disfigures the furnishings of houses and the atmosphere of our soul—as it is to define urbanization. It goes far beyond the limits of the city, consisting, according to Groulx, of "the moral empire of large agglomerations, an empire with multiple tentacles and with borders that are too elusive."[23] Urbanization spreads the American microbe to the four corners of the province. "The great majority of us now live in the city; the city has itself transported its morals to the countryside, and here all the ramparts of yesteryear have collapsed, and the American microbe floats in the air everywhere."[24]

And just as the French language does not make a French Canadian, the United States does not make Americanism, and the city does not make urbanization, the English language, Groulx reiterates, does not make Anglicization:

> That this mockery is severe in the urban milieux, more or less invaded by cosmopolitanism, goes to a certain point. But when it spreads to the countryside, the last refuge of our French homogeneity...nothing is more disconcerting and painful!...I think of our customs and our morals, I think of our roadsides, of our public bridges, of our buildings, of our churches, of our country houses in particular, which reveal, for the last fifty years, such a retreat of the French taste and art.[25]

Wherever he looks, Groulx sees only:

> Economic, social, moral, intellectual penetrations, one cannot truly talk of an area where one does not feel the busy and dissolving presence of the foreigner. In a word, we are in the process of becoming an American colony.[26]

We note the usage by Groulx of this rather unusual term "dissolving" and of its derivatives, which would be taken up by certain Action nationale writers. It seems that the first to use it in an ideological context was Friedrich Nietzsche:

> What I warn people against: confounding the instincts of decadence with those of humanity;

> Confounding the dissolving means of civilisation and those which necessarily promote decadence, with culture, "confounding debauchery, and the principle of 'laisser-aller' with the will to Power (the latter is the exact reverse of the former)."[27]

The national-socialist ideology would take up the same term—which became one of its key words—attributing, for example, to Judaism all the dissolving trends at work in the German nation, including Communism.[28]

The United States, "tomorrow leader of the white race and master of the world," led "toward an atheistic civilization, admitting no other god but material progress, no other law but the hard law of economic supermen, no other goal than sensual enjoyment in which the best races of the human animal are bred."[29] Groulx cannot avoid asking, with anguish, "What gruesome and rapid ravages will then be sown, in its too quickly growing adolescent body [French Canada], the microbes of its neo-paganism [that of the United States]?"[30] And then there are the "seeds of death" propagated by this same civilization:

> Almost always, the wealth, the opulence, have been the seeds of
> death for peoples...Every day, do we not witness the lamentable
> spectacle of too many of our compatriots for whom coming of
> wealth is accompanied by a familial decadence and a total or par-
> tial renouncement of the Catholic and French ideal?[31]

The American infection, which can already be easily dis-
cerned, is alarming:

> How can we not be alarmed when we think of what it has already
> brought us: the appalling rot of its theatre, the moral looseness of
> its magazines, the licentiousness of its monstrous newspapers and
> tabloids, the brazen articles raised to the level of industrial ex-
> ploitation, the frenetic craving for criminal dramas, the passion for
> exploiting them carried to sadism, and with the manifest conse-
> quence of this dissolution, amoralism in business and politics, the
> cult of wealth that is an end in itself, the slackening of family ties,
> the rapid decline of education.[32]

The evils caused by Americanization did not stop there: there
was the "unhealthy feminism" that "attacked the foundation of
the family." In the following sentence, Groulx linked, as if it
were obvious, feminism to the theatre and the movies: "It has as
an ally, admitted or not, the dregs of the theatre, the demoraliz-
ing cinema that, in our large and small cities, and sometimes
even reaching our countryside, has become the most vast, the
most catastrophic vehicle of contemporary paganism." Then the
sentence that follows evokes French-Canadian "worker activity":
stained with socialism because under the thumb of the foreigner,
"our worker activity is, as well, dominated, directed in large part,
by a power that has its seat in a foreign land and whose strongly
socialist tendencies increase the threat of coming conflicts."[33]
Understand that if you can...

As if these ravages were not enough, the style of urban living
in North America enfeebled the race physically; the city, fashion,
and sport undermined the French-Canadian race:

> Our being swallowed up in the cities, life in the slums, the
> prolonged misery resulting from unemployment will undermine
> and consume many structures. Our absence of child hygiene and
> food hygiene, constitute permanent threats. Good doctors under-
> stand the degeneration of the woman, of the young girl, by tobacco
> abuse, sports, alcohol, fashion, in particular winter fashion.[34]

In short, we find ourselves in the presence "of a inevitable, invasive evil, which no quarantine could artificially check."[35] Survival, for the French-Canadian nation, would thus require strict moral-hygiene measures against the fevers and poisons that intoxicate it:

> Survival, for us, what is it then, if not, in the first place, forbidding ourselves the doctrines and works of death and keeping people from propagating them among us. An elementary measure of moral hygiene. There are fevers and poisons that Catholics do not have the right to introduce into national life, not even under the pretext of art or liberty, there is an art, a literature, a journalism, a novel, a poetry, an economy, a politics that we do not have the right to make or let be made. And with my eyes on our flowering youth and our little people, I add: there is a theatre that we do not have the right to tolerate.[36]

Notes

1. Lionel Groulx: *Directives*, pp. 233-234.

2. *Ibid.*

3. *Ibid.*, pp. 235-236; *Ibid.*, p. 66; Lionel Groulx: *Orientations*, p. 235.

4. Lionel Groulx: *Orientations.*, p. 236

5. *Directives*, p. 20.

6. *Ibid.*, pp. 60-61; *Ibid.*, p. 102.

7. Lionel Groulx: *Orientations*, pp. 95-96. The situation evokes for Groulx "...the accusing image...of an entire people dying on its own dunghill, just *that* close to a gold mine that it has neither the desire nor the understanding to exploit." Lionel Groulx: *op. cit.*, p. 154; Lionel Groulx: *Directives*, pp. 248-249.

8. Lionel Groulx: *Directives*,p.22.

9. Jacques Brassier (pseudonym of Lionel Groulx): "Pour qu'on vive.," *Action nationale*, (November 1933), p. 189.

10. *Ibid.*

11. Lionel Groulx: *op. cit.*, p. 106.

12. *Ibid.*, p. 201; On the "canker of the proletariat" cf.: André Marois (pseudonym of Lionel Groulx): "Réforme d'un parti ou réforme d'une politique," *Le Devoir*, 21 September 1932, p. 1; Lionel Groulx: *L'enseignement français au Canada*, tome 1, p. 313.

13. Lionel Groulx: *La déchéance incessante de notre classe moyenne*, Montréal, *Le Devoir*, December 1931, p. 1. (Coll. "Le document."); "How many have no other desire but, as if it was a natural vocation, to go and beg a job from the foreigner, a paper-pusher's job that dispenses them from the effort of creative thought or the rewarding risks of individual enterprise." Lionel Groulx: *Orientations*, pp. 131-132. *Ibid.*, p. 253.

14. Lionel Groulx: *Directives*, p. 71.

15. *Ibid.*

16. Lionel Groulx: *Orientations,* p. 130.

17. Lionel Groulx: *La déchéance incessante de notre classe moyenne,* p.15.

18. Lionel Groulx: "De la matière à réflexion," *Le Devoir,* 19 August 1932, p. 2.

19. Lionel Groulx: "Pays français, visage anglais," *Le Devoir,* 2 December 1932, p. 1, editorial.

20. Lionel Groulx: *Orientations,* p. 253.

21. Lionel Groulx: *L'Appel de la race,* p. 197.

22. Lionel Groulx: *La bourgeoisie et le national,* pp. 102-103.

23. *Ibid.,* p. 104.

24. Lionel Groulx: *Orientations,* pp. 229-230.

25. Lionel Groulx: "Pays français, visage anglais," *Le Devoir,* 2 December 1932, p. 1, editorial; Lionel Groulx: "De la matière à réflexion," *Le Devoir,* 19 August 1933, p. 1; Lionel Groulx: *Directives,* p. 160.

26. Lionel Groulx: "L'éducation nationale.," *Action nationale,* (January 1934), p. 12.

27. Friedrich Nietzsche: "The Will to Power", in Stephen J. Taylor, ed.: *National Socialism: Conservative Reaction or Nihilist Revolt?,"* New York, Holt, Rinehart and Winston, 1961, p. 8.

28. Ernst Nolte: *Les mouvements fascistes. L'Europe de 1919 à 1945,* Paris, Calmann-Lévy, 1969, p. 68.

29. Lionel Groulx: *Orientations,* p. 37.

30. *Ibid.,* p. 38.

31. Lionel Groulx: *Directives,* p. 19; Jacques Brassier(pseudonym of Lionel Groulx): "Pour qu'on vivre [sic] ", *Action nationale,* (October 1935).

32. Lionel Groulx: *Orientations,*pp. 44-45; *Ibid.,* p. 126.

33. Lionel Groulx: *Méditation patriotique,*p.4.

34. Lionel Groulx: *Directives,* p. 226.

35. *Ibid.,* p. 100; *Ibid.,* p. 239.

36. Lionel Groulx: *Orientations,* pp. 23-24;
"There is a kind of economics and social legislation that we must be forbidden to practise or to permit;...there is a kind of journalism, an art, a theatre, literature, poetry, which we cannot infect with poisons and sickness, at the risk of being doubly criminal." *Ibid.,* p. 35.

6

THEIR MASTER'S VOICE

L'Action nationale, Jeune-Canada and Le Devoir faithfully parroted Lionel Groulx's extremist right-wing nationalist views. Their new catechism included the myth of origins, the evil totality, the Traitor and the Other.

L'Action Nationale

"French Canada," l'Action nationale explains in an editorial column, "is struggling for its life in a hostile environment."[1] As Wilfred Guérin had so succinctly put it several years earlier, this environment was "teeming with the nefarious, materialistic influences of the North American continent."[2] It permitted the Other to "impose economic tyranny which crushes our people."[3] Such tyranny, Groulx had taught him, was "the child of liberalism and eighteenth century libertarian doctrine,"[4] and was transforming French Canadians into "a servant class in a plutocratic society."[5]

Liberalism was turning French Canadians into proletarians who "congregate in the cities where plagues concentrate, and detritus of both a physical and moral nature piles up."[6] Unrestrained competition engendered political tyranny which, in turn, bolstered "a shady and irresponsible economic dictatorship. Left to itself, this economic dictatorship would develop into financial internationalism and cosmopolitan capitalism...The country would be swallowed up by international financiers."[7] Capitalism, the carrier of all social ills, was synonymous with the Other. In an article evocatively entitled The Scourge of our Times, François-Albert Angers suggests that the Other also comprised the various races which had taken over the province.

> Unemployment is a hideous scourge which sucks the country's lifeblood dry, ravages its children's bodies and souls and leads us down the path to physical, intellectual and spiritual decay as well as to turmoil the likes of which we have never known. In Quebec, this fatal disease infects mainly French Canadians and is laying the way for the ultimate victory of already flourishing foreign races.[8]

The province of Quebec seemed to be languishing permanently in the mire. It had become a "mass grave for mediocrity in which our flesh was putrefying,"[9] and where politicians bustled about "trying to divide us artificially into enemy camps."[10] Their rhetoric fuelled civil strife. "The anger is there for all to see. One half of the country must rise up against the other."[11] But politics was not the only evil, the editorial went on to say. "Politics is only a tool. Behind the *de jure* country lies the *real* country."[12]

The opposition between the *de jure* country and "real country" was a phrase made famous by Charles Maurras. The "real nation" would survive for better or worse amidst "widespread cowardice and dereliction, the violence of alcoholism and petty betrayal."[13] Political parties and personalities might come and go, but the situation would stay much the same.

> It goes without saying that nothing ever changes in the parliamentary circus where puppets are manipulated by the powers of damnation hovering in the shadows, and where ill-prepared men of unbridled ambition are responsible for tasks exceeding their capabilities. It is not at all surprising that the healthier elements of the population are rebelling against this worm-eaten, pernicious thing called democracy.[14]

It is only a small step from democracy to partisan spirit and individualism, Anatole Vanier noted, accusing many of his fellow citizens of unconsciously committing treason. "Personal and party interests prevent a great number of well-meaning people from grasping the fact that when they refuse to be openly nationalistic in their own country, they serve foreign national interests."[15]

Everyone was betraying the nation: the élite who could not pull themselves out of "the mire of coarse, material pleasures;"[16] the "exasperating"[17] middle class "the very sight of whom sickens one;"[18] the "hawkers of universal suffrage and their astonishing knack for treason;"[19] young people "who only give their support to individual endeavours;"[20] college students obsessed with their "silky mustaches,"[21] "the pleats in their pants,"[22] "girlfriends"[23] and "sports;"[24] "yesterday's convent girls" who parade through the streets, "emptying their tankards and leaving lipstick-stained cigarette butts in the ashtrays."[25] Everyone was falling victim to the same fallacious reasoning: "If the only way to achieve the easy life is to trample over the interests of my nation, then so be it."[26]

The Jeune-Canada movement

L'Action nationale cheered when the Jeune-Canada movement began, demonstrating its active support by publishing the group's manifesto.[27] Over the next few years it welcomed their written contributions and reports of the group's events.[28] Le Devoir was similarly supportive, faithfully publishing accounts of every one of the group's meetings.[29] Furthermore, "the Jeune-Canada made a habit of submitting the texts of their speeches to a group of advisors consisting of Louis Dupire, Omer Héroux, Georges Pelletier, Papin Archambault of l'Ecole sociale populaire and Canon Groulx."[30] Le Devoir also printed 3000 copies of Jeune-Canada pamphlets in Montreal.[31]

Jeune-Canada was founded when four young men, including André Laurendeau and Pierre Dansereau, decided to protest the appointment of English-speaking civil servants to the Montreal Customs Office and the federal Department of Revenue, and the lack of French technical staff at the Imperial Conference of 1932 held in Ottawa. One autumn day, the four young men asked Groulx to suggest an effective course of action. Groulx replied, "Publish a manifesto denouncing the shame and abuse in which we're wallowing. Try to strike your young friends and compatriots where you suspect they're the most vulnerable."[32]

A movement was born. On 19 December 1932, a group of young people organized a public meeting in the Gesù meeting hall during which they launched their manifesto. In it, they denounced the unilingualism of certain federal government documents and of printed money. These blows to French Canada were all the more painful, as Groulx pointed out, because "the French Canadian nation is a pure race without a trace of crossbreeding."[33]

Echoing Groulx's belief that French Canadians are a chosen people, Thuribe Belzile predicts that the French Canadian nation, "issuing forth beneath the shadow of the cross, would be blessed by God."[34] The United States of America—literally Satan incarnate—served as a perfect foil for a homogeneous and vigorous Catholic French Canada:

[They are] worn down by forces they could never master and by weaknesses which will only worsen with time: different races and nations living within the same State (Blacks and Chinese, Germans, Italians, Jews, Irish, French and the like); cancerous growths (atheism, widespread materialism and its repercussions of divorce, family breakdown, and the primacy of money or, more correctly, of credit).[35]

In the French original of the above quotation, the word "faisceau" describes what is required to master this chaos, a uniting of forces, a single blinding beam, and it is not pure chance that the French "faisceau" and its Italian equivalent constitute the etymological root of the term "Fascism."[36]

Was French Canada really any better than the United States? Had not its population also been seduced by the superficial glitter of society's evils? André Laurendeau launched a vitriolic attack against an élite composed of "traitors, except for a handful of exceptions." They were, in his words, "a bunch of rootless egotists, exotic plants and dried fruits, cynics and idiots" groaning under the "yoke of individualism and servility."[37]

The ordinary masses hardly fared any better, according to Laurendeau. They invariably elected inept representatives and had an "obsession for things English," even though they "were obviously growing poorer while foreigners prospered. They rant against the Jew while lining his pockets." The greatest proof of the people's treason was that "Montreal has a Catholic school commission and a Protestant one. The city does not have a French Canadian school commission and Mr Victor Doré thus forbids education of a truly national nature."[38] The Catholic school commission, it appears, was not considered French Canadian because it did not offer a truly national education. Neither language nor religion were the defining characteristics of the "true" French Canadian. He or she seemed to be a part of an amorphous mass, guilty of a list of offences which similarly lacked form and substance.

Jeune-Canada dwelt at length in its pamphlets on the decay of the national ideal. In *Nos déficiences, conséquences, remèdes*,*[39] for example, Thuribe Belzile composed a list of his countrymen's weaknesses: intellectual sloth, lack of discipline, instability, wastefulness, absence of judgement, routine-minded-

---

* Our deficiencies, their consequences and remedies

ness, defeatism and a predisposition to use words instead of action.

Politicians betrayed the nation time and time again. "The provincial liberal government of Mr Alexandre Taschereau, which should be exercising control from above, is really under the rule of others. Did he not display servility of the worst sort by delegating responsibility for two legislative assembly committees to Israelites?"[40] After assisting Jews to enter the National Assembly, the Liberal government let Jews and Americans walk all over it by allowing "over-exploitation of our forests, our water power and, to top it all off, our very selves."[41]

Dollard Dansereau concludes that, by their very temperament, French Canadians are not suited to the parliamentary system which is "at odds with the Latin idealism we inherited from France." He deplores the effects of this system both here and elsewhere, claiming it "pushes us headlong into the kind of indifference, apathy and political materialism into which democracy lures people all over the world."[42]

Political partisanship was "an open wound on our forehead which would soon weaken and infect our entire body."[43] André Laurendeau describes it as "this germ which makes us ill,"[44] and elsewhere, "this putrid disease with which we have been infected for three quarters of a century."[45]

The city was the evil empire of the Other, a place where immorality and weakness flourished due to his very presence.

> It is clear that immorality is becoming ever more prevalent. The French and English are living side by side and constantly mingling. At the time of the secession, four fifths of our people lived in the countryside. Today, over 60 percent are city-dwellers, rubbing shoulders on a daily basis with the English, who, in Canada at least, have almost always lived in cities.[46]

In short, French Canadians were abasing themselves, "grovelling willingly at the feet of the English,"[47] and allowing themselves to be snugly "caged by the pagan civilization of the American dollar."[48]

The retail business had been wrested from the hands of innocent, non-profit-minded French Canadians by "chain stores, department stores and general stores," which happened to be 95-percent owned by "foreigners, Americans, English-speaking Canadians, Syrians and Jews." The French Canadian population did nothing but encourage these foreigners. "What weakness in our nature," Thuribe Belzile thunders, "permits us to shower privileges on these pillagers of our national resources? We have no right to undermine our nation in this way."[49]

French Canadians wrongly exercised this right in every economic sector, betraying their nation without batting an eyelid. In the men's clothing industry, for instance, there are only "two truly French Canadian companies," and as for other sectors, you just have to look around you to see the decay, Belzile observes. Montreal's cafés and restaurants belonged "to Greeks, Chinese or foreign chains," and the movie theatres devoured "the money we shell out every day, feeding the cash registers of foreigners who are, more often than not, Jewish."[50]

The mysterious, enemy forces were often referred to as "trusts," and were closely linked to the Other. "The trusts, which monopolize our people's money and bleed us dry, are managed by foreigners, Englishmen, Yankees and Jews."[51] They mesmerized the people, the politicians and, most of all, the newspapers into dancing to their tune.

> The enslavement of our newspapers by the trusts is one of the most repulsive scourges of our political life. It is certainly encouraging the spread of perfidious ideas which, in turn, encourages idolatry and political partisanship.[52]

Those who partook of "Jewish or American financing" or disguised themselves behind "institutions bearing venerable French Canadian names," were routinely threatened. "The day will come when names must be revealed, and we will post them up for all to see," Thuribe Belzile declares. The object was to discourage betrayals of this nature, and "most importantly, to stigmatize those who had the audacity to advertise and grow rich at our expense."[53]

If nothing is done to shake off "the yoke of the heartless, mostly foreign forces" which are crushing Quebec, "we will slip fatally into anarchy and revolution," Gérard Filion predicts. "This is exactly what happened in the Cuban revolution,"[54] he explains.

André Laurendeau concurs and elaborates. "The influence of trusts, or foreign capital, is ubiquitous. The trust rules Ottawa. It cracks the whip in Quebec..." One day the people would wake from their slumber and "do to the people running the trusts what the Germans did to the Jews. Throw them out. Too bad for them if they do not manage to emerge unscathed."[55]

Too bad indeed.

Le Devoir

On the occasion of Le Devoir's twenty-fifth anniversary, Canon Groulx paid it homage by publishing a flattering article in its pages. He points out that French Canada is indebted to the institution for its steady "nationalistic and Catholic loyalties" and its indefatigable "propagation of wholesome thought."[56] l'Action national also showers it with praise. "Born of the same creed, loyal to the same traditions and sharing the same goal, our modest magazine cannot help but applaud the achievements of this proud Montreal daily newspaper."[57] Le Devoir, in turn, expresses the esteem it feels for the Canon. Those who cultivate and propagate "wholesome" ideas, "are more needy of salubrious truths than ever before. Certain truths, uttered by wise and august lips, have already exerted a positive influence."[58]

Between the years 1929 and 1939, Le Devoir printed 41 articles and speeches by Lionel Groulx. It publicized in 60 first-page advertisements, often in the *Bloc-notes* column, courses offered by the Canon, books he published and patriotic demonstrations he organized. In 1935, Le Devoir published Groulx's books, *L'appel de la race* and *Au Cap Blomidon*, in comic-book form; Groulx referred to them as "picture novels." During that year, 27 articles or editorials also discussed the writings and activities of Groulx and his entourage.

Le Devoir also offered Groulx material resources: publication in brochure-form in the "Document" series, and sale through its mail-order service, of the following list of Groulx's speeches: *La déchéance incessante de notre classe moyenne*,*[59] *Nos positions*,**[60] *Le national et l'économique*.***[61] In the same series, 3 000 copies of the Dollard file[62] were printed and distributed. In 1932, *Au Cap Blomidon* was published, and the mail-order

*   The coming collapse of our middle class
**   Where we stand
***   Nationalism and Economics

service also made *Orientations*[63] available to readers. Omer Héroux congratulated himself on the fact that the first 3 000 copies sold out[64] and he had to print an additional 2 000 copies, bringing the grand total to 5000 barely three months after it first appeared.[65] The same service also distributed *L'Education nationale,*[66]* *Notre maître le passé,*** second edition[67], and *Directives.*[68]

Under the pseudonym of André Marois, Groulx published diatribes in Le Devoir denouncing the "canker" and "cancerous tumour"[69] on the state, an umbrella term denoting the provincial Liberal Party, the provincial police ("the militia of liberal Fascism, if common ground can be found linking the conglomeration of appetites and egos of a political herd and the ideals of the Fascist Party.") and the "brainless federal Conservative party" which, he writes, "is riddled with appalling egos, and has become a dumping ground for false partisans—blue in Ottawa, red in Quebec—and men from various financial clans all stuck together so they can betray their nation with greater ease." Groulx-Marois further denounces "the growing number of urban centres, the destruction wrought by capitalism and unemployment, and the vertiginous explosion of poverty."[70] Foreign control of the economy, he writes, has caused "a plague of unemployment which has spread among them [the French Canadians] as rapidly as a cancer. Young [French Canadian] people—technicians and engineers groomed in the best schools for future economic leadership—are languishing without jobs or else must leave the country to find work."[71] Omer Héroux openly supported the tenor of Groulx's editorials. "This is, indeed, food for thought!" he writes. "How many newspapers in the province would dare to publish a letter attacking both the left and the right with such impartiality, and posing so many serious questions?"[72]

Le Devoir and Groulx both raised the spectre of absolute independence which would somehow remain above reproach with regards to political parties.[73] Their ideological similarity did not end

---

*   National education
**   History is our Master

there. "As Catholics living among 100 million Protestants and materialists, we alone are privileged to have access to the truth, to the words of life eternal."[74] The entire North American continent conspired against the continued existence of French Canada, chants Le Devoir, which was certainly as dedicated a catechumen as either l'Action nationale or Jeune-Canada.

> It is impossible not to worry when one thinks of current trends of thought in North America, where a handful of Catholics are surrounded by hordes of people infected with materialistic greed and heresy, where morals are sliding back to pagan times and where falsehoods are daily printed in newspapers and books distributed by the millions.[75]

The degeneration of the middle class, accompanied by social problems of incalculable proportions, greatly worried the newspaper which claims the change occurred "before our very eyes without most of us even realizing what was happening."[76] Groulx was to be thanked for having shed light on the issue.

Omer Héroux takes frequent potshots at democracy, which "all too often leads to political partisanship, and in extreme cases resulted in the tyranny of the majority. Death to political partisanship!"[77] Party loyalty is "detestable and harmful, dividing French Canadians and turning them against each other."[78] In the same vein, Albert Rioux castigates the performance of governments which seem unaware of the fundamental fact "that their ancestors discovered, colonized and nurtured the better part of America with their sweat and blood. As the descendants of pioneers, our roots are more deeply embedded in this country than anyone else's. Do our elected representatives pay sufficient heed to this fact?" No indeed, Rioux replies, citing Groulx as an authority.

> 'I cannot understand why,' Groulx observed, 'the 2 300 000 French Canadians living in Quebec who have ruled the province for 300 years as well as all the province's big business, financial institutions, large-scale manufacturers, insurance companies, water power, forests and mines are owned by a minority of 300 000 people.'[79]

Did this minority of 300 000 people reside in the province? Did they constitute the elusive "international capital?" Who were they?

Omer Héroux elaborates on the theme of the Other's achievements in an editorial discussing a certain issue of l'Action nationale. The similarity with Groulx's writing and that of his ideological disciples is striking. He thanks Groulx for recalling the "brutal fact," that "our group is one of the most threatened worldwide in terms of the preservation of its own identity." If it is true that a century ago North America constituted a "separate entity" from French Canada:

> Today, we are in constant, immediate contact with it. Protestant or materialistic English-language newspapers and magazines have infiltrated and bogged our country down. It is the same story with the theatre and, to an even greater extent, with radio. We are under siege from all sides.[80]

The city greatly exacerbated the danger, which "had become predominantly urban," of modern heresy. By migrating to the city, French Canadians "lost a good part of their natural means of defence and found themselves confronted with unprecedented problems of great magnitude. The fact that foreign influences are particularly strong in some of our larger cities adds to the gravity of the situation."[81]

This perilous situation elicits the following heartfelt cry from Omer Héroux. "The Iroquois of today live in the cities!"[82] Dollard had come to symbolize, more strongly than ever before, "the eternal battle which rages, in various guises, in and around us."[83] Elsewhere he writes, "The eternal Iroquois symbolizes those elements around us and, more importantly, within us which diminish and weaken our worth, and our capacity to act."[84] Héroux predictably concludes, "We are realizing that the list of enemies against whom we must continually fight is regrettably long. All too often the Iroquois resides within us."[85]

Héroux makes it clear that the hostile Other dwells right inside the Traitor. Groulx, the man who originally coined the terms Traitor and Other, never stated the case so succinctly.

Mentions of Groulx in l'Action nationale are fewer in number and more discreet than those in Le Devoir, which reproduced in its entirety Groulx's plan of action for the new magazine[86], and whose mail-order service solicited subscriptions.[87] In the Blocnotes column, Omer Héroux drew attention to the magazine's first[88] and third[89] anniversaries, and celebrated Mr Harry Bernard's (the magazine's editor) recovery from ill-health[90] as well as the appointment of Mr André Laurendeau to the editorial board.[91]

Le Devoir lavished still more generosity on the Jeune-Canada. It announced their meetings on 11 occasions and, between the years 1932 and 1938, printed 39 articles furnished by the group. Between December 1932 and 23 December 1935, it published 25 pieces of varying length praising the group's activities and ideological stances. It also published the group's pamphlets and promised its "wholehearted" and willing assistance.[92]

On the day that Jeune-Canada held its inaugural public meeting, Omer Héroux cheers "the existence of a group of young people who take national interests seriously."[93] The following morning he returns to the subject. "[The Jeune-Canada's manifesto] was signed by almost 500 young people. In a spirit of brotherhood appropriate to a national movement, names that are known in the most diverse circles find themselves together. This is no partisan or clan undertaking."[94]

Placing the nation ahead of party interests was of paramount importance. Of the Jeune-Canada's Dollard Dansereau, Le Devoir writes, "he [Dansereau] so clearly exposed the stupidity of the two-party system and its incompatibility with the logical, pragmatic Latin temperament. It is pure idiocy to create an opposition whose only purpose is to block the initiatives of our elected representatives."[95]

The Jeune-Canada's creation could hardly have been more timely, given "how far we have sunk into moral decadence, political tomfoolery and spinelessness."[96] After quoting Pierre Dansereau in an editorial piece, Omer Héroux writes, "We will not be able to cleanse society with rosewater. If it takes vitriol to save ourselves from the viruses of speculation and trusts, then this is what we must use." He concludes that, "When it comes to the province's well-being, vitriol is a better option than gangrene."[97]

As Albert Rioux writes, "[Groulx] knows that God gave nations the capacity to cure themselves."[98] Wounds could always be cauterized.

Notes

1. "Réponse à quelques fols.," *Action nationale*, editorial, (March 1938).

2. Wilfrid Guérin:" La XIième Semaine sociale du Canada," *Action nationale*, (January 1933), p. 44.

3. "Le péril communiste.," *Action nationale*, editorial, (October 1934); "Le régime capitaliste.," *Action nationale*, editorial, (April 1933).

4. Eugène L'Heureux: "La dictature économique dans la province de Québec.," *Action nationale*, (January 1933), p. 67.

5. Paul Leblanc: "Problèmes gaspésiens.," *Action nationale*, (February 1938), p. 133. Les dictateurs économiques n'ont pas fini "...d'immoler le peuple sur l'autel du veau d'or" Adrien Gratton: "Avant que ne vienne le Grand soir.," *Action nationale*, (March 1938), p. 198.

6. Hermas Bastien: "Corporatisme et liberté." , *Action nationale*, (April 1938), pp. 307-308.

7. *Ibid.*

8. François-Albert Angers:"La plaie de notre siècle.," *Action nationale*, (September 1939), p. 64.

9. Guy Frégault: "Pour un ordre laurentien.," *Action nationale*, (March 1937), p. 148.

10. Roger Duhamel: "Abattus? Jamais!," *Action nationale*, (January 1938), p. 56.

11. "Guerre civile.," *Action nationale*, editorial, (September 1935), p. 3; Arthur Laurendeau: "La situation est-elle acceptable?," *Action nationale*, (February 1937), p. 68-80.

12. *Ibid.*, p. 4.

13. *Ibid.*, p. 3.

14. Roger Duhamel: "Chroniques.," *Action nationale*, (September 1938) p. 58.

15. Anatole Vanier: "Politique extérieure.," *Action nationale*, (February 1937), p. 99.

16. Arthur Laurendeau: "L'Education nationale.," *Action nationale*, (May 1934), p. 277.

17. Guy Frégault: "Où est la Révolution?," *Action nationale*, (February 1937), p. 86.

18. *Ibid.*

19. Guy Frégault: "Pour un ordre laurentien.," *Action nationale*, (March 1937), p. 149.

20. Paul Dumas: "En marge d'un beau livre.," *Action nationale*, (November 1935), p. 186.

21. *Ibid.*, p. 186.

22. *Ibid.*, p. 187.

23. *Ibid.*

24. *Ibid.*

25. *Ibid.*

26. *Ibid.*, p. 188. On the many acts of treason committed by French Canadians: Paul Gouin: "Refrancisons la province.," *Action nationale*, (April 1933), pp. 195-205; "La vie courante.," *Action nationale*, (May 1933), p. 310.

27. "Les jeunes s'en mêlent.," *Action nationale*, (February 1933), pp. 117-120.

28. Among others: Pierre Dansereau: "Jeune-Canada.," *Action nationale*, (May 1933), pp. 267-274; Arthur Laurendeau: "Les Jeune-Canada à Carillon.," *Action nationale*, (June 1933), pp. 357-360; Jacques Brassier (pseudonym of Lionel Groulx): "Pour qu'on vive...Les Jeune-Canada et l'éducation nationale.," *Action nationale*, (November 1934), pp. 241-247; Lionel Groulx: "Les échos d'une campagne.," *Ac-*

tion nationale, (January 1935), pp. 44-56; Arthur Laurendeau: "Ce que dit la jeunesse." *Action nationale*, (February 1935), p. 125-128; André Laurendeau: "Pour mettre dans l'âme de la jeunesse à la place du culte de l'esprit de parti. Extrait du dernier des Jeune-Canada: André Laurendeau: Notre nationalisme.," *Action nationale*, (December 1935), p. 262; André Laurendeau: "Explicitation.," *Action nationale*, (February 1936), pp. 120-122; Thuribe Belzile: "La ruralisation de l'école rurale.," *Action nationale*, (January 1938), pp. 11-18; Dostaler O'Leary: "Directives.," *Action nationale*, (January 1938), pp. 70-78; Roger Duhamel: "Saint-Henri, morne plaine...," *Action nationale*, (February 1938), pp. 159-162.

29. Lucienne Fortin: *Les Jeune-Canada*. Dans: Fernand Dumont, Jean-Paul Montminy, Jean Hamelin: *Les idéologies au Canada français*, p. 218.

30. *Ibid.*, p. 229.

31. *Ibid.*, p. 217.

32. Lionel Groulx: *Mémoires*, Montréal, Fides, 1974, tome 3, p. 275.

33. Paul Dumas: *Nos raisons d'être fiers*, Tracts Jeune-Canada no.1, Montréal, November 1934, no. 1, pp. 14-15; *Ibid.*, pp. 26-27; For a faithful rehashing of Groulx's stereotypes of New France, cf.: Gérard Filion: *Les Canadiens français sous l'ancien régime*, dans: *Sur les pas de Cartier*, Les Cahiers des Jeune-Canada II, Montréal, 1934, p. 11-27.

34. Thuribe Belzile: *Sur les pas de Cartier*. dans: *Sur les pas de Cartier*, Montréal, Les Cahiers des Jeune-Canada, 1934, II, p. 6.

35. André Laurendeau: *Notre nationalisme*, p. 50.

36. "In fact, the very word Fascism* well translates the nature of this historical phenomenon: a convergence of *many different forces* , **whose unity, even whose definition comes from this fait accompli.**"

37. André Laurendeau: *ibid.*, p. 34.

38. *Ibid.*, pp. 34-35; "La trahison est partout..." Gilbert Manseau: *Notion du fait national*, dans: *Le Canadien français, ses droits, son idéal*, Tracts Jeune-Canada, no. 3, Montréal, April 1935, p. 4.

39. Thuribe Belzile: *Nos déficiences, conséquences, remèdes*, Tracts Jeune-Canada, no.4, Montréal, May 1935, p. 6 à p. 19.

40. Thuribe Belzile: *Vue d'ensemble de notre vie nationale*, dans Les Jeune-Canada: *Qui sauvera Québec?*, p.43.

41. Dollard Dansereau: *Les Canadiens français et la Confédération*, dans: *Sur les pas de Cartier*, pp. 50-51; "Les politiciens, vampires du sang du peuple." René Monette: *Commerce juif et commerce canadien-français*, dans: Politiciens et Juifs, p. 41.

42. Dollard Dansereau: *Ibid.*, p. 51.

43. Thuribe Belzile: *op. cit..*, p.20.

44. "...ce triste microbe nous a rendus malades, c'est la politique de parti ou mieux, la triste politicaillerie de nos hommes publics, bleus ou rouges." André

---

* Etymologically, from "faisceau," the gathering of rifles into a bundle, or the fasces of the lictor in ancient Rome. Henri Michel: *Les fascismes*, Paris, Presses Universitaires de France, 1983, p. 3. (Coll. "Que sais-je?").

Laurendeau: *Partisannerie politique*, dans: *Politiciens et Juifs*, Les Cahiers des Jeune-Canada, I, Montréal, 1933, p. 55.

45. *Ibid.*, p. 58.

46. Jean-Marie Fortin: *Notre position au Canada*, Tracts Jeune-Canada, no.6, Montréal, March 1936, pp. 16-17.

47. *Ibid.*, p. 16.

48. Thuribe Belzile: *Sur les pas de Cartier*, dans: *Sur les pas de Cartier*, p. 8

49. Thuribe Belzile: *op. cit.*, p. 27; Gilbert Manseau: *op. cit.*, p. 8

50. Thuribe Belzile: *Vue d'ensemble de notre vie nationale*, dans: *Qui sauvera Québec?*, p. 43.

51. Thuribe Belzile: "Les conséquences de la dictature." , *Le Devoir*, 11 November 1932, p. 1.

52. Gérard Filion: "Cartels et Trusts," *Le Devoir*, 7 November 1933, p. 2.

53. Thuribe Belzile: *Vue d'ensemble de notre vie nationale*, dans: *Qui sauvera Québec*, p. 42.

54. Gérard Filion: op. cit.

55. André Laurendeau: "Le trust, danger social et national.," *Le Devoir*, 14 November 1933, p. 2.

56. Lionel Groulx: "Une lettre de M. l'abbé Groulx.," *Le Devoir*, 18 January 1930, p. 2.

57. *Action nationale*, (January 1935), p. 124.

58. Omer Héroux: "Des pages qui feront réfléchir.," *Le Devoir*, 23 April 1934, p. 1, editorial.

59. Lionel Groulx: La déchéance incessante de notre classe moyenne, Montréal, Le Devoir, 1931. (Coll."Le Document")

60. Omer Héroux: "Pour qu'on pense.," *Le Devoir*, 22 March 1935, p. 1, Bloc-notes.

61. Omer Héroux: "Bonne nouvelle.," Le Devoir, 3 March 1936, p. 1.

62. Omer Héroux: "Dollard," *Le Devoir*, 26 May 1932, p. 1.

63. Annonce publicitaire, *Le Devoir*, 8 October 1935, p. 1., 18 August 1936, p. 3.

64. Omer Héroux: "Signe des temps.," *Le Devoir*, 9 January 1936, p. 1.

65. Annonce publicitaire, *Le Devoir*, 10 January 1936, p. 3.

66. Clarence Hogue: "Pour les éducateurs et les parents.," *Le Devoir*, 9 November 1935, p. 10.

67. Annonce publicitaire, *Le Devoir*, 26 May 1937, p. 3.

68. Annonce publicitaire, *Le Devoir*, 3 January 1938, p. 6.

69. André Marois(pseudonym of Lionel Groulx): "Réforme d'un parti ou réforme d'une politique.," *Le Devoir*, 20 September 1932, p. 1.

70. André Marois(pseudonym of Lionel Groulx): "Réforme d'un parti ou réforme d'une politique" *Le Devoir*, 21 September 1932, p. 1.

71. *Ibid.*

72. Omer Héroux: "La lettre d'André Marois.," *Le Devoir*, 22 September 1932, p. 1.

73. *Ibid.*

74. Albert Rioux: "Orientations. En lisant le dernier livre de M. l'abbé Groulx.," *Le Devoir*, 3 December 1935, p. 1, editorial.

75. Omer Héroux: "Le Père Doncœur et les jeunes.," *Le Devoir*, 20 April 1934, p. 1, editorial.

76. Omer Héroux: "Des faits qui feront réfléchir.," *Le Devoir*, 23 April 1934, p. 1, editorial; Omer Héroux: "Bons signes.," *Le Devoir*, 28 December 1931, p. 1, editorial; Omer Héroux: "Deux hommages.," *Le Devoir*, 21 April 1933, p. 1; Omer Héroux: "Lisez ce livre!," *Le Devoir*, 25 October 1935, p. 1, editorial; Albert Rioux:"Orientations.," *Le Devoir*, 3 December 1935, p. 1, editorial.

77. Omer Héroux: "L'esprit de parti.," *Le Devoir*, 15 June 1938, p. 1; Omer Héroux: "M. Ashley W. Cooper nous donne de dures mais salutaires leçons." *Le Devoir*, 10 June 1938, p. 1, editorial; 78. Omer Héroux: "Le sursaut," *Le Devoir*, 12 April 1933, p. 1.

79. Albert Rioux: "Orientations.," *Le Devoir*, 3 December 1935, p. 1, editorial; Georges Pelletier: "Ploutocratie.," *Le Devoir*, 23 July 1934, p. 1.

80. Omer Héroux: "De quoi faire réfléchir.," *Le Devoir*, 22 September 1934, p. 1, editorial.

81. *Ibid*

82. Omer Héroux: "Les Iroquois, c'est là qu'ils sont maintenant!," *Le Devoir*, 24 May 1938, p. 1, editorial.

83. *Ibid.*

84. *Ibid.*

85. *Ibid.* Sur l'apologie de Dollard des Ormeaux: Omer Héroux: "Dollard.," *Le Devoir*, 26 May 1932, p. 1; Lucien Desbiens: "La fête de Dollard.," *Le Devoir*, 23 May 1934, p. 1; Omer Héroux: "La fête de Dollard.," *Le Devoir*, 24 May 1939, p. 1.

86. *Le Devoir*, 3 January 1933, p. 2.

87. *Ibid.*

88. Omer Héroux: "Etude nécessaire," *Le Devoir*, 20 December 1933, p. 1.

89. Omer Héroux: "L'Action nationale.," *Le Devoir*, 7 January 1935, p. 1.

90. Omer Héroux: "M. Harry Bernard.," *Le Devoir*, 21 June 1934, p. 1.

91. Omer Héroux: "M. André Laurendeau.," *Le Devoir*, 8 September 1937, p. 1.

92. *Ibid.*

93. Omer Héroux: "Bravo!," *Le Devoir*, 19 December 1932, p. 1, editorial

94. Omer Héroux: "Continuez!," *Le Devoir*, 20 December 1932, p. 1, editorial.

95. Georges Pelletier: "L'assemblée d'hier.," *Le Devoir*, 23 January 1934, p. 1; "They first gave us a show which aroused a most hearty reaction: young men, who could have been distracted by so many things, disciplined themselves to fathom the most profound questions, to investigate them and find solutions outside of any partisanship." Omer Héroux: "Au Monument National.," *Le Devoir*, 3 December 1934, p. 1.

96. Paul Anger: "Les Jeune-Canada.," *Le Devoir*, 14 November 1933, p. 1.

97. Omer Héroux: "M. Taschereau et les Jeune-Canada.," *Le Devoir*, 18 December 1933, p. 1, editorial.

98. Albert Rioux: "Orientations. En lisant le dernier livre de M. l'abbé Groulx.," *Le Devoir*, 3 December 1935, p. 1, editorial.

7

GOLDBERG'S NOSE

"People fear their own likeness; that is the source of racism."

—Jean-Pierre Dupuy

It soon became clear that for Lionel Groulx and his followers, "Other" was synonymous with "Jew." The Jew's physical distinctiveness was for them an indelible "mark;" it was impossible for them to miss him, with his pendulous, crooked nose and twisted fingers, his circumcision and repulsive odour. Certain of the jew's most salient personality traits were manifested in his physiognomy. They thought his nose, for instance, suggestive of criminal tendencies.

The second "mark" distinguishing the Jew from other people was his surname. Given that Jews possessed such a panoply of clues as to their identity it should have been easy to pick them out, but this did not appear to be the case. Certain journalists from Le Devoir fearfully noted the way Jews adopted French names and mastered the French language; they regarded this as fraud and usurpation. Identifying the Jew was becoming increasingly difficult; this was in fact the biggest cause of consternation. A distinction—whether it was arbitrary, grotesque, patronymical or caricatured—had to be maintained at all costs. On the other hand, since no one seemed to know exactly what a French Canadian was, there was always definition-by-exclusion: Jews were *not* French Canadians.

ACCORDING TO LE DEVOIR, two things distinguished Jews from other members of society. First of all, there were certain idiosyncratic physical traits. In response to a Russian Jew who asserted that "the Jews themselves are disappearing, merging with the masses to the point that young people can no longer say whether they are Russian or Jewish,"[1] Le Devoir, which had become an expert on the matter, replies, "Nevertheless, there are physical signs."[2]

The most obvious sign was the Jew's nose which, according to classic anti-Semitic iconography, was crooked. "The Dutch people we are thinking of bringing over to settle in Canada might turn out to have crooked noses and hail from Hamburg."[3] And did not Paul Anger meet "a certain Abraham, whose exceedingly long nose got lost in his beard, thus bearing witness to his ethnic origins?"[4] Anger warns French Canadians travelling to the United States, "If by chance you end up in a ritzy American hotel, you will be infuriated by the number of crooked-nosed people milling about whose fingers are heavily, or at least visibly, covered with rings."[5]

The shape of a nose could determine criminality. "All these shady deals in which the crooked noses are involved demonstrate that the bulk of police-work consists in disciplining foreigners." The practical-minded journalist suggests a handy solution to the problem:

> Why don't these people pay the costs themselves? Every Oriental immigrant ought to pay a police tax of $100 upon entering the country. Of course, exclusion would be even more practical and less costly.[6]

And was it not true that "certain financial transactions were just as crooked as the noses of the men orchestrating them?"[7] As Le Devoir observes on the subject of names and noses, "Why bother to change your name when you cannot change your nose?"[8]

If the truth be told, the Jew's entire face betrayed him. "Look carefully at the photograph of last Saturday's anti-Fascist demonstrators with their Yid features, carrying signs saying 'Down with Fascism'. It is clear that people from around here are responsible."[9]

Le Grincheux, writing in Le Devoir, was as interested in Jews' feet "which, by some genetic fault, turn out at right angles"[10] and their circumcised penises—as if circumcision was a trait unique to Jews—as he was in their crooked noses. "All this praise Israel has been receiving of late practically makes one want to rush out and get circumcised."[11] "People have said that Hitler was Jewish. It could be true. He did, after all, perfect circumcision."[12] Circumcision, whose secondary meaning is purification, became the butt of many puns."The German Jews, whom the Nazis recently stripped of citizenship, have been cut down to size. Of course, they've already been cut before."[13] The anonymous writer obviously found nothing wrong with this puerile brand of humour.

The Jew also had a distinctive body odour. "The nose does not make the Jew," Pamphile writes, seeming to retract earlier statements, "but it often smells him."[14] The odour was garlic. Writing about a man named Aisenbud who supported the entry of

Jewish refugees into Canada, Le Grincheux observes, "The good Aisenbud smells a little too much of garlic. Baptiste is worried and doesn't intend to suffocate."[15] Even Jews' names apparently stank of garlic. "A New York judge, who does not happen to be Jewish like all the others who spring to mind, has a name which reeks of garlic: Rudich."[16] Sometimes Jews emitted a combination of smells: garlic, caviar and vodka. "Ivan Issemmocski. Does not this name carry a distinct odour of caviar, garlic and vodka?"[17]

Topping off this very particular list was the Jew's lack of hygiene. Even though Jews now liked bathing, after having been forced into the habit by the Nuremberg laws,[18] they still lived in flea-ridden ghettos so it actually did them little good. "Saint Lawrence Boulevard is described as 'very French,' words that boggle the minds of both Jews and Canadians. This may give some idea of the value of the information [contained in a certain tourist guide], but foreigners should be aware that the squalor of the ghetto will spread and affect us."[19]

Filthy, stinking and residing in their flea-ridden ghettos, Jews could not help but soil the public places they frequented.

> It remains to be seen what effect these signs will have on the Jews in Jeanne Mance Park, where more greasy garbage is in evidence than grass. To be fair, I am told that Jews treat Lafontaine Park with the same disregard, and that they treat English Canadians in the west island in exactly the same manner as they treat French Canadians in Montreal's east end.[20]

Other parks fared no better. Mount Royal, for instance, "two or three years ago, was a splendid retreat. It allowed one to forget the city's ugliness and dirt, emerging out of the polluted waters like a paradisiacal island. Today, it lies submerged."[21] Who is responsible for this desecration?" Orientals," who clutter the mountain in great numbers.

> Everywhere you look—in alleys and in clearings—you will find greasy heads, torsos shamelessly bared, exposing themselves to the sun's rays, crooked noses and sagging chests. The Jewish race may have certain redeeming social qualities, but unfortunately cleanliness is not among them.[22]

The stereotype of the Jew propagated by Le Devoir was so crude, it is not surprising that the newspaper was occasionally forced to admit exceptions to the rule. "For a Hebrew (sic), Sir

Herbert Samuel does not have many Semitic traits."[23] It also occasionally confessed its confusion and inability to determine ethnicity on the basis of conflicting physical signs. "The binding of two biblical names, Mardochée and Ézechiel, leads one to suspect that the bearer of these names is Jewish. But Mr Mordecai Ézekiel's physical appearance is not even the slightest bit Semitic." The author is more inclined to think that Mr Ézekiel is the "offspring of a venerable puritan family."[24]

This must have greatly reassured readers. Mr Samuel Untermeyer, on the other hand, was not quite so lucky. "There is a successful lawyer living in New York. His name is Samuel Untermeyer so, unlike most Americans, he probably does not claim to have descended from those who crossed the ocean on the Mayflower."[25]

Surnames were the second indelible sign of the Jew, in the opinion of certain Le Devoir journalists. "According to Doctor Albert Hyman—if he is not Jewish then Einstein is Scottish[26]—Jewish quacks cannot accept a smaller remuneration." Similar remarks are made about Mrs Muriel Jacobson, "whose name betrays its ethnic or racial roots,"[27] "another individual with a typically Yid name"[28] and Algernon O'Stifsky, "whose name is half-Irish, half-Polish, and gives off a strong, alliaceous Jewish stench."[29]

Like the nose, names also suggested criminality. Of a woman involved in a financial scandal in France, Georges Pelletier writes, "The instigator of the whole affair is Mrs Hanau. Her ex-husband—for she is a divorcee—is Jewish like she is, with a name commonly associated with jailhouses...This certainly does little to weaken anti-Jewish sentiment in Paris or anywhere else."[30] How could one avoid being an anti-semite when Jews were dirty, smelly, circumcised foreigners who harboured criminal tendencies?

Two weeks later, Georges Pelletier again stresses the involvement "of several foreigners" in the scandal, and names them, as if this in itself will prove their unfamiliar origins. Meanwhile, in a story involving three Montreal brothers who received thousands of dollars' worth of stolen merchandise, and some New Yorkers implicated in a huge fraud operation, Le Grincheux simply writes, "the names of the accused smell strongly of garlic and Galicia. What a coincidence."[32]

The game of peering behind a criminal's name to find the hidden Jew seems never to have tired Le Grincheux. He unmasks "Chapereau, Mrs Edgar Lauer, Jack Benny, Paul Cheyskens," all of whom were implicated in international fraud. "Chapereau claims to be Nicaraguan, but his name—which is really Shapiro—gives him away. Mrs Lauer's Israelitic origins...are obvious, as are Cheyskens's, and Jack Benny absolutely reeks of garlic." Then Le Grincheux starts in on the special tax theme." If we have to keep importing Jews, the least we can do is insist they pay for the increases in police costs caused by their presence."[33]

While on the one hand a Jewish surname indicated criminal tendencies, it did not, on the other hand, suggest that one was Canadian. "Bronfman...Bronfman...it is amazing how un-Canadian this name sounds."[34] "The Musicas and Kantors, the Sam Reichbachs and Costers are all local names. It goes without saying that some of them are Canadian; but how did they become Canadians and in what year?"[35] Prosper created the generic Jewish surname "Machinsky,"[36] much like in Germany from 1938 onward, Jewish men were called Israel, and Jewish women, Sarah. "Following the Fuhrer's decree, there were an estimated 500 000 Israels and an equal number of Sarahs. One could liken it to the Scottish 'Mc' or the Irish 'O'."[37]

None of these formulas provided a foolproof method for identifying a Jew. "According to recent statistics, there are 126 196 Jews living in Canada. This does not take into consideration the Whites, Rosses and Smiths whose origins are not Anglo-Saxon. Of these, there are several thousand."[38]

Perhaps Le Devoir made such a fuss about names because the identification of physical traits was so unreliable. The fact that Jewish Canadians could legally alter their patronymics made certain journalists tremble with fear. Something was not right in the racial cosmogony. Two editorials violently denounced the way Harold Arnold Goldberg, Lilian Goldberg, Herman Goldberg and Max Goldberg changed their surnames to Gordon. Would it become possible in Quebec for "one hundred thousand people of both Christian and Jewish origin," by means of a legal sleight of hand, "to rid themselves of their names and previous personalities, and deck themselves out in completely new

skins?" Changing one's name was akin to existential trans-
mogrification. "Given that there is no legal difference between a
first and a tenth name-change, could these same individuals use
this elementary procedure to evolve successively from Goldberg
to Gordon to Taschereau to Duplessis to Carroll to Bennett and
Dandurand?"[39]

Names were so closely tied to identity that legally altering
them entailed a personality change and quasi-genetic mutation.
The changes were so profound that they were best described
using biological terms. Ironically, Le Devoir journalists were not
so much frightened by the differences distinguishing Jews from
French Canadians as by the fact that they would no longer be
able to identify Jews. It was the lack of differentiation rather
than the differences (no matter how grotesque their portrayal)
which rankled.

Le Devoir considered the risks serious enough to organize "a
public order campaign"[40] to stop people from changing their
names. During this campaign, Omer Héroux denounced
Schwarzes and Smilovitches who tried to turn themselves into
Swards and Smileys,[41] and the Horowitz family who wanted to
adopt Harvey as their patronymic.[42]

Pierre Kiroul devoted a column to a merchant named Jacques
Saint-Pierre who lived in a small town on the lower Saint
Lawrence River." His real name was Jacob Rocksterg. He cut
Rocksterg in half and pulled Saint from Sterg, Pierre from Rock.
Jacques Saint-Pierre was a direct translation of Jacob Rock-
sterg."[43]

Name changing began to seem like an epidemic. "In the good
city of Montreal, we can no longer keep track of the number of
Lévys, Bercovitches, Tannenbaums and Cohens who have
changed themselves into Gordons, Browns, Murphys, and even
Labertés."[44]

The most deplorable consequences of the practice were com-
mercial, because Jewish store-owners could dupe their clients.
Paul Anger tried to dispel the illusions of naive Montrealers who
applauded the proliferation of French Canadian businesses along
Ste. Catherine Street. Do not be fooled, he warns. "French
Canadian places of business should really be called Oriental."
They are not a sign of progress, he goes on, but rather of "regres-

sion," as the following anecdote reveals. A shopkeeper, a "Levan-tin, who had taken a venerable French Canadian name, one which 'figured prominently in the Church's history,' refused to allow a disgruntled client to return a piece of merchandise. The latter glared at him and let fly the following comment, 'That's what I get for trying to encourage French Canadians. From now on, I'll buy from the Jews.'"[45]

One reflective journalist remarks, "The Jews steal our names because they are worth something. They are the only thing we have left."[46] The root of the Jews' propensity for name-changing lay in their criminal nature. "Why should the ease with which Israelites change their names be so surprising? Surely there are precedents. Since the dawn of time, bandits have created alibis."[47]

Religious differences exacerbated the hostility. Certain jour-nalists at Le Devoir seemed pleased by the fact that French Canadians occasionally sported Scottish surnames. The dif-ference was that Scots were Christian.

> There are quite a few Scots in French Canada. In fact, certain families who are French Canadian to the marrow of their bones have last names harkening back to their ancestors in the hills of Scotland...Harvey is not the only example. How many Mac-Nichols, Murphys and MacDuffs around here are Scottish in any-thing but name?[48]

The author deplores the loss of "intimate contact" between the two groups and suggests that l'Association franco-écossaise be revived.

The only way to solve this very serious name-changing problem was to enact a law obliging "every immigrant doing business in Ca-nada to post his real name and that of his country of origin in a visible place in his establishment or business place, so that the pu-blic and his customers can know with whom they are dealing."[49]

In an article in l'Action nationale, Gratien Gélinas laid into Jews who learned French and spoke it fluently, and suggested people reject attempts made by certain Jewish citizens to in-tegrate. These attempts, he feared, were motivated solely by malice and treason. "Making your purchases at an English or Jewish shop is never patriotic—even if you do it in French. We should keep our business among ourselves. Without knowing it, we may even be acting unpatriotically."[50]

Gélinas dwelt for a while on the new form of treason he had just identified. "It has already been said that French Canadians must possess pride in themselves in order to demand the ubiquitous use of the French language...Throwing millions and millions of our dollars to foreigners who slyly claim to be of our stock can hardly be called pride."[51] At the head of this list of foreigners was the Jew.

> Are we managing to increase the use of French? The answer is yes, to the point that in a few years the Jews, who are cunning, will be fluent in our language and will thank our people for their services. The public will not know the difference. They will still be proud whether or not it is a Jew speaking to them in the language of Dollard des Ormeaux.[52]

Spelling mistakes on public billboards had a certain advantage, as long as they were made by Jews. "It is all right if Jewish shopkeepers massacre the French language. It simply allows us to ferret them out more easily. If our fellow French Canadians pick up the habit, however, I will not know what to do."[53]

Notes

1. Pamphile: Carnet d'un grincheux, *Le Devoir*, 7 September 1933, p. 1.

2. *Ibid*.

3. Pamphile: Carnet d'un grincheux, *Le Devoir*, 29 September 1933, p. 1.

4. Paul Anger: "Tribunaux comiques.," *Le Devoir*, 4 August 1933, p. 1.

5. Paul Anger: "L'avenir d'Israël.," *Le Devoir*, 4 November 1936, p. 1.

6. Pamphile: Carnet d'un grincheux, *Le Devoir*, 28 August 1934, p. 1.

7. Le Grincheux: Le carnet du grincheux, *Le Devoir*, 30 December 1938, p. 1.

8. Pamphile: Carnet d'un grincheux, *Le Devoir*, 28 February 1934, p. 1; Pamphile: Carnet d'un grincheux, *Le Devoir*, 21 March 1934, p. 1; E.B.: "Pourquoi ne pas se prendre pour la S.D.N.?," *Le Devoir*, 30 November 1937, p. 1.

9. Le Grincheux: Le carnet du grincheux, *Le Devoir*, 2 May 1938, p. 1.

10. "Trois Israélites.," *Le Devoir*, 8 September 1934, p. 1.

11. Pamphile: Carnet d'un grincheux, *Le Devoir*, 7 December 1933, p. 1.

12. Pamphile: Carnet d'un grincheux, *Le Devoir*, 23 December 1933, p. 1; Sur la circoncision: Pamphile: Carnet d'un grincheux, *Le Devoir*, 8 January 1934, p. 1; Pamphile: Carnet d'un grincheux, *Le Devoir*, 24 March 1934, p. 1; Louis Dupire: "L'ogre creuse sa tombe avec ses dents.," *Le Devoir*, 12 January 1931, p. 1; Nessus:"Le bill Bercovitch.," *Le Devoir*, 1 February 1932, p. 1.

13. Le Grincheux:Carnet d'un grincheux, *Le Devoir*, 18 September 1935, p. 1; Le Grincheux: Carnet d'un grincheux, *Le Devoir*, 24 March 1934, p. 1.

14. Pamphile: Carnet d'un grincheux, *Le Devoir*, 6 July 1933, p. 1.

15. Pamphile: Carnet d'un grincheux, *Le Devoir*, 6 June 1936, p. 1.

16. Paul Anger: "Avis à la police." *Le Devoir*, 9 May 1934, p. 1.

17. Nessus: "Mettez-y des dents.," *Le Devoir*, 5 February 1932, p. 1; Jean Labrye: "L'ail vainqueur.," *Le Devoir*, 11 March 1936, p. 1; The Jew also smells of onion: Le Grincheux: Le carnet du grincheux, *Le Devoir*, 24 November 1938, p. 1.

18. "The city of Nuremberg was obliged to decree obligatory baths for the Israelites, but then having discovered they actually began to *like* to wash, because everything changes, even the most marked racial mores, the civil authorities there today order the police: Get rid of the bath, they like it!" Paul Anger: "Quand Israël se baigne.," *Le Devoir*, 8 August 1933, p. 1.

19. Paul Anger: "Pauvre touriste!," *Le Devoir*, 19 June 1930, p. 1.

"On both sides of the former city hall, two other fountains, also dried up and in a state of dilapidation that would even disgust a Jew from the ghetto." Paul Anger: "Malpropreté municipale.," *Le Devoir*, 13 June 1934, p. 1.

20. Paul Anger: "En rentrant des États-Unis.," *Le Devoir*, 23 June 1937, p. 1.

21. Paul Anger: " Le Mont-Royal.," *Le Devoir*, 25 September 1931, p. 1.

22. *Ibid.*

23. Émile Benoist: "Sir Herbert Samuel.," *Le Devoir*, 8 August 1933, p. 1.

24. Émile Benoist: "M. Mordecai Ézekiel.," *Le Devoir*, 13 October 1933, p. 1.

25. Paul Anger: "Le droit fait vivre son homme.," *Le Devoir*, 14 April 1930, p. 1.

26. Paul Anger: "Quand on est mort, c'est pour peu de temps.," *Le Devoir*, 4 July 1933, p. 1.

27. .E.B.: "La propagande se poursuit.," *Le Devoir*, 24 October 1938, p. 1.

28. Paul Anger: "Americana.," *Le Devoir*, 13 August 1935, p. 1.

29. Paul Anger: "Le maire statufié.," *Le Devoir*, 5 March 1935, p. 1.

30. Georges Pelletier: "Scandale.," *Le Devoir*, 10 January 1929, p. 1.

31. Georges Pelletier: "Etrangers.," *Le Devoir*, 22 January 1929, p. 1; The name betrays the foreigner's state": A man "named Leo Kerwin and who mjst have, unless we are very mistaken, a marked Semitic profile." Paul Anger: "Extrêmes.," *Le Devoir*, 12 March 1935, p. 1; Pamphile: Carnet d'un grincheux, *Le Devoir*, 11 January 1934, p. 1; Pamphile: Carnet d'un grincheux, *Le Devoir*, 9 October 1934, p. 1; Pamphile: Carnet d'un grincheux, *Le Devoir*, 10 October 1934, p. 1; Le Grincheux: Le carnet du grincheux, *Le Devoir*, 7 January 1939, p. 1.

32. Le Grincheux: Le carnet du grincheux, *Le Devoir*, 14 June 1939, p. 1.

33. Le Grincheux: Le carnet du grincheux, *Le Devoir*, 10 January 1938, p. 1; Jean Labrye: "Parlez plus bas...," *Le Devoir*, 2 February 1939, p. 1; Le Grincheux: Le carnet du grincheux, *Le Devoir*, 2 February 1939, p. 1.

34. Le Grincheux: Carnet d'un grincheux, *Le Devoir*, 15 December 1934, p. 1.

35. Le Grincheux: Le carnet du grincheux, *Le Devoir*, 21 December 1938, p. 1; Pamphile: Carnet d'un grincheux, *Le Devoir*, 17 November 1933, p. 1.

36. Prosper:"Propos de palais.," *Le Devoir*, 23 January 1932, p. 1.

37. Le Grincheux: Le carnet du grincheux, *Le Devoir*, 20 August 1938, p. 1.

38. Pamphile: Carnet d'un grincheux, *Le Devoir*, 26 June 1933, p. 1; Le Grincheux: Carnet d'un grincheux, *Le Devoir*, 30 August 1935, p. 1; Omer Héroux: "Comme chez nous.," *Le Devoir*, 20 September 1935, p. 1.

39. Omer Héroux: "Suite de l'affaire Goldberg Gordon.," *Le Devoir*, 22 February 1934, p. 1; Omer Héroux: "Comment ces Goldberg se muèrent en Gordon," *Le Devoir*, 15 February 1934, p. 1.

40. Omer Héroux: "Ces changements de noms.," *Le Devoir*, 10 March 1933, p. 1.

41. Omer Héroux: "Témoignage.," *Le Devoir*, 12 March 1934, p. 1; Omer Héroux: "Ces changements de noms.," *Le Devoir*, 14 March 1934, p. 1; Omer Héroux: "Pourquoi MM. Schwartz et Smilovitz veulent changer de noms.," *Le Devoir*, 15 March 1934, p. 1; Omer Héroux: "Ces changements.," *Le Devoir*, 5 April 1934, p. 1.

42. Omer Héroux: "Un autre.," *Le Devoir*, 14 October 1937, p. 1. Omer Héroux is troubled: "If tomorrow morning, by the will of the provincial parliament Horowitz becomes Harvey, how many Harveys will be taken for Jews? It is obvious that it is better that everyone keep his own name."

43. Pierre Kiroul: "Un précurseur.," *Le Devoir*, 16 February 1934, p. 1. Sur les changements de noms: Georges Pelletier: "Leurs noms vrais.," *Le Devoir*, 6 May 1939, p. 1; Omer Héroux: "Pourquoi?," *Le Devoir*, 29 November 1939, p. 1.

44. Paul Anger: "Quand Murphy devient Lévy.," *Le Devoir*, 22 July 1937, p. 1

45. Paul Anger: "Quand tromper ne paye pas.," *Le Devoir*, 30 November 1936, p. 1; Paul Anger: "Gogoïsme.," *Le Devoir*, 18 April 1933, p. 1.

46. Pamphile: Carnet d'un grincheux, *Le Devoir*, 19 July 1934, p. 1.

47. Le Grincheux: Le carnet du grincheux, *Le Devoir*, 28 August 1937, p. 1. 48. E.B.: "Nos amis les Écossais.," *Le Devoir*, 1 December 1937, p. 1.

49. Paul Anger: "Les alias.," *Le Devoir*, 27 March 1934, p. 1; Georges Pelletier: "Abus d'hospitalité." *Le Devoir*, 27 March 1939, p. 1; *Ibid.*; Omer Héroux: "Il faut en finir avec cet abus!," *Le Devoir*, 1 March 1934, p. 1; Omer Héroux: "Comment on change de nom.," *Le Devoir*, 7 March 1934, p. 1; Georges Pelletier: "L'affaire Bethléem.," *Le Devoir*, 6 April 1934, p. 1.

50. Gratien Gélinas: "Du patriotisme, ça?," *Action nationale*, (May 1935), p. 292.

51. *Ibid.*, p. 293.

52. *Ibid.*, p. 294.

53. Maurice Huot: "Le français qu'on affiche.," *Le Devoir*, 24 July 1933, p. 1.

8

THE UNTOUCHABLES

Groulx and his followers thought that by his very nature, the Jew was incapable of assimilation. Set apart from others by race and religion, he remained a perpetual, hostile stranger. Anti-Judaism and anti-Semitism fed symbiotically off of each other, the former providing a foundation for the latter. Jews were hostile to Christendom. Lambert Closse preached this gospel, reminding readers that the Jews murdered Christ and would reap their just reward. "Furthermore, the Jewish people is damned to eternal exile. When they left their homeland, their hearts brimmed with hatred for Christ."[1] The Jew did not limit himself to violent hatred of Christianity, he was also the worst of the viruses attacking the national traditions of the French Canadian people.

The Jew was the driving force behind capitalism, and democracy's close friend—presumptuous, spineless, rotten, avaricious, foreign, a criminal, a mental patient, and at the same time a fomenter of social upheaval. Faced with such a formidable enemy, French Canada had no choice but to defend itself.

The situation was aggravated by rapid secularization—one of the most serious side effects of the 20th century—and by the fact that now Jews were being blamed for French Canadians' loss of religious faith. the Traitor was never far removed from the Jew, it seemed, or vice versa.

Rarely had the Jew been so blatantly used as a scapegoat. But Lionel Groulx, l'Action nationale, Jeune-canada and Le Devoir also issued endless decrees against their own people, a race which steadfastly somehow eluded their grasp. This phenomenon tends to support the theory that racism is the product of groups which perceive themselves as threatened, regardless of the threat's actual size.

Despite this group's despair, there was still room for optimism: Nazi Germany was showing the way.

L'ACTION NATIONALE'S ANATOLE VANIER claimed Jews were a virus eroding the nation's health. They constituted "one of the worst viruses to attack our religious and national traditions."[2]

This virus was particularly tenacious because "Jews are never the first inhabitants of the countries in which they live—not even in the Promised Land," and when they settle somewhere, "it is always as immigrants incapable of assimilation. They want to compete, but above all, remain Jews within the host-nation."[3]

As we are all well aware, having lived with them for so long, "their international solidarity, which can be considered a virtue, and their nomadic tendencies, are the enemies of love of the fatherland."[4]

The presence of this virus—this group of immigrants who refused to assimilate and were incapable of loyalty to any flag—provoked violent reactions in many countries, including Nazi Germany, with whom l'Action nationale deeply sympathized. Is anyone to blame, Anatole Vanier asks, "if Germans or French Canadians want to live as they wish in their own homes? The Jews should not be so surprised when original occupants defend what is rightfully theirs in their own country."[5]

God and instinct demanded a strong national reaction to the Jewish peril.

> Instead of bearing a grudge against the active strength of the people whose character, aspirations and most sacred beliefs they are trying to thwart, why do they not turn their minds to the divinely inspired, if tragic, struggle for life waged instinctively since the beginning of time by people attacked, or simply jostled, by newcomers?[6]

It is the Jew's attitude that creates all his current problems, Vanier continued philosophically. "They perpetuate their own unhappiness by the habit of dispersion and by the way they elbow themselves into other people's countries." It explained the rising movement in new (Nazi) Germany, a movement which Vanier hoped to see duplicated in Quebec. "It is because of this that Jews live in ghettos and will continue to live in them in Germany and elsewhere. The current movement in the new Germany is spreading wherever Jews are regarded as invasive or burdensome. One might ask if they are ever regarded as anything else."[7]

Vanier was using the exact postulate upon which Groulx had constructed his racial cosmogony. God deliberately created different races and the skirmishes in which they indulged. Their evolution did, however, have biological roots in the "instinct" each race invariably manifested. Groulx's myth of origins directly linked French Canadians of his day to the first French colonists, excluding all other groups and designating his people, even though several centuries had passed, "first occupants." It also allowed Vanier to question the right of Jewish French Canadians to live in Quebec. With Groulx's theory in hand, Vanier could reasonably conclude that Hitler's edicts of 1933 concerning German citizens of Jewish extraction were part of a "movement in new Germany," one which could take root in any country—Canada included—in which Jews were considered "burdensome."

André Laurendeau of Jeune-Canada does not mince words on the subject of Jews who "do not allow themselves to assimilate anywhere. No race has successfully absorbed the occult rites of this eastern civilization."[8] They have only themselves to blame for their misfortunes, he recites, parroting Vanier.

> You insinuate yourselves among us myopically; your obnoxious lack of tact, your presumption when you are strong and your spinelessness when you wax eloquent will get you into trouble. If you could only feel the exasperation your presence everywhere provokes, and which ideologues and demagogues excessively exploit.[9]

Laurendeau's mild criticism of ideologues and demagogues at the end of this quotation hardly weakens the substance of his threat. Pierre Dagenais of Jeune-Canada denies that he belongs to a movement which openly admits its hatred of Jews, but quickly adds that "when one people threatens the national and economic life of another people, it is only just and fair for the latter to protect itself."[10]

When Dagenais writes, "They remain Jews, wherever they are and whatever they do,"[11] he articulates more clearly than Groulx, l'Action nationale or Le Devoir ever did, the founding principle of racism: differences are immutable and permanent.

Many Le Devoir journalists were convinced that Jews, by their very nature, were precluded from joining any nation. Charlie Chaplin was not English, he was Jewish;[12] from 1910 to 1930, Montreal was inundated with Austrians, Russians and Poles who were "no more Austrian, Russian or Polish" than you or me;[13] the writer Joseph Kessel is not a Frenchman, but a naturalized Russian Jew;[14] Mr Jean Zay, France's national minister of education, was "a Jew, first and foremost;"[15] Jewish blood flowed in the veins of New York Mayor Fiorello La Guardia;[16] Judges Louis Brandeis and Cardozo of the United States Supreme Court were Israelites and not Americans[17] and "Freud was as Jewish as his brothers in Germany."[18]

While Mussolini "fires the imagination, builds his country," Paul Poirier thunders, Léon Blum "desperately tries to discredit and destroy everything that formerly contributed to France's greatness." This is not inordinately surprising given that he "is not French...belonging as he does to the tribe of the wandering Jew, who went from the central European ghettos to Germany, then Alsace and, finally, tried to conquer France." Despite having been pushed into the abyss, there was still a glimmer of hope for France, Anger concludes. "God does not abandon nations who stood for centuries at the vanguard of Christendom."[19] Pamphile edifies readers with the news that "Léon Blum is of Oriental extraction."[20] "In Paris," he continues in an ironic vein, "Blum claims he can make the rain fall and the sun shine. His counterpart in Quebec is Bercovitch—yet another true-blooded Frenchman."[21] The caustic reference is to liberal Member of the provincial parliament Peter Bercovitch.

In England,[22] the United States,[23] Switzerland,[24] France,[25] Germany,[26] the Sudetenland,[27] Romania[28] and Hungary,[29] it appeared that Jews remained totally, exclusively and immutably Jewish. Le Devoir never once considered them English, American, Swiss, French, German, Romanian, Hungarian or, for that matter, French Canadian. Omer Héroux froths at the thought that a business run by Samuel Breitholz and Benjamin Schulman could operate under the name "La Maison Champlain Incorporée." The owners "could not possibly be more antithetical to everything Champlain loved, lived and fought for."[30]

Le Devoir frequently registered the fact that someone was Jewish. It recounts the story, for instance, of "a passenger aboard a steamship, a cripple of Jewish stock who had stuffed his artificial limb with eight thousand dollars' worth of diamonds"[31] and was arrested upon arriving in Quebec. We never learn his name or nationality. His Jewishness—and perhaps also his lameness!—suffice to describe him; the tenets of racism permit him no identity apart from ethnic affiliation.

Le Devoir applies the same reasoning to a variety of individuals. "A young Israelite," living in the United States is described as "a Jewish genius;"[32] "The Jew Einstein, has convinced us to accept the theory of relativity on trust."[33] On the topic of sports, Le Devoir informs us that "the Jewish boxer Bauer is formidable."[34]

After positing the "stateless" and disloyal nature of the Jew, Le Devoir draws a logical conclusion. "The Jews," it states pithily, "who have taken the whole planet as their home, will be hurt no matter which country is under attack."[35] When four countries refused to allow the ship Saint-Louis and its cargo of 907 refugees to enter their harbours, Le Devoir dubbed the incident a modern variant on the medieval legend of the wandering Jew. In that legend, God condemned Jews to wander the earth as penance for the crime of deicide.

But the planet was no longer a willing home. "Wandering Jews" is one of the headlines in Le Devoir, 3 June 1939. "Cuba, Paraguay, Mexico and Argentina turn away hundreds of German refugees. Santo Domingo accepts them."[36] If it were up to Le Devoir, Jewish refugees would continue to wander. Canada could not welcome "more or less unassimilable people, unaccustomed to working the land anywhere in the world."[37] Following the lead of l'Action nationale, Georges Pelletier reiterates this theme, quoting the English writer Hilaire Belloc. "The Jewish nation, with its insular tradition and social spirit, is necessarily at loggerheads with the people among whom it lives." "What has happened in Europe will happen to an even greater degree here in Canada."[38]

For these reasons, Jewish immigration had to be halted. André Laurendeau took this one step further. We cannot open our doors to "useless mouths, strangers...who do not even try to settle, social revolutionaries, creatures who refuse to assimilate into any other race and who, by virtue of their religion, interests and traditions, constitute a state within a state."[39]

The effects of immigration on the nation are analogous to those of a bacterial infection in the human body.

> If it persists in opening its doors to anyone who comes knocking, strangers will invade its lands, minorities will threaten the national well-being, the country will be poisoned, its temperature will rise, and because it failed to heed those who tried to give advice, it will be wracked by wild hallucinations.[40]

Pierre Dagenais of Jeune-Canada also favoured the prophylactic approach, counselling the greatest caution regarding the immigration "of unassimilable souls whose presence threatens the nation's health."[41]

In its arguments against immigration Le Devoir sometimes invoked economic reasons like unemployment,[42] or fears such as immigrants' lack of hygiene and well-known criminal tendencies,[43] or even the disruption of demographic balance between the two founding peoples[44] which would ultimately lead to the disappearance of French Canadians.[45] The disappearance of Catholicism was more worrisome than that of the French language. If Canada welcomed people without any idea of their religious persuasion, "did it not risk bringing a strong non-Christian influence into the province?"[46]

It is clear that objections to Jewish immigration raised by Le Devoir, l'Action nationale and Jeune-Canada have nothing to do with present-day official nationalist interpretation of events. It is difficult to believe these objections were simply the "reaction of a little-people-whose-survival-was-threatened-by-Jewish-immigration." What concerned these writers was not the number of Jews admitted or to be admitted, but the Jew's anti-patriotic, unassimilable character, not to mention his nebulous "insular tradition" and "social spirit" which would undoubtedly feed the fires of "social revolution." They are not interested in real, flesh and blood Jews, but in a demonic symbol which they never tire of vilifying.

With regards to the "stateless naturalized Canadian foreigners"* of 1938, to whom he attaches the medieval and now-derogatory term *aubain*, Georges Pelletier indignantly exclaims, "We do not ask them for any information except the name of their country of birth. There is never any indication of their race or religion."[47] Anti-Semitism in this century often harkens back to the legends and terminology of the Middle Ages. In this case an aubain cannot, by definition, be a naturalized citizen. When Georges Pelletier writes about "the list of naturalized aubains," he is referring to people who are Canadians in name only; those who must, by nature, remain foreigners.

The epithets used by various writers at Le Devoir, l'Action nationale and Jeune-Canada to refer to European refugees whom they believe, rightly or wrongly, to be Jewish are similarly telling. Under the very particular circumstances of the 1930s, the term "refugee" came to be equated with Jew.

---

* The word "aubain" used in the French original of the above quotation dates back to medieval times. Larousse Dictionary (1973) defines the term as "a person without naturalized status living in a foreign country." (Translator's note)

These wretches and newly arrived immigrants (ex-refugees) were labelled "Europe's exiles,"[48] "thousands of abandoned Europeans,"[49] "foreigners and, all too often, spoiled goods,"[50] "foreigners and dubious characters,"[51] "criminals and mentally ill," "this poorly regulated flood [which] has increased the incidence of crime as well as the number of weak-minded people incarcerated at the expense of both federal and provincial governments."[52] The mysterious Lambert Closse elaborated on the theme of criminals and lunatics:

> The moment the Jews entered the order of Freemasons, murders and gruesome assassinations began. It should come as no surprise when Police Chief Bingham tells us that Jews make up 50% of the criminal population. And how many lunatics are locked up in asylums, victims of Jewish materialism?[53]

Czechoslovakian refugees were "impossible to deport"[54] because their country had been wiped off the map. "Anti-Nazi refugees, whether they were Jewish or not," were turning Canada into "Europe's dumping ground."[55] The country would soon become a mirror image of "the Commonwealth, a vast dumping ground for the feverish emigration of any race whatsoever." Waste products in this unfortunate enterprise were the "Jewish population and advocators of democracy" whom England was preparing to jettison.[56] Immigrants arriving in Canada in 1913 were nothing more than "the refuse of other nations."[57]

Jews were set apart as much by race as by religion, and these two factors reinforced each other in attempts to justify their exclusion. Religious differences fuelled Jews' supposed hostility towards Christians in all kinds of ways. Lambert Closse promoted Jews to the rank of the greatest enemies of Christ, on a par with Satan himself. In *La Réponse de la Race*, the "French Canadians' national catechism," he writes:

> Who are Christ's greatest enemies?
>
> Lucifer and the Jews. They must be linked if we are to advance in our study of the social question...The Jews! World history objectively instructs us that the Jews refused to recognize Christ who had been appointed by God to be the Messiah. Evidence of their attitude consists in their killing Jesus and calling him an imposter."[58]

"When they mix with Christians, Jews must subdue a natural antipathy," Le Devoir asserts. "When he manages to overcome his handicap, it is proof that he is extraordinarily decent."[59]

Jeune-Canada was of the opinion that Jews' lives were rendered intolerable by "the public nature of religion and Christianity here. Throughout history, wherever Jews have lived they have sought to destroy this public aspect..."[60]

Paul Anger of Le Devoir, uses a fictional Jewish character to show the ultimate goal of Jews domiciled in Quebec. The fable he recounts brings to mind the Protocols of the Elders of Zion because in it Jews openly and painstakingly express their insatiable desire to rule.[61] Writing from the Jew's point of view, Anger lays the story's groundwork. "Money is the God of modern times just as it is our God of old. We have worshipped it for so long!" He then enters into the heart of the matter. "Do you know what our aim is? We will take over every troubled church and transform it into a Jewish institution." Mount Royal and its huge illuminated cross were obvious targets for Jewish covetousness and hatred. "Tonight you will see the mountain's head encircled by a halo of light. To the Jew, this is an insult. But the Jew will be avenged." The Jew avenges himself by transforming Mount Royal with the help of money (his beloved God) and the Traitor. "Very soon, thanks to two French Canadian allies, Mr Bray and La Presse, the mountain will have a casino. The cross can shine all it likes, but who will notice it in the glare of a thousand casino lights: the temple of the golden calf?"

Saint Joseph's Oratory would also fall victim to the heinous, insatiable Jew. "If you walk to the other side of Mount Royal, you will find an immense basilica. This basilica will soon be a synagogue." Warning signs of Jewish designs on the Oratory were already in evidence. "We are already crouching at its feet where we built our splendid, brazen hospital.* And when enough time has passed, we will rebaptize the mountain as Mount Sinai."

Paul Anger reminds readers that this dialogue between a Jewish man and an American woman is fictional, but this does not mean their words should be taken any less seriously. "How can we be sure," he wonders, "that after nightfall, in the smoky kitchens of the ghetto, patriarchs in green greatcoats do not

---

* This is a reference to the Sir Mortimer B. Davis Jewish General Hospital of Montreal, which now serves one of the most multi-ethnic neighbourhoods in the city.

speak of such things while twining their long, stained beards?"

The Jews' right to work on Sunday, enshrined in a provincial statute, detracted from the province's Christian character and provided additional evidence of Jews' "love of money," and "passion for capital."[62] Furthermore, they violated the law by bringing in Christian employees to operate their stores on the Christian Sabbath.[63]

Jews were not alone in refusing to care about Sunday and the Christian character of Quebec. They were not the only ones working on the Christian Sabbath and employing Christians to do the same. The practice of working Sundays was spreading to the last bastion of the Catholic faith: French Canadian farmers. They set up roadside stands and offered their produce to city-dwellers out for a Sunday drive. And it did not end there. The very same day of the week, infected with mercantile fever, they welcomed their most important urban customers and bustled about, filling the latters' trucks with fruit and vegetables. What part did the Jews play in all this? They made their appearance during the finale, just as one was beginning to think they will never be called on stage. "Didn't a journalist write last year that on Sundays certain parts of the countryside bear an uncanny resemblance to Jewish neighbourhoods in Montreal?"[64]

If the Jew's culpability only ended there, it would have been a meagre thing indeed. He had to be proven directly responsible for the unprecedented taste for easy money spreading among Catholic farmers. "Alas, these sinful habits often originate there [in the Jewish areas of Montreal]. Jewish shopkeepers drive out to the countryside on Sundays to stock up for the week."[65]

Other religious holidays followed in Sunday's wake, and were treated with increasing indifference by Catholic businessmen and consumers. It goes almost without saying that the Jews were held to be the root cause of this trend.

Omer Héroux quoted the *Comité des Oœvres Catholique de Montréal* with approval when it urged Catholic shopkeepers to close their establishments, and customers to confess their sins rather than emptying their wallets on December 8, the day honouring the Immaculate Conception. French Canadians had sunk to this depth of religious contempt because merchants were so "fearful that their customers would abandon them for the competition next door, which was less scrupulous or of a different religion."[66]

The truth was that a growing number of French Canadians were remorselessly abandoning the celebration of the Sabbath. In addition to farmers, businessmen and consumers, pulp and paper workers entered the fray[67] as well as the entire working class, who had been debased by "large foreign companies" before being forced to desecrate the holy day. As l'Action nationale laments, "These days, they willingly offer their services in many places, simply because it pays."[68] The annulment of article seven, requested and obtained by the *Ligue du Dimanche*, Le Devoir[69] and l'Action nationale[70] did little to curb what these groups regarded as a wave of secularization. Jewish citizens had to respect a day which the nationalists themselves admitted was respected by a dwindling number of Catholics. It is but one of the many ironies punctuating the history of anti-Semitism in Quebec.

Notes

1. Lambert Closse: *La réponse de la race.*, 1936, p. 507.
2. Anatole Vanier: "Les Juifs au Canada," *Action nationale*, (September 1933), p. 6; *Ibid.*, p. 13; Hermas Bastien: "Pages documentaires.," *Action nationale*, (March 1936), pp. 191-192.
3. Anatole Vanier: *Ibid.*, p. 19; "En deux mots, l'immigration juive." *Action nationale*, (December 1938), p. 373.
4. *Ibid.*, p. 6.
5. *Ibid.*, pp. 7-8.
6. *Ibid.*
7. *Ibid.*
8. André Laurendeau: *Partisannerie politique*, in: Les Jeune-Canada: *Politiciens et Juifs*, p. 62.
9. André Laurendeau: "Les Jeune-Canada et l'antisémitisme.," *Le Devoir*, 30 January 1934, p. 2.
10. Pierre Dagenais: *L'immigration au Canada et le commerce*, in: Les Jeune-Canada: *Politiciens et Juifs*, p. 27.
11. *Ibid*, p. 28.
12. Georges Pelletier: "Nul n'est prophète.," *Le Devoir*, 6 April 1931, p. 1; Maurice Huot: " Fidèles jusqu'à la moustache.," *Le Devoir*, 17 November 1935, p. 1.
13. G. Pelletier: "Ces immigrants.," Le Devoir, 29 September 1933, p. 1; Anatole Vanier: "Les Juifs au Canada," Action nationale, (September 1933), p. 5; Roger Duhamel: "Quand Israël est candidat.," Action nationale, (December 1938), p. 325; Maurice Huot: "An English-speaking country.," Le Devoir, 18 May 1938, p. 1.
14. Pamphile: Le carnet d'un grincheux, *Le Devoir*, 8 February 1934, p. 1.

15. Omer Héroux: "Du cardinal Pacelli, de la France et de l'Allemagne.," *Le Devoir*, 14 July 1937, p. 1.

16. E.B.: "Persécutions et propagande.," *Le Devoir*, 17 November 1938, p. 1.

17. Omer Héroux: "L'affaire Frankfurter.," *Le Devoir*, 12 January 1939, p. 1, editorial.

18. Le Grincheux: Le carnet du grincheux, *Le Devoir*, 25 September 1939, p. 1.

19. Paul Poirier: "Inquiétude.," *Le Devoir*, 16 September 1936, p. 1.

20. Pamphile: Carnet d'un grincheux, *Le Devoir*, 13 February 1934, p. 1; Le Grincheux: Carnet d'un grincheux, *Le Devoir*, 23 May 1936.

21. Le Grincheux: Carnet d'un grincheux, *Le Devoir*, 8 June 1936, p. 1; The provincial liberal Member Joseph Cohen receives similar treatment. Cf.: Le Grincheux: Carnet d'un grincheux, *Le Devoir*, 18 March 1936, p. 1; On Léon Blum who is not French: Le Grincheux: Le carnet du grincheux, *Le Devoir*, 21 December 1936, p. 1; Le Grincheux: Carnet d'un grincheux, *Le Devoir*, 16 June 1936, p. 1; Le Grincheux: Carnet du grincheux, *Le Devoir*, 24 April 1937, p. 1; Le Grincheux: Le carnet du grincheux, *Le Devoir*, 15 June 1937, p. 1.

22. Le Grincheux: Le carnet du grincheux, *Le Devoir*, 28 December 1939, p. 1.

23. Georges Pelletier: "Radio ou journaux?," *Le Devoir*, 4 September 1935, p. 1.

24. G. Pelletier: "Une opinion nette.," *Le Devoir*, 9 May 1935, p. 1.

25. Georges Pelletier: "Réfugiés.," *Le Devoir*, 9 May 1933, p. 1; Georges Pelletier: "Les cent jours de Stavisky.," *Le Devoir*, 28 April 1934, p. 1; Paul Anger: "Le faux cheval de course.," *Le Devoir*, 19 September 1934, p. 1; Le Grincheux: Carnet du grincheux, *Le Devoir*, 20 June 1938, p. 1.

26. Georges Pelletier: "Comme les autres.," *Le Devoir*, 23 June 1933, p. 1; "Le Juif n'aura plus de droits politiques en Allemagne.," *Le Devoir*, 16 September 1935, p. 1; Le Grincheux: Le carnet du grincheux, *Le Devoir*, 19 July 1937, p. 1; E.B.: "Des réfugiés juifs en Chine.," *Le Devoir*, 22 June 1939, p. 1.

27. Le Grincheux; Le carnet du grincheux, *Le Devoir*, 18 October 1938, p. 1.

28. Le Grincheux: Le carnet du grincheux, *Le Devoir*, 21 January 1938, p. 1.

29. "Imredi démissionne parce qu'il a du sang juif.," *Le Devoir*, 15 February 1939, p. 1, Headline; Le Grincheux: Le carnet du grincheux, *Le Devoir*, 24 December 1938, p. 1.

30. Omer Héroux: "Le cas "La Maison Champlain Incorporée.," *Le Devoir*, 4 March 1937, p. 1., editorial; On the exclusion of Jews from various nations: Le Grincheux: Carnet d'un grincheux, *Le Devoir*, 11 March 1935, p. 1; Le Grincheux: Le carnet du grincheux, *Le Devoir*, 29 May 1937, p. 1; Le Grincheux: Le carnet du grincheux, *Le Devoir*, 2 December 1938, p. 1; Le Grincheux: Le carnet du grincheux, *Le Devoir*, 2 November 1939, p. 1.

31. G. Pelletier: "Contrebande.," *Le Devoir*, 23 August 1929, p. 1.

32. Nemo:"Faiseurs de nouvelles.," *Le Devoir*, 25 November 1929, p. 1.

33. Paul Anger: "A chacun son métier.," *Le Devoir*, 15 February 1932, p. 1.

34. Pamphile: Carnet d'un grincheux, Le Devoir, 15 June 1934, p. 1.

35. Le Grincheux: Le carnet du grincheux, *Le Devoir*, 25 August 1939, p. 1.

36. On the wandering Jew: Paul Anger: "M. Ford derrière les barreaux.," *Le Devoir*, 20 July 1929, p. 1; Pierre Kiroul: "Le plus grec...," *Le Devoir*, 9 March 1933, p. 1; Le Grincheux: Carnet d'un grincheux, *Le Devoir*, 3 May 1934, p. 1; Le Grincheux: Le carnet du grincheux, *Le Devoir*, 1 December 1938, p. 1; Le

Grincheux: Le carnet du grincheux, *Le Devoir*, 14 March 1938, p. 1; Paul Poirier: Le Juif errant, *Le Devoir*, 11 November 1938, p. 1.

37. Georges Pelletier: "A chacun ses Juifs.," *Le Devoir*, 3 December 1938, p. 1, editorial.

38. *Ibid.*

39. *Ibid.*

40. Georges Pelletier: "Doser avant, non pas après.," *Le Devoir*, 14 March 1935, p. 1.

41. Pierre Dagenais: *op. cit.*, p. 27.

42. Omer Héroux: "Immigration.," *Le Devoir*, 15 August 1933, p. 1; Omer Héroux: "L'Ouest n'en veut pas plus que nous.," *Le Devoir*, 22 August 1933, p. 1., editorial; Georges Pelletier: "Un autre projet.," *Le Devoir*, 12 April 1935, p. 1; Georges Pelletier: "Attendons.," *Le Devoir*, 31 January 1936, p. 1; Omer Héroux; "A propos d'immigration.," *Le Devoir*, 30 June 1938, p. 1, editorial; Georges Pelletier: "Pas de cela.," *Le Devoir*, 4 July 1938, p. 1; Le Grincheux: Le carnet du grincheux, *Le Devoir*, 19 November 1938, p. 1; Omer Héroux: "L'attitude du Star.," *Le Devoir*, 23 December 1938, p. 1; Léopold Richer:"Deux députés s'opposent net à l'immigration juive au Canada.," *Le Devoir*, 25 January 1939, p. 1.

43. Alvarez Vaillancourt: "L'exploitation de notre industrie minière et l'immigration.," *Le Devoir*, 25 February 1939, p. 12.

44. G. Pelletier: "Doucement.," *Le Devoir*, 14 October 1933, p. 1.

45. Georges Pelletier: "Ne soyons pas des autruches.," *Le Devoir*, 4 April 1936, p. 1, editorial.

46. G. Pelletier: "Naturalisation," *Le Devoir*, 9 December 1938, p. 1; E.B.: "Le dire ailleurs.," *Le Devoir*, 15 December 1938, p. 1.

47. Georges Pelletier: "Naturalisation.," *Le Devoir*, 9 December 1938, p. 1; Georges Pelletier:"Est-ce une tour de Babel que le Canada bâtit?," *Le Devoir*, 18 March 1939, p. 1, editorial.

48. Paul Poirier: "Le Juif errant.," *Le Devoir*, 11 November 1938, p. 1; Le Grincheux: Le carnet du grincheux, *Le Devoir*, 22 December 1938, p. 1.

49. Georges Pelletier: "Le nom de cette agence.," *Le Devoir*, 12 June 1933, p. 1.

50. André Marois (pseudonym of Lionel Groulx): "Pour vivre!," *Action nationale*, (April 1936), p. 230.

51. Georges Pelletier: "Immigration.," *Le Devoir*, 17 July 1935, p. 1; Pierre Kiroul: "L'invasion.," *Le Devoir*, 1 March 1935, p. 1.

52. Georges Pelletier: "En marge des bagarres à Toronto.," *Le Devoir*, 19 August 1933, p. 1.

53. Lambert Closse: *op. cit.*, p. 521

54. Georges Pelletier: "Est-ce une tour de Babel que le Canada bâtit?," *Le Devoir*, 18 March 1939, p. 1.

55. E. B.:"Dépotoir des nations.," *Le Devoir*, 18 October 1938, p. 1.

56. Léopold Richer: "Non, non et non!," *Le Devoir*, 20 October 1938, p. 1.

57. Pierre Dagenais: *L'Immigration au Canada et le communisme*, in: Les Jeune-Canada: *Politiciens et Juifs*,p.25.

58. Lambert Closse: *op.cit.*, p. 506.

59. Paul Anger: "Bercovitch et les "Slush Fund Brothers.," *Le Devoir*, 5 October 1938, p. 1; Le Grincheux: Le carnet du grincheux, *Le Devoir*, 10 October 1938, p. 1.

60. Gilbert Manseau: *Les Juifs sont-ils une minorité au Canada?*, in: Les Jeune-Canada: *Politiciens et Juifs*, p. 21; Paul Anger: "Quand Israël est roi.," *Le Devoir*, 15 January 1930, p. 1.

61. Paul Anger: "Ainsi parlait Abraham...," *Le Devoir*, 4 August 1934, p. 1.

62. P. Poirier: "Une traite...oubliée.," Le Devoir, 5 July 1933, p. 1.

63. La Ligue du Dimanche: "Pour une meilleure observation du dimanche.," *Le Devoir*, 14 May 1934, p. 8; René Monette: *Commerce juif et commerce canadien-français*, in: Les Jeune-Canada: *Politiciens et Juifs*, pp. 50-51. La Ligue du Dimanche: "Pour la répression du travail le dimanche.," *Le Devoir*, 30 September 1929, p. 2; The celebrated Article seven of Chapter 199 of the Revised Statutes of 1925 reads as follows:
"Notwithstanding any dispositions to the contrary contained in the present section, whomsoever conscientiously observes the seventh day of the week as the Sabbath and really abstain from working on this day, shall not be subject to being pursued for having worked on the first day of the week, inasmuch as this work does not interfere with other persons in their observance of the first day of the week as holy day, and if the place where such work takes place is not open for business on that day." S.R.(1909), 4471, cited in: Omer Héroux: "Travail et" Commerce," *Le Devoir*, 10 April 1934, p. 1; La Ligue du Dimanche: *op.cit.*, p. 8;"Dieu ou Mammon.," *Action nationale*, (April 1934), p. 194.

64. Joseph-Papin Archambault, o.s.j.: "Le précepte dominical.," *Le Devoir*, 3 May 1933, p. 1; "Dieu ou Mammon": *Action nationale*, (April 1934), pp. 193-194.

65. *Ibid.*

66. O. Héroux: "Simple équité.," *Le Devoir*, 1 December 1931, p. 1.

67. Omer Héroux:" Le travail du dimanche.," *Le Devoir*, 26 March 1936, p. 1., editorial; La Ligue du Dimanche: "Pour la répression du travail le dimanche.," *Le Devoir*, 10 March 1931, p. 2; Joseph-Papin Archambault: "Le précepte dominical.," *Le Devoir*, 3 May 1933, p. 1, editorial; La Ligue du Dimanche: "Pour une meilleure observation du dimanche.," *Le Devoir*, 14 May 1934, p. 8; Joseph-Papin Archambault, o.s.j.: "Le respect du dimanche.," *Action nationale*, (April 1933), pp. 236-237.

68. "Dieu ou Mammon: *Action nationale*, (April 1934) p. 193.

69. "L'arrêt de la Cour d'Appel au sujet du privilège juif de travailler le dimanche.," *Le Devoir*, 9 December 1935, p. 10; Omer Héroux: "Le travail du dimanche.," *Le Devoir*, 26 March 1936, p. 1, editorial; The other articles published by Le Devoir on respecting Sunday are listed in Appendix B of the French edition of this book.

70. Léo Pelland: "Pour une politique nationale.," *Action nationale*, (April 1937), p. 204.

9

THE INTERNATIONAL JEWISH CONSPIRACY

Ugly, malodorous and incapable of assimilation despite his best efforts to blend in, the Jew is nonetheless using all his wiles to take over the world. And succeeding, according to Lambert Closse. "The Jewish spirit" and "Jewish internationalism," which ultimately had nothing at all to do with Jewish faith or identity, were eroding the foundations of western civilization. The Jew was endowed with unparalleled ideological breadth; at one and the same time he was a dedicated capitalist and a die-hard Communist. With his bellicose nature he set the world ablaze, leaving a trail of bloody conflict, war and revolution. Closse suggested that along with their sidekicks the freemasons, Jews controlled the League of Nations. they had also, apparently, infiltrated the presidential office of the United States of America. Was not the real name of Theodore Roosevelt—who was also a freemason—*Rosenfeld*? "God gave the Jews power over the property and lives of all other peoples,"[1] Closse writes, allegedly quoting from the Talmud. Nevertheless, the governments of Germany, Austria and Italy were demonstrating that opposition to the International Jewish Threat was feasible.

THE JEW HAD ONLY ONE EARTHLY AMBITION. "He had sworn that one day he would take over the world and become a rich and powerful ruler to all people,"[2] Lambert Closse asserts. How was he planning to realize his dream? Not one to be subjugated, Closse has an answer at the ready. The Jew's passion for money was his most powerful tool. "The Jew is interested in one thing, and one thing alone: making money. That is why he can be found wherever business is being transacted. It is the source of his internationalism. He does not care a fig about his hosts' traditions and customs. It is money, the profits he can reap from any given place, which interests him."[3]

The issue was really very simple. Jewish economic domination in Quebec, responsible for "our present economic inferiority," was caused by the *fact* that "Jewish internationalism corresponds perfectly with the internationalization of world finance. The Jew hunts for gold, and gold follows him."[4]

By labelling the Jew an international creature it was possible to dissociate him from the Jewish race and religion which are usually his defining features. There was a "Jewish spirit," which had nothing to do with either race or religion: a Jew without the Jews!

L'Action nationale did its best to guide the ignorant masses through the maze of the Jewish question. One has to understand, it maintains, that "the international Jewish spirit is not the same thing as the Jewish race and religion." Even if he did not properly exist, the Jew was still western civilization's most wanted enemy. "No one can contest the fact that a great number of Jews, who have no interest in religion, exert a pernicious influence in every area of modern life." What is this "pernicious influence" to which l'Action nationale refers? "The economy, trade, business, competition, the Bar Association, medicine, social interactions and the political arena are often infiltrated and, indeed, shaken by materialist and liberal principles originating, for the most part, in Jewish circles."[5]

Jeune-Canada drives this point home. The Jewish people cannot help it, "they exude international spirit in spite of themselves." It also chants hatred's refrain, observing, "The Jewish international spirit is much more harmful than the Jewish race or religion itself."[6]

Under the pseudonym of Jacques Brassier, Lionel Groulx also denounces "Jewish internationalism as one of the most dangerous forces of moral and social decay on the planet."[7]

Jewish international spirit is thus responsible for the ills of liberalism, materialism, and moral and social decay.

Jews band together, but they also spread throughout the world. "This makes it impossible to step on the Jew-bitch's tail in Germany without provoking a round of barking in Canada,"[8] writes a member of Jeune-Canada. André Laurendeau expressed the same opinion in equally harsh terms. Resisting the forces of oppression for over two thousand years has imparted to the Jews "bitter tenacity, an iron will and unbreakable cohesion."[9] Jewish fellowship is an unwavering phenomenon of international proportions, according to Le Devoir. "Neither borders nor oceans can disturb their solidarity."[10]

According to prevailing myth, the power emanating from this solidarity was played out on an international scale. A European correspondent confirms Le Devoir's opinion that "the anti-Semitism of Hitler's supporters alienated them from the whole world due to the Jews' international power."[11] The power of *Il*

Duce himself paled beside that of the Jews. "Mussolini can only
strike the Jews in Italy, while the Jews can retaliate from every
corner of the globe."[12] Lambert Closse carefully outlines the
ramifications of world-wide Jewish power. "They infiltrate
everywhere in their search for gold: banks, trade, government,
behind the scenes in Parliament if they cannot be elected as
Jews. They proceed noiselessly while they are not yet strong
enough to bare their teeth."[13]

According to Le Devoir, protests sparked throughout the
western world by Hitler's persecution of German Jews constituted additional evidence of Jewish international strength.
Citing the views of a Parisian columnist, Le Devoir ponders
whether Jewish demonstrations against Nazi persecution merely
reflect "this excessive power which Hitler rightly denounced."
After all, "Nothing like this happened when Mussolini instituted measures against the Freemasons. It seems to prove that
Judaism is much stronger than the lodge."[14]

Lambert Closse, who followed every twist and turn of the international Jewish conspiracy, disagreed. "Entire book stores
could be filled with volumes attesting to the fact that the
Freemasons are an organization run by Jews."[15] The allegiance
was inevitable. "If you think about it, what could be more
natural than this association between Jews and Freemasons?
Both of them harbour the same hatred of Christianity—
civilization's indisputable, and undisputed, foundation."[16] The
League of Nations spearheaded the assault on Christian civilization. "One cannot reiterate often enough," Closse writes, the
"Judeo-Masonic nature" of the League of Nations.[17] The United
States had already fallen victim to the Judeo-Masonic plot. Its
president, Theodore Roosevelt, was "Jewish and Masonic
through and through," born of "a Jewish Dutch family" which
changed its name from Rosenfeld to Roosevelt the instant it
landed in America.[18]

Anatole Vanier followed suit, quoting parts of a letter written
by Monseigneur Gfoellner, the Bishop of Linz, Austria, which
had already been published in its entirety by l'Action nationale.
The assortment of crimes imputed by the Catholic prelate to the
strange creature, Judeo-Masonry, sways the inattentive reader or
hurried Christian, who was unaware of the extent of the danger.

> Together with Freemasonry, degenerate Judaism above all else propagates the worship of Mammon—capitalist self-interest—while simultaneously founding and preaching socialism and Communism, the forerunner and harbinger of Bolshevism.

In his warning to his flock, Gfoellner recalls the basic principles of Christianity. "Doing battle against and breaking Judaism's pernicious influence is not merely the legitimate right of every upstanding Christian, it is an imperative, conscientious duty."[19]

It comes as no surprise that Canon Groulx, Le Devoir and Jeune-Canada did not deign to take seriously the Nazi atrocities which were the focus of so many popular demonstrations. Groulx refers to them as "persecutions occurring at the other end of the world, which may or may not be true,"[20] and André Laurendeau calls them "supposed" atrocities "which have not been proven."[21] How could they write otherwise when, as Laurendeau puts it, "it is difficult not to be sceptical about the authenticity of these persecutions when one remembers that all, or practically all, news agencies are owned by Jews."[22]

In any event, the "supposed" persecutions harmed only "the Jewish plutocracy," Pierre Dansereau of Jeune-Canada asserts and then goes on to castigate Canadian politicians who denounced the Third Reich. "They cried out for tolerance, but, Ladies and Gentlemen, there is no such word in the Christian lexicon. We do not tolerate good; we encourage it. Nor do we tolerate evil; we condemn it."[23]

The fact that when Mexican Catholics were mistreated people the world over barely batted an eyelid demonstrated that:

> In the world of business, finance, trade and international banking, Catholics are not worth much. This explains why they cannot muster the powerful influences international Jewry relied on to counter Hitler and the Nazis.[24]

The lack of public interest in the persecution of German Catholics[25] and Spanish insurgents[26] could be similarly explained. Le Grincheux challenges Jews to "say whether their people in communist Spain had been on the side of the pillagers or the pillaged, the persecutors or the persecuted, the killers or those murdered."[27]

Of the 22 articles included in the Protocols of the Elders of Zion which Lambert Closse re-printed in his book *La réponse de la race*, article 16 is one of the more inflammatory: "Create 'events' to stir up international mistrust, aggravate enmity between different races, cultivate hatred and increase weapons production."[28] Closse later alleges that, "Jewish influence is present in every conspiracy and at the base of all revolutions which always have the same goal: the obliteration of Christianity. It breeds the corruption of values and traditions in every country which allows Jews entry."[29] In light of this, how could one turn a blind eye to the fact that the Jew's hideous form was crouching behind contemporary wars and conflicts? Le Devoir and Jeune-Canada were not to be fooled!

In Le Devoir, Pamphile maintains Jews like using their international power to sow the seeds of war and destruction. The real name of weapons manufacturer Sir Basil Zaharoff—Basileos Zacharias—"smells pungently of the ghetto." He is "an Israelite. This explains his remunerative internationalism."[30] There were also "certain quasi-industrialists" working under this same Zaharoff, whose only goal was "to push the nations of the world into declaring war, or preparing for it."[31]

André Laurendeau throws in his two cents, alleging that "Their vanguard is conquering unassailable countries all over the world. Israeli might is international in scale. Yesterday it helped Germany fight the Allies; tomorrow it might help France vanquish Germany. It intercedes wherever its interests dictate."[32] The fact that France was dragged into the war was the fault of "this internationalist club," "this Judeo-Masonic-Bolshevist clique"[33] which ruled it.

On the eve of the Second World War, with the signing of the German-Soviet non-aggression pact, Le Devoir's fury against Jews was at its zenith. "Perhaps during this eight-day period of appeasement western nations will ruminate upon the fact that the enemies of their civilization—Christian civilization—are Tartars infected with Semitism. These Tartars, alas, are allied with the 'Huns' only because the 'others' [England, France, etc.] were unable to get them."[34]

Le Devoir's editor never made light of these serious matters. Pierre Anctil describes how "Le Devoir's editor, a man of penetrating intelligence, took pains to inform himself. At the close of 1937 he travelled to Europe for several weeks" in order to study the "Jewish question"[35] first-hand. The following is what this "penetrating intelligence" gleaned from his European tour.[36] In England, "Jews do not have any cares or enemies" because half of the country's newspapers belong to them. The situation was worse in France due to revelations in Edouard Drumont's magazine, *La Libre Parole*, and the "ill-considered behaviour" of Léon Blum who "filled the most important positions in his government with an unprecedented number of Jews, many of whom have lived in France for only one or two generations," much too short a time to become true Frenchmen.

Compared to this, the situation in Belgium was relatively calm despite the fact that the fraud committed by a certain Jew "greatly annoyed clear-sighted people" in that country. According to the logic of racism, the crimes of one individual became the crimes of his people. Individuals were merely indistinguishable clones of the mythical group to which they belonged.

In Germany, Jews made their presence known loudly and clearly. "In Cologne, Berlin, Munich and Leipzig, on streets where professionals set up their offices, firms and residences, Le Devoir's representative saw signs of lawyers, doctors and dentists with Jewish first and family names." In Austria and Hungary, which "also brim with Jews," Jewish citizens "amass growing fortunes." In Vienna, one learns that "There are 600 000 Jews in a total population of about 1 800 000, constituting a third of the city...They are in evidence everywhere, at the most beautiful and prestigious places." What does it matter that German refugees are fleeing across the border penniless and stripped of their property? "We have not managed to stop them from bringing along their money-making talents. And make money they will. "Jewish greed was absolutely insatiable. Jews were not content simply to grow grotesquely rich; they had to take over "an entire newspaper"—the *"Neue Frei Presse."*

And their influence did not stop anywhere near there. "They also lead the socialist rank and file, and occupy prominent places in the capitalist order." Jewish invasiveness prompts Le Devoir's editor's "penetrating intelligence" to inquire, "How long can this state of affairs persist? No one can be sure. But latent anti-Semitism, nourished on the one hand by German propaganda, and on the other by the tactlessness and insolence of Jewish people living in new Austria, is rearing its head and flourishing."

Jews hardly behaved any better in Hungary, where their future prospects were growing dimmer with each passing day. Jewish refugees from Poland and Germany flooded its borders, making their fortunes "in trade, industry and banking." In Budapest and in Vienna, "they acted as if they were in conquered territory." But it was not for this alone that Hungarians hated them. "In Budapest, where Jews will soon comprise two fifths of the city's population, Jews are reviled primarily because one of their people, Bela Kun, imposed a bloody communist regime on the country for several months in 1920. The mere mention of his name still sets people trembling." Their arrogance was dampened, however, with "the election of Goga in Romania, who openly declared the need to effect a quick purge of his country's Jewish population."

In Czechoslovakia, Jews are enjoying "a first-rate situation." "The Czechoslovakian Republic's humanitarian constitution, a proverbial thorn in Germany's side, has transformed the country into a refuge for every Jew who hastens to its door." As a result, "Prague is...objectively the European city where Jews are most numerous and feel most at home." This had been true for over a thousand years.

"Have their ancestors not lived there since before the year 1000? And how many of today's most important Jewish families living in Paris and London, not to mention New York; or in the Berlin, Frankfurt and Cologne of yesterday originally came from Prague's ghetto?"[37]

The idea that Prague was the birthplace of the Jewish world conquest caught the imagination of another journalist at Le Devoir. "Will every Israelite hoping to immigrate to Canada come from Czechoslovakia? A convenient departure point...Prague formerly sent its Jewish families out to every corner of the world. Will this phenomenon be repeated?"[38]

In what could easily be qualified as the understatement of the century, Georges Pelletier concludes his summary of the European situation by noting "the Nazis' determination to put a definitive end to Jewish competition with Europeans, wherever it exists..."

Other journalists parroted the views of Le Devoir's editor that in Europe Jews control newspapers, finance and the entire economy[39], thereby demonstrating that in Europe, as in Canada, Jews are possessed of a distinctive dishonesty and wiliness.[40] Was it not true that the Jewish leader Isaacovitch forced the federal government to effect "great changes in our commercial laws, substituting trickery, fraud and theft for probity?"[41] Furthermore, their numbers everywhere exceed the quotas—never clearly determined—adjudged suitable for each individual country.[42]

It is not just in Austria, Georges Pelletier observed in his "penetrating" editorial on the situation of the Jews in Europe, that Jews engaged in socialism and capitalism with equal frenzy. In fact, this had been going on for many years. "The name Rothschild derives from the red shields that decorated the Frankfurt house where Rothschild's ancestors started their small business. The Jewish people have always had a penchant for shields and for the colour red. Just think back to the Russian revolution."[43]

Pierre Dansereau also sounds the warning bell. "If we were merely enslaved by Jewish money, we would have less to complain about. Every day, however, Jewish internationalism (which some people refer to as Communism) advances a few more steps, even here in Canada."[44] His colleague René Monette uses a familiar biological metaphor to describe the effects of Jewish Communism. "Orientals, European imports and immigration carry with them the fatal virus of Communism."[45]

The evidence, Pierre Dagenais writes, is irrefutable. "Karl Marx, creator of the Communist utopia which bears his name, is Jewish. Most party leaders, from the founders to those in power today, are Jewish." The author then summarily converts Lenin for argument's sake. "Consider the following examples: Trotsky, Kerensky, Lenin." At any rate, "Jews are to be found in all modern-day revolutions. Whether it be Poland or Russia, they can be found working away in every enterprise whose goal is to destroy the traditional foundations of Christianity."[46]

Le Devoir proceeds to quote Goering, one of the foremost experts on the international Jewish conspiracy. The following headline adorned the newspaper's first page on November 30,

1936: *"Goering accuses the 'band of Moscow Jews.' The Prus-sian prime minister attributes the spread of the Communist threat throughout the world to Soviet agitators."*

From 1933 on, Groulx warns his readers about Jewish Com-munism. "It is true that Jews are not the only ones cultivating the seeds of Communism in their hot-houses. But many reputable authorities believe that they cultivate in larger quan-tities than others, and this gives us sufficient grounds for wari-ness."[47] It would be apparently easier to criticize the anti-Semitism of Nazis if the Jews were not such revolutionaries.

> After roundly denouncing Nazi anti-Semitism the other day (the April 15, 1933 edition), political columnist at the *Revue des Deux Mondes*, René Pinon, a man not given to frivolous utterances, did not hesitate to add, "Events in Germany can teach people a second, completely different lesson. Israel should be much more discreet about embracing revolutionary ideals and propagating them in other countries."[48]

Three years later Lambert Closse, the mysterious, pseudo-nymous historian, explained that the evil went deeper and fur-ther than people realized. The French Revolution, during which "the evils of liberalism and socialism" were born, was really the work of the *Illuminés*, a "Freemason secret society" founded in 1778 by a Jew named Weisshaupt.[49] The predecessor of this ter-rible organization was the *"Empire Suprême Occulte Juif,"* also known as *"La Main Cachée,"* directed since 1770 by Rothschild. Not even the leaders of the Communist Party were immune to this group's schemes.

> Conclusive evidence in the form of the interest shown by the Central Executive—'l'Alliance Israélite,' Bruyère Street—in the Rothschild dynasty, as well as the latter's satellites and Masonic lodges points to the existence in Paris of a mysterious Jewish emperor delegating leadership in various countries to men like Lenin, Stalin, Trotsky and the like, and even having them ex-ecuted, if need be...[50]

Despite the fact that they were capitalists, Jews were held responsible for the economic ruin of the 1930s. "Times are hard. The economic crisis, a product of Judeo-Masonic machinations, is breeding hatred by crushing large companies and throwing millions of men into the street."[51]

Jews had nothing to lose by waiting. Their power was crumbling under Fascism's thrusts. "The Jews, who had experienced the triumph of the Bolshevik Revolution in Russia and central Europe, were now sensing defeat in the winds blowing through Austria, Germany and Italy. Communism was being crushed."[52] Closse deals this final trump to people who doubt Jews' abhorrence of Fascism:

> The two Socialist Internationals who have been rivals until now have formed a "common front," as their meetings "Against War and Fascism" easily prove. They are using indirect means to continue their endangered revolutionary work. [53]

Le Devoir's Paul Anger shared Closse's optimism. The Jew's triumph in Russia was absolute, and the revenge the entire world would wreak would be equally impressive. "In order to propagate their anti-Christian and antisocial views, Jews did not mind suppressing their love of money. Their triumph was substantial, overly substantial and far too blatant because people all over the world today are rising up against Communism, and its corollary, the Jew."[54]

Confiscation of the property of German Jews was nothing more than retaliation for the fortunes they had grabbed in Russia.

> In Germany, the confiscation of one fifth of the Jewish fortune is regrettable. But it must be remembered that Trotsky and others, Jew rulers in Russia, confiscated one fifth of the fortunes of the aristocracy and middle class, and more often than not, their lives as well.[55]

Would victory over the Jew-Freemason-capitalist-liberal-Communist-socialist-Bolshevist ever be achieved? What good did it do to deport them if they simply repeated their infiltration and took over another country? Le Grincheux reflects that "If Austria chased out its Jews as Germany had done before it, the Jews could always go and pick the pockets of England and France."[56] "'The Jews have beaten me,' says Mr Goga,"[57] Le Devoir trumpets in bold type. The Jew's wide-reaching power would be felt even in the province of Quebec.

Notes

1. Lambert Closse: *La réponse de la race,*. p. 508.

2. *Ibid.*

3. *Ibid.*

4, René Monette: "Commerce juif et commerce canadien-français," in: Les Jeune-Canada: *Politiciens et Juifs*, p. 46.

5. Mgr. Gfoellner: "L'internationalisme juif.," *Action nationale*, (June 1933), p. 381.

6. Pierre Dagenais: *L'immigration au Canada et le communisme*, dans: Les Jeune-Canada: *Politiciens et Juifs*, p. 31.

7. Jacques Brassier(pseudonym of Lionel Groulx): "Pour qu'on vive.," *Action nationale*, (September 1933), p. 1.

8. René Monette: *op. cit.*, p. 47.

9. André Laurendeau: *Partisannerie politique*, dans: Les Jeune-Canada: *Politiciens et Juifs*, p. 62.

10. Omer Héroux: " Solidarité.," *Le Devoir*, 27 May 1930, p. 1; Omer Héroux: "L'affaire de l'Emden.," *Le Devoir*, 1 May 1936, p. 1; Le Grincheux: Carnet d'un grincheux, *Le Devoir*, 1 May 1936, p. 1; Le Grincheux: Le carnet du grincheux, *Le Devoir*, 17 March 1938, p. 1; Le Grincheux: Carnet du grincheux, *Le Devoir*, 5 December 1939, p. 1.

11. Alcide Ebray: "Les débuts du IIIe Reich allemand.," *Le Devoir*, 13 May 1933, p. 1.

12. Omer Héroux: "Les étonnements de M. Glass, député et organisateur du boycott juif contre la marchandise allemande.," *Le Devoir*, 26 October 1938, p. 1, editorial.

13. Lambert Closse: *op. cit.*, p. 508

14. Georges Pelletier: "Réflexions d'un Français.," *Le Devoir*, 16 May 1933, p. 1; "Bela Kun a plongé la Hongrie dans le sang. Il n'y a pas eu de protestation. Bela Kun n'était pas Hongrois. Il était juif." Pamphile: "Carnet d'un grincheux, *Le Devoir*, 27 April 1933, p. 1.

15. Lambert Closse: *op. cit.*, p. 521.

16. *Ibid.*, p. 525.

17. *Ibid.*

18. *Ibid.*, pp. 526-527.

19. Mgr.Gfoellner: "Lettre.," cité dans: Anatole Vanier: "Les Juifs au Canada.," *Action nationale*, (September 1933), p. 15.

20. Jacques Brassier(pseudonym of Lionel Groulx): "Pour qu'on vive.," *Action nationale*, (June 1933), p. 361.

21. André Laurendeau: *op. cit.*, pp. 55-56.

22. *Ibid.*

23. p. Dansereau: *Politiciens et Juifs.*, pp. 10-11; The headline of Le Devoir on 24 March 1933 reads as follows: "Une enquête britannique sur les prétendues atrocités commises contre les Juifs en Allemagne."

24. Georges Pelletier: "Et les catholiques mexicains?," *Le Devoir*, 13 November 1934, p. 1; Georges Pelletier: "Silence au Mexique, clameurs en Palestine.," *Le Devoir*, 6 September 1929, p. 1; Émile Benoist: "Persécutions et propagande.,"

Le Devoir, 17 November 1938, p. 1; Le Grincheux: Le carnet du grincheux, Le Devoir, 27 January 1939, p. 1; André Laurendeau: op. cit., p.57.

25. Pamphile: Carnet d'un grincheux, Le Devoir, 30 June 1933, p. 1; G. Pelletier: "Réfugiés catholiques.," Le Devoir, 30 July 1934, p. 1.

26. Pamphile: Carnet d'un grincheux, Le Devoir, 14 June 1933, p. 1; G. Pelletier: "Juifs et Espagnols.," Le Devoir, 15 June 1933, p. 1; Omer Héroux: "Espagnols et Juifs. Le formidable contraste. Pour se renseigner.," Le Devoir, 29 June 1933, p. 1; Omer Héroux; "En Espagne.," Le Devoir, 21 November 1934, p. 1; Le Grincheux: Le carnet du grincheux, Le Devoir, 21 November 1938, p. 1.

27. Le Grincheux: Le carnet du grincheux, Le Devoir, 16 January 1939, p. 1.

28. Lambert Closse: op. cit., p. 516.

29. Ibid., p. 511.

30. Pamphile: Carnet d'un grincheux, Le Devoir, 24 January 1934, p. 1.

31. G. Pelletier: "Larrons en foire.," Le Devoir, 25 October 1934, p. 1; G. Pelletier: "Zaharoff.," Le Devoir, 8 September 1934, p. 1.

32. André Laurendeau: op.cit., pp. 62-63.

33. G. Pelletier: "Bêtise catastrophique," Le Devoir, 27 April 1935, p.; Le Grincheux: Le carnet du grincheux, Le Devoir, 7 July 1937, p. 1

34. Le Grincheux: Le carnet du grincheux, Le Devoir, 4 December 1939, p. 1.

35. Pierre Anctil: Le Devoir, les Juifs et l'immigration., p.92.

36.Georges Pelletier: "Sur l'antisémitisme en Europe centrale," Le Devoir, 22 January 1938, p. 1. editorial.

37. Ibid.

38. Le Grincheux: Le carnet du grincheux, Le Devoir, 25 October 1938, p. 1; 39. Georges Pelletier: "La Pologne juive.," Le Devoir, 9 June 1937, p. 1; 40. E.B.: "La propagande se poursuit.," Le Devoir, 24 October 1938, p. 1; There are numerous criminals in the ranks of the Jews, whether it be in Germany: Georges Pelletier: "Tactiques.," Le Devoir, 15 September 1933, p. 1.; or in France, where the Stavisky affair is taking place: Georges Pelletier "Escroquerie.," Le Devoir, 23 July 1929, p. 1.; Pamphile: Carnet d'un grincheux, Le Devoir, 25 August 1934, p. 1.; and the Levy affair has everyone talking: Le Grincheux: Carnet d'un grincheux, Le Devoir, 28 November 1934, p. 1; in the United States: Pamphile: Carnet d'un grincheux, Le Devoir, 29 June 1933, p. 1.; and in Canada where the four Bronfman brothers are accused of having defrauded the Tax department of a sum of 5 million dollars: Le Grincheux: Carnet d'un grincheux, Le Devoir, 12 December 1934, p. 1.; Le Grincheux: Carnet d'un grincheux, Le Devoir 13 December 1934, p. 1.

41. P. Anger: "Ces messieurs du "bootleg," Le Devoir, 14 December 1934, p. 1.

42. Le Grincheux: Le carnet du grincheux, Le Devoir, 3 September 1938, p. 1.

43. Le Grincheux: Carnet d'un grincheux, Le Devoir, 3 November 1934, p. 1.

44. Pierre Dansereau: op. cit., p. 13.

45. René Monette: Commerce juif et commerce canadien-français, dans: Les Jeunes-Canada: Politiciens et Juifs, p. 39.

46. Pierre Dagenais: L'immigration au Canada et le communisme, dans: Les Jeune-Canada: Politiciens et Juifs, pp. 30-31.

47. Jacques Brassier(pseudonym of Lionel Groulx): "Pour qu'on vive.," Action nationale, (June 1933), p. 365; Anatole Vanier: "Lettre adressée à Sir Georges Perley, Premier ministre intérimaire.," Action nationale, (September. 1933), p. 85; "La menace

rouge.," *Action nationale*, (May 1936), pp. 1-2, editorial; Carmel Brouillard, o.f.m.: "Problèmes.," *Action nationale*, (November 1936), p. 211; Roger Duhamel: "Les Jeux de la politique.," *Action nationale*, (April 1939), p. 351.

48. Jacques Brassier (pseudonym of Lionel Groulx): *ibid.*

49. Lambert Closse: *op. cit.*, p. 523.

50. *Ibid.*, p. 522.

51. *Ibid.*, p. 537.

52. *Ibid.*

53. *Ibid.*

54. Paul Anger: "L'avenir d'Israël.," *Le Devoir*, 4 November 1936, p. 1; Sur Les Juifs et le communisme: Omer Héroux: "Cause abandonnée.," *Le Devoir*, 31 January 1929, p. 1; Omer Héroux: "Livitnoff.," *Le Devoir*, 16 August 1929, p. 1; Omer Héroux: "Témoignage.," *Le Devoir*, 12 August 1933, p. 1; Paul Anger: "Passim.," *Le Devoir*, 17 August 1933, p. 1; "Les Juifs et le communisme.," *Le Devoir*, 10 May 1935, p. 3; Le Grincheux: Carnet d'un grincheux, *Le Devoir*, 15 October 1936, p. 1; Le Grincheux: Carnet d'un grincheux, *Le Devoir*, 10 April 1937, p. 1; Le Grincheux: Carnet du grincheux, *Le Devoir*, 30 July 1938, p. 1; Le Grincheux: Carnet d'un grincheux, *Le Devoir*, 22 October 1938, p. 1; Le Grincheux: Carnet d'un grincheux, *Le Devoir*, 12 November 1938, p. 1; "La terre promise des Juifs, n'est-ce pas la Soviétie?" le Grincheux asks rhetorically. Le Grincheux: Le carnet du grincheux, *Le Devoir*, 19 November 1938, p. 1; Le Grincheux: Le carnet du grincheux, *Le Devoir*, 17 March 1939, p. 1; Le Grincheux: Le carnet du grincheux, *Le Devoir*, 31 May 1939, p. 1; Le Grincheux: Le carnet du grincheux, *Le Devoir*, 22 August 1939, p. 1.

55. Le Grincheux: Le carnet du grincheux, Le Devoir, 16 December 1938, p. 1.

56. Le Grincheux: Le carnet du grincheux, Le Devoir, 19 February 1938, p. 1.

57. *Le Devoir*, 11 February 1938, p. 1.

10

THE ENEMY IN OUR MIDST

Jews reigned supreme in the Province of Quebec just as they did all over the world. Capitalism and democracy laid the groundwork for the French Canadian people's economic and political enslavement. The most unrealistic figures were quoted as proof of this double yoke, but speakers and journalists hardly noticed, so insulated were they from reality.

The Jew would never have managed to achieve such power without the connivance of the Traitor in the person of the politician. L'Action nationale maintained that political rights were redundant for citizens of Jewish persuasion in Canada, because they were well-treated. What was more, they hurt the Catholic majority, painfully robbing it of its dignity. It would be best simply to relieve them of these rights.

Jews were held responsible for all the evils of modernity. Montreal was beginning to look like Warsaw; entire neighbourhoods were infested with Jews. Jews were taking over the city and exposing its inhabitants to the eroding influences of their materialism. Their impudence knew no bounds. They dared to clutter the tramways, for instance. They were behind the media, advertising, theatre, the movie industry, jazz, vile dance-hall music and trends in fashion, spreading the cancer of American influence.

Even the low French Canadian birthrate was attributable to the Jews. We are informed that "sensual materialism," so common among members of the Jewish race, leads to "excessive and harmful" immorality.

CAPITALISM WAS LOOKED UPON askance because it led inevitably to economic subjection and the "inhuman civilization" that we have come to accept as our own. It was considered a doubly heinous system because Jews both organized and embodied it. "The soulless world in which we live learned the hard lesson that economic dictatorship is accompanied by dangerous social evils. The fact that Jews are not the only ones implicated in this type of dictatorship is of little consequence."[1]

Jews remained the primary target for attack despite a clumsy distinction articulated by Groulx.

To what end are all these absolutely unjustifiable privileges being accumulated if not to encourage the establishment of a veritable Jewish commercial tyranny—a tyranny which Israel's international influence ensures will be formidable and easily implanted—in Quebec and, first and foremost, in Montreal.[2]

According to Lambert Closse, Israel's hold over capitalism would be the death of the French Canadian people. "Here is a brief description of the economic system which has been unable to kill us over the past 30 years: it is unjust, antisocial, unpatriotic, a Jewish creation of international scope, anti-Christian and murderous. This is our master, despite the fact that we are living in our own country!"[3]

Anatole Vanier faithfully echoed his master's voice. Ravaged by ambition, Jews "coveted the best positions in Germany, the United States, Canada, Quebec and everywhere else." How would they eventually obtain them? "To realize their goals, they made occasional use of liberal 'principles,' which some of our people naively and unpatriotically espouse, and for which they are exploited."[4]

Liberalism became synonymous with the Jew and the Traitor, the latter receiving a leg up from the former and comfortably installing himself at the top of the economic hierarchy. According to Anatole Vanier, liberalism acts as a corrosive "solvent" on the "basic national feelings" of French Canadians. "Liberalism—sometimes considered superb, at other times merely useful, but always corrosive—abounds."

Anglo-Saxon and Jewish crimes dated back to the Conquest. If the Americans were guilty of exploiting natural resources, "the Jews and Anglo-Saxons on Saint James Street were guilty of just about everything else. These two groups have been grinding us beneath their heels since the time of the Conquest." They were only too glad to ride on the backs of French Canadians. "The fact that our people are nothing more than good labourers and docile flunkies is fine as long as it serves their interests." French Canadian debasement at the hands of this Jewish-Anglo-Saxon duo transformed "Montreal into the megalopolis it is today, and tragically disrupted the local demographic balance."[6]

The soft drink business did not manage to escape the clutches of the Jews or the English. "In days gone by, our people were in charge of it...The English, followed by the Jews, gradually deposed them (these companies). Coca Cola reigned unopposed."[7]

One member of Jeune-Canada tried to translate the Jewish hegemony into numbers.[8] Without ever revealing his data sources, and apparently without noticing their unreasonableness, he states that "although we make up two sevenths of Canada's population, we own a mere one seventh of Canadian wealth; the Jews, approximately numbering 150 000, possess a quarter of the Dominion's assets." This was not overly surprising as Jews had helped themselves to "farm produce, fisheries, meat, drinks and the grocery trade." Industry was one of the Jew's strongholds. "Jews are firmly rooted in industry. Their industrial capital is between 400 and 600 million. Fisheries, the clothing industry, milk products, and pulp and paper constitute their private preserves." It was impossible to begin to describe the extent of Jewish finances. "Let us not even talk about Jewish finances. They grow so quickly that it is impossible to estimate their exact worth." According to this self-appointed expert, Jews had only one occupation. "One hundred percent of the population engages in business. Jews are never labourers, producers or inventors. They are distributors and businessmen."[9]

The proposition that an entire group would exclusively concentrate its energies in a single sector of economic activity is palpably absurd. Racist determinism, however, does not put much stock in numbers and does not mind if they are far-fetched. François-Albert Anger also believed in the Jew-as-economic-intermediary, and used this fact as justification to refuse him entry into the country. "All over the world Jews engage in parasitic, artificial activities; they graft themselves onto work done by others." These parasites were dishonest as well. "Simply by living in a place, Jews lower morality levels. Respect for contractual obligations, business ethics, and the most elementary forms of trust are demolished; the law of the jungle replaces rules of good conduct."[10]

Jews strangled French Canadian farmers by imposing iniquitous mortgages and buying produce exclusively from growers in Ontario and California.[11]

Neither business, nor the professions, nor any other sector escaped the Jews' formidable clutches. "They have taken over our businesses and industries, and have brought in new methods and customs which do nothing but harm society...Their numbers in our universities and professions are shooting above population norms...out of 92 non-Catholic students in this university [the University of Montreal], 82 are Jewish."[12]

And that was not the end of it. "The wave of Jews flows from this university into the professions." The ever-vigilant Anatole Vanier observes that, "The Montreal Court House sometimes seems preponderantly Oriental due to the number of Jewish lawyers and assistants of the same religion crowding about them." Continuing his detailed account of Jewish students enroled in the University of Montreal, Vanier predicts that this is but the beginning of a growing trend. "The wave keeps on growing. During the month of May of this year, out of 42 bachelor degrees and diplomas from the University of Montreal, 12 were handed out to Jews."[13]

With a touch of what it takes to be irony, Le Devoir echoes the positions taken by Groulx, l'Action nationale and Jeune-Canada on the question of Jewish hegemony.[14] Paul Poirier flips through a Montreal telephone book and exclaims, "What surprised me was not that there are Israelite lawyers in Montreal, but that there are still Canadian and English ones." The retail business was suffering a similar fate. Jewish shops were multiplying on both St. Lawrence Boulevard and on the eastern part of Ste. Catherine Street.

One Le Devoir journalist came up with this line on Jewish tolerance towards the uncircumcised: "The Israelite is quite tolerant. He allows gentiles to buy from him as they wish and he deigns to take money from uncircumcised men." Even English Canadian businesses on Ste. Catherine Street West are being replaced by "booths and bazaars frequented primarily by French Canadian fanatics who persecute Jews by handing over all their money. What a cruel form of persecution!" The fruit and vegetable trade, the clothing sector, big business, finance and alcohol are run "uniquely by the circumcised." To the fictional French Canadian who defensively replies, "I will recite a long list of companies belonging to us..." Poirier rejoins, "You are only proving Jewish tolerance—for the moment they are allowing others to work alongside them. Let us give thanks!"

Paul Anger also invents a Jewish straw man who asserts, "the future is ours because money is ours; it sniffs us out, hunts us down and comes to us. We attract it magnetically. And money, my dear lady, can do anything, open any door, break into any mind, excite anyone's blood."[15]

The Jew's dishonest business habits made him invincible, as the following tale attests. A Craig Street pawnbroker named Isaac put a filthy, stinking fur coat up for sale. "A customer from the town of Sainte-Emilie-de-l'Energie came into the shop, tempted by the low price on the store's sign." The customer noticed the fur's smell. "He mentioned it to Isaac who cried happily, pointing at his own chest, 'No, it's not the coat that stinks, it's me.' This exchange took place at a heroic time when Jewish businessmen were considered invincible."[16]

Paul Anger believed that Israel's power was weakening. As proof of its waning invincibility, he cites Jewish protest against a song published by the Postal Board:

A thousand rebellious Jews
Cruel murderers
Spit at the feet
Of the great God of Love.

The Jews' sensitivity revealed their weakness. "Their shield of invulnerability has fallen. We are at an historical turning point."[17]   But Israel's power was not so easily rattled. Democracy, which was growing continually stronger, would ensure the perpetuation of Jewish hegemony.

Lionel Groulx lets fly a volley of his own by supporting Jeune-Canada who "denounced another, more serious abuse." The intolerable abuse to which he refers is, "The elevation to the rank of privileged class of an ethnic minority of no particular significance which does not warrant this extraordinary distinction." Who are the members of this culpable class? "This is the way we are treating Jews in Canada and, more than anywhere else, in Quebec." Groulx elaborated on this criminal state of affairs.

> In Montreal we have drawn safe electoral districts for him, veritable private grounds where the sons of Israel can use and abuse their voting rights as they wish. If they feel like it they can turn out only 10 percent of the population without the slightest risk of worry, and also without the unpleasant necessity of taking oath, a rule or safeguard reserved for the false voters of other races.[18]

According to the above passage, the Jewish minority was profiting unduly from a biased electoral map. They lived in constituencies where election results were inevitably and criminally skewed. The Jew's political influence, which was as huge as it was illegitimate, was made possible by collusion with the Traitor. The position French Canadians found themselves in was due to, "the complacency of self-interested, tolerant politicians who allow Jewish electoral preserves to infiltrate our 'democracy' almost on principle. Let us kneel before these golden ghettos."[19]

The collusion between Jews—who carried the Freemasons in their pockets—and politicians had astonishing ramifications. Bolstered by "blind politicians, Jews and Freemasons have managed to transform the province of Quebec. One simply has to ask the old guard. But Jews and their friends stand by each other. They will say the allegations go too far." Lambert Closse stifles any possible objection by attributing the longevity of Alexander Taschereau's liberal government to Judeo-Masonic dealings.

> Without the help of mysterious powers, how could a man sustain a government which ruled the roost for 15 years, abusing everyone and allowing Jews to work Sundays in the world's most Catholic province, run all the trusts and assume the directorship of the country's wealthiest companies?[20]

The politicians hypocritically turned a blind eye to the cancer knawing away at their province. "Judeo-Masonry is, beyond the shadow of a doubt, the cancer which is ravaging us. Our politicians refuse to admit it."[21]

A Jewish party existed in French Canada which had little to do with the Jewish religion or race, much like the "Jewish spirit" mentioned in a previous chapter. L'Action nationale's Roger Duhamel quoted and commented on an excerpt published in Le Caada. In Quebec, has there not always been "outside the two mainstream political parties, a Jewish party without any particular political ideology, whose sole purpose is the realization of Jewish ambitions? No one needs to found this party; it has always existed." Its so-called policy platform "consists of two objectives: 1. unite to elect Jewish representatives; and 2. organize matters so as to remain always in the vicinity of power.[22]

"Foreigners are well-treated here," Anatole Vanier asserts. "They enjoy a high degree of civil liberty. What need do they have for political rights?" The fact that Jewish electoral constituencies were breeding grounds for democracy in Quebec made these rights even more redundant. "Everyone knows they only serve party interests." Radical measures were needed to contain the Jewish mob. "Because they harm us and attack our dignity, we must suppress them." This enlightened political commentator concludes that if Quebeckers do not abolish constituencies swarming with Jews, the latter will "force us, sooner than we imagine, to adopt hitlerian attitudes."[23]

In short, Vanier's plan was to deprive citizens of Jewish persuasion of the political rights normally universally accorded, and to forbid the election of Jewish representatives to the provincial legislature. If this was not done immediately, "hitlerian attitudes" would rear their ugly heads. Having read the outpourings of this same author on the "movement in new Germany," it is hard not to suspect he is simply wanted a convenient justification for Fascist acts.

In a similar vein, André Laurendeau attacks Jews as the perpetrators of political partisanship. After fulminating against "party politics, this putrid illness which has ravaged us for three quarters of a century," he writes that the reason why Canadian politicians protested Hitler's persecution of the Jews and attended "meetings of unassimilated and unassimilable immigrants" was obvious. "They were honouring an old political tradition: flattering a powerful group of voters..." Furthermore, these shady politicians were not unaware of the maxim, "Prayers do not win elections." Jews had "economic might" to offer, and their "nice little nest-egg" made them irresistibly seductive.[24]

Democracy and "political partisanship" had enslaved French Canadians, and would continue to do so. "There is but one oppressor. We are the victims of finance, of gigantic trusts which use political partisanship to oppress us." Defining the problem in this way made it imperative to protest "caresses meant to flatter a certain powerful group of voters."[25]

Le Devoir dwells at length over a type of "political partisanship" of which Jews were especially fond: electoral fraud. In a series of articles published between November 1935 and the end of 1936, the newspaper describes fraudulent practices occurring in the Saint Laurent riding during the provincial elections and gives eye-witness accounts of voter beatings.[26] Constituency representative Josef Cohen was forced to resign in the face of this damning accumulation of evidence, but not before Le Devoir repeatedly charged that he enjoyed the "full support" of Alexander Taschereau's liberal government.[27]

Le Devoir was not simply questioning the dishonesty of certain of Josef Cohen's supporters, its target was the alleged fraudulent comportment of 'Jewish' French Canadians in several constituencies. Le Devoir contends that the Mercier riding's liberal candidate, Anatole Plante—a good Christian and French Canadian—owes his seat "to five hand-picked Jewish election return officers..."[28] "who stuffed the ballot boxes with 705 Plante votes against 48 for Cormier,"[29] and to "police imposters working hand in glove with candidate Plante's Jewish assistants...."[30] These policemen mingled with the voters, pushing and shoving, and Yiddish became "the official language in certain polls."[31]

Ironically, Jewish electoral preserves—those privileged grounds of criminal electoral practices—did not actually contain many Jewish voters.

> Jews seem to dominate certain Montreal neighbourhoods. If the truth be told, their apparent dominance is due more to the brazen criminality of a minority than to the size of their population. You just have to look at the electoral lists in the three Montreal constituencies popularly referred to as Jewish to realize that the great bulk of people living there are Christian.[32]

"Jewish electoral preserves," the stronghold and jewel of "political partisanship," we learn, were predominantly Christian! Unfortunately, myth carried infinitely more weight than reality. Émile Benoist used the worn-out biological metaphor to warn that "the criminal boldness" of certain Jewish politicians could spread throughout the electoral body like gangrene through human flesh. "A wound which is left to suppurate will poison the entire body," he cautions. "Odious and violent demonstrations took place in the Maisonneuve riding," he reports, adding that "two days after the ballot, loud and threatening crowds moved through the Laurier riding. Proof that the disease was spreading."[33]

What did it matter that the so-called "Jewish ridings" actually comprised few Jewish denizens; or that the vote had been tampered with in the ridings of Abitibi, Gaspésie and Berthier, as well as "10 to 15 other ridings;" or that less than 50 percent of the Jewish electorate in the Mercier riding voted; or that, again in the Mercier riding, 60 percent of Jews voted for the liberal candidate while 40 percent supported the Union Nationale;[35] or that apologies poured forth from the Canadian Jewish Congress for the criminal acts attributed to citizens of Jewish descent?[36] Georges Pelletier of Le Devoir wrote that when the time was ripe the government ought to deprive an entire "group of voters and candidates" of their voting rights. He also advised it to limit the number of people sharing the religious convictions of this "group of voters"[37] allowed entry into the country.

The subject of so many of Le Devoir's attacks was a symbol of its own making: the elusive, mythical Jew. During the 1936 inquiry into public spending which eventually brought down the provincial liberal government, Le Devoir's Paul Anger wrote an article about liberal MNA Peter Bercovitch who had been chosen to defuse the scandal. Anger writes that Bercovitch "has great presence, a nice voice, good manners and remarkable parliamentary skill and experience given that he has occupied his seat since 1916. The role he has accepted, however, makes him odious."

The above quotation is not all that revelatory, but in the very next sentence the myth rears its head, devouring Bercovitch in no time at all. "First of all, he is Jewish—Jewish to the depths of his soul and in every fibre of his body...." During his campaign against the Liberal Party, Duplessis used Bercovitch as a valuable trump card, knowing full well that he could play on his audiences' emotions. "Nothing irritates them more than this Jew trying to cover up the truth, particularly in an era in which his people are hated more universally than they have ever been before."[38]

Israelites reigned supreme in Quebec[39] and throughout America,[40] and this elevated them above the law.[41] It is not hard to recognize in these phrases the hackneyed anti-Semitic theme song of Quebec's Fascist nationalists.

More was yet to come. Jews were so presumptuous that they actually began to feel at home in Canada. They had ingratiated themselves so thoroughly that the federal Radio Commission appointed an Israelite to its board of directors[42]; and "Yiddish, Czech and Communist Spanish were heard on Radio Canada; it was only a matter of time before Moscow became an ally and the Russian dialects joined them."[43] Furthermore, "in many (federal government) departments, typists, clerks and inspectors are hired because of their Yiddish fluency,"[44] and federal Liberal Member of Parliament Samuel W. Jacobs was Quebec's representative in London, on the dubious pretext that he was "elected in a largely French Canadian riding." "He was already on foreign soil in Ottawa where he had taken over the territory of another," fumed Le Devoir. "But this was not sufficient. Give an Israelite an inch, and sooner or later he will take four feet."[45] "Abraham, Isaac and Jacob want a tenth Canadian province: New Palestine."[46]

The tenacious Hebrew people, who would not be scared off, went so far as to clutter the tramways. "Time and time again we hear that gentiles, for example, have a lot of trouble finding a seat on Sundays on the Cartierville tram because the Hebrews crowd into the cars, shoving everybody out of the way."[47]

The Jewish invasion was such that Montreal was beginning to look like Warsaw. The two cities were drowning beneath "this Jewish mob, these Levites, these boots and visored black skullcaps, these beards, these heads with corkscrews adorning their jowls, these bizarre human specimens who are unique unto themselves," to such an extent that "while entire Montreal districts are ruined just like in Warsaw, smaller municipalities like Plage Laval are also complaining that Jews have destroyed real estate values."[48]

Groulx laments that the city now belongs to the Other. Paul Anger takes a ride on a Montreal tramway and describes the passengers as having "high cheekbones, olive skin, piercing eyes...woolly hair, chocolate complexions, thick lips, white teeth, pug noses." He also sees "blond-haired men, sober and stiff, rosy-cheeked, hardly moving,..."and "Chinese with stained fingers, velvet eyes in faces burnt by the sun and wind, others reeking of garlic and speaking Italian, sporting waxed mustaches, hair greased down with vaseline, smelling of cheap perfume." Then there were the "sordid, dubious characters from the slums of some city in Europe," not to mention "the cucumber-noses, hand-wavers, flat feet, mouths that loudly spit out foreign sounds and the occasional, mangled English word, eyes that stare menacingly at you. Behold the Jew."[49]

For his part, Pierre Dagenais melted all the city's immigrants into a single threatening mass. "Where are the descendants of the 10 thousand French colonists who created this

country?...They are in the crowd here, practically submerged by
the foreign races which trample all over them, and threaten to
crush them if they refuse to defend themselves."[50]

Blissfully ignorant of the threat stalking them, "seduced by
the city's glitter, the good farming people allowed themselves to
be swept along to try their fortunes there. In their new neighbourhoods they encountered the Communist virus, imported
from southern Europe."[51]

Communism was not the only menace capable of killing
French Canadians. Materialism, a by-product of urbanization
and thus associated with the Other and the Jew, was just as
dangerous. "The destruction of our ethnic character by excessive
urbanization and by debilitating contact with Jewish
materialism has been one of most unfortunate occurrences of
the last 50 years."[52]

Le Devoir never tired of linking Jews to the city. "It is of note,"
Georges Pelletier writes, "that Jews tend to favour big cities.
More than half of their population lives there."[53] While fishing
for reasons to block the entry of Jewish refugees into Canada Le
Grincheux observes, "In Canada, Jews have settled in the cities.
Too many of our people are also flocking to the cities to mix
with the quantities of foreigners."[54] Montreal, he says, echoing
his colleagues, is turning into a Jewish town. "In the not too distant future, some official wanting to beautify Montreal will
probably suggest importing the Wailing Wall from Jerusalem and
setting it up in Saint Louis Square."[55]

Groulx had already warned French Canadians that daily life in
a largely urban, industrialized society would bring them into
contact with the Other and would encourage the eruption of all
kinds of social cankers. L'Action nationale agreed, and then
proceeded to finger the guilty parties.

> One frequently finds evidence in the media, advertising, theatre
> and movies of the frivolous or indecent attitudes which have
> penetrated to the very depths of Christian souls and poisoned
> them. Jews are the main instigators and most zealous pedlars of
> these influences.[56]

André Laurendeau, who was then still a member of Jeune-
Canada, uses numbers—which invariably bolster credibility—to
make the same case.

The ritual impregnability of the Jews in a country where they make up barely one thirtieth of the population is sustainable because these same Jews are wealthy, and 55 to 70 percent of commercial advertising as well as the entire international film industry are controlled by them. And we call ourselves free?[57]

"In a study published in August of 1924 by l'Action nationale, Mr Harry Bernard proved that Jews rule the cinematic world. They own 80 percent of all film companies."[58]

Louis Dupire quotes an American expert as saying, "These days most animated cartoons depict crime and sow the seeds of vice and perfidy."[59]

A few Le Devoir journalists vented their anger against sensationalist tabloids—otherwise known as "yellow rags"—which they regarded as "crime's henchmen."[60] These publications were poisonous. "Nevertheless, in most homes...one can find these papers along with their perfidious influence."[61] If parents and teachers refused to take action, the cancer of Americanism would spread, infecting the souls of French Canadian youth. With "...lightning speed our children will succumb to profound, incurable American contamination. Language is not the only thing that will suffer. The very health of our young people will be undermined."[62]

"Crude advertisers, intimately linked with Judeo-American interests," worked in tandem with yellow journalism. "Publicity for theatrical events and, even more importantly, for movies was one of their primary sources of daily revenue."[63]

Every form of entertainment and amusement in North America was Jewish-owned. "Jews controlled theatre in Canada and throughout the world. They ruled Broadway and dominated Hollywood." According to the same journalist, their sphere of influence did not stop there. "Entertainment of almost every conceivable form...is controlled by Israelites. Whether indirectly or directly, they control radio in the United States. In Canada they control it to the extent that it is not government-owned." They also spread a type of music Le Devoir held in contempt. "They use radio to recruit people to jazz halls where the music is very often composed by Jews. Everyone is familiar with the most famous Jewish jazz composer, Irving Berlin, but there are a great many others."[64] Had jazz been the only problem,[65] there would have been hope. Unfortunately, via the intermediary of their old friend, the Jewish-infiltrated daily La Presse, Jews were able to introduce another kind of music into the mainstream. "If you tune in around 11 o'clock to the radio station belonging to La Presse—that family newspaper purporting to defend Catholic interests—you will hear vile dance hall music." The nation's moral spirit would suffer greatly from Jewish monopolization of the entertainment industries, the journalist continued. "Entertainment has an undeniable influence on a country's morality. As I have said before, these industries belong in large part, if not completely, to Israel."[66]

"Shh! Don't you dare say the word 'Jew.' All the radio stations will close down."[67]

When the provincial police arrested members of a French operatic company for indecency, Georges Pelletier raged against the foreigners and circumcised men who were spoiling French art forms. It is a "...shame that French men and women would stoop to act in this—when it's not a Jew who wrote it, it's a Greek, or a Frenchified German Jew, or a foreigner who, 10 years ago did not know a word of French but spoke Russian or Yiddish, or pidgin French mixed with the language of the ghetto."[68]

It was impossible for French playwrights of Jewish persuasion[69] or German-Jewish film directors living in Paris[70] to create French works of art. The French movie industry was run by "adventurers, foreigners, corrupt individuals and exploiters who only recently received naturalized French status."[71]

Jewish influence did not stop at the media and entertainment, it extended to the fashion industry, encouraging an indecency "which women themselves had never really asked for." And just when the trend seemed to be turning back to decency,

These days, Israelites in the fashion industry are returning to long dresses. They are not propelled by any concerns over decency. They judge all things by one standard alone. If a product does not make money, it is bad; if it makes money, it is good." Just how did longer dresses fit into the picture of the Jew's passion for profit? "With dresses getting shorter every year, women of modest means tended to alter them themselves. It is easy to shorten a hem; it is quite another thing to lengthen one..." Women would be forced to go out and buy. To top it all off, indecency was still thriving. "Lack of decency in the form of light, transparent fabrics and daring, low-cut, often bare-backed designs spiced up women's apparel.[72]

Jews used similar forms of sexual exploitation in advertising. "Advertising, a field dominated by our Judeo-American rulers, has decided that sex appeal sells. They use it all the time, without the slightest concern for relevancy."[73]

Jews had no sense of decency concerning even their own bodies. One Le Devoir journalist writes about a trip to Saint Agathe where he encountered "two women out walking and doing their grocery shopping at the corner store in swimsuits—suits that were too scanty even for bathing." To add insult to injury, this was right in the middle of the pristine Quebec countryside! "The women were Jewish. I have nothing to say about their religion, as this they cannot help." He then advises town councils to "adopt by-laws prohibiting such revolting exhibitionism. We beseech them in the name of our people's religious beliefs, the dignity of our race and our traditions of decency and modesty."[74]

This chapter will conclude with the words of René Monette who believed that "Jewish sensuality" was directly responsible for the falling French Canadian birthrate. "Sensual materialism, which afflicts the great majority of the Jewish race, manifests itself among our people by an immorality which is excessive and harmful. Our birthrate, which was 41 percent at the end of the 18th century, has fallen to 21.7 percent."[75]

Notes

1. Jacques Brassier (pseudonym of Lionel Groulx): "Pour qu'on vive.," *Action nationale*, (June 1933), p. 364-365.

2. *Ibid.*

3. Lambert Closse: *La réponse de la race.*, p. 35.

4. Anatole Vanier: "Les Juifs au Canada.," *Action nationale*, (September 1933), p. 7;

5. *Ibid.*, p. 16; René Monette: *Commerce juif et commerce canadien-français*, in: Les Jeune-Canada: *Politiciens et Juifs*, pp. 47-48; François-Albert Angers: "La conquête économique.," *Action nationale*, (February 1939), p. 162; Arthur Laurendeau: "Éducation nationale.," *Action nationale*, (March 1936), p. 182.

6. Maurice Tremblay: "Régionalisme.," *Action nationale*, (May 1937), pp. 276-277; E.M.: "Si l'on voyait clair.," *Action nationale*, (April 1933), p. 248; Dominique Beaudin: "Capitalisme étranger et vie nationale.," *Action nationale*, (June 1933) p. 324; "Montréal, ville...française.," *Action nationale*, (June 1937), p. 345.

7. La vie courante., *Action nationale*, (December 1933), p. 272.

8. René Monette: *op.cit.*, p. 45.

9. *Ibid.*, p. 46.

174 THE TRAITOR AND THE JEW

10. François-Albert Anger: "Quo vadis Israël.," *Action nationale*, (January 1939), p. 50.

11. *Ibid.*, p. 43.

12. Anatole Vanier: *op.cit.*, pp. 8-9.

13. *Ibid.*, p. 9.

14. Paul Poirier: "Il a raison.," *Le Devoir*, 9 July 1935, p. 1; "They have only one way of judging things. It's bad if its not profitable, it's good if it pays." Paul Anger: "Mussolini triomphera-t-il?," *Le Devoir*, 10 October 1929, p. 1; For the articles in Le Devoir about the Jew and commerce, see Appendix C. of the French edition of this book.

15. Paul Anger: "Ainsi parlait Abraham..," *Le Devoir*, 4 August 1934, p. 1.

16. Paul Anger: "Israël faillit.," *Le Devoir*, 31 December 1934, p. 1.

17. *Ibid.*

18. Jacques Brassier(pseudonym of Lionel Groulx): "Pour qu'on vive.," *Action nationale*, (June 1933), pp. 363-364.

19. Anatole Vanier: "Les Juifs au Canada.," *Action nationale*, (September 1933), pp. 11-12.

20. Lambert Closse: *op. cit.*, p. 539.

21. *Ibid.*

22. Roger Duhamel: "Quand Israël est candidat.," *Action nationale*,(December 1938), p. 327.

23. Anatole Vanier: *op. cit.*, pp. 13-14; "The most basic decency demands however that those who adopt Canada as their home, but intend to maintain their traditions, their religion, their language—as is the case with the Jews—abstain from participating in political life." Roger Duhamel: *op. cit.*, p. 328.

24. André Laurendeau: Partisannerie politique.: *op.cit.*, pp. 58-59.

25. *Ibid.*, p. 61.

26. Cf. Appendix D., French edition of this book.

27. Cf. Appendix E., French edition of this book.

28. "Cinq polls cuisinés à l'ouest de Saint-Denis, ont à peu près élu Plante.," *Le Devoir*, 11 January 1936, p. 1.

29. *Ibid.*

30. "Il y a eu jusqu'à des faux policiers provinciaux.," *Le Devoir*, 20 January 1936, p. 1.

31. "Le yiddish était la langue officielle dans certains polls.," *Le Devoir*, 22 January 1936, p. 1; On this matter: "Comment les vrai électeurs juifs de Mercier ont voté.," *Le Devoir*, 10 January 1936, p. 1; "Plante, tout comme Cohen, eût plus de voix qu'il y avait d'électeurs inscrits.," *Le Devoir*, 13 January 1936, p. 1; Le Grincheux: Carnet d'un grincheux, *Le Devoir*, 23 January 1936, p. 1; Le Grincheux: Carnet d'un grincheux, *Le Devoir*, 2 March 1936, p. 1; "La journée du 25 novembre sur le front Plante.," *Le Devoir*, 4 July 1936, p. 1.

32. E.B.: "Mœurs électorales.," *Le Devoir*, 14 December 1935, p. 1.
Georges Pelletier: "Cette majorité.," *Le Devoir*, 24 March 1936, p. 1.

33. *Ibid.*

34. G.Pelletier: "Cette majorité.," *Le Devoir*, 24 March 1936, p. 1.

35. "Comment les vrais électeurs juifs de Mercier ont voté.," *Le Devoir*, 10 January 1936, p. 1.

36. "Déclaration du "Canadian Jewish Congress" au sujet de la corruption électorale." *Le Devoir*, 26 December 1935, p. 1; G. Pelletier: "Cette déclaration.," *Le Devoir*, 30 December 1935, p. 1.

37. G. Pelletier: "Six mois et l'amende.," Le Devoir, 22 March 1939, p. 1.

38. Paul Anger: "Maladresses.," *Le Devoir*, 2 June 1936, p. 1.

39. Pamphile: Carnet d'un grincheux, *Le Devoir*, 21 June 1933, p. 1.

40. Pamphile: Carnet d'un grincheux, *Le Devoir*, 13 June 1933, p. 1.

41. Pamphile: Carnet d'un grincheux, *Le Devoir*, 21 September 1934, p. 1; Le Grincheux: Le carnet du grincheux, *Le Devoir*, 2 August 1939, p. 1.

42. Louis Dupire: "Pourquoi M. King retardait.," *Le Devoir*, 12 September 1936, p. 1; Le Grincheux: Carnet d'un grincheux, *Le Devoir*, 11 September 1936, p. 1.

43. Le Grincheux: Le carnet du grincheux, *Le Devoir*, 2 July 1939, p. 1.

44. Albert Rioux: "Encore le Service civil.," *Le Devoir*, 24 March 1936, p. 1, editorial.

45. Le Grincheux: Le carnet du grincheux, *Le Devoir*, 1 April 1937, p. 1; Le Grincheux: Le carnet du grincheux, *Le Devoir*, 6 April 1937, p. 1.

46. Le Grincheux: Carnet d'un grincheux, Le Devoir, 10 March 1936, p. 1.

47. Le Grincheux: Le carnet du grincheux, *Le Devoir*, 2 August 1939, p. 1.

48. Anatole Vanier: "Les Juifs au Canada.," *op. cit.*, pp. 10-11.

49. Paul Anger: "Cosmopolis.," *Le Devoir*, 7 September 1934, p. 1.

50. Pierre Dagenais: *L'immigration au Canada et le communisme.*, in: Les Jeune-Canada: *Politiciens et Juifs*, pp. 24-25.

51. *Ibid.*, p. 30.

52. René Monette: *Commerce juif et commerce canadien-français*, in: Les Jeune-Canada: *Politiciens et Juifs*, p. 38.

53. Omer Héroux: "M. Jacobs aussi.," *Le Devoir*, 26 October 1933, p. 1, editorial; "Quelle sorte d'immigrants entrent au Canada?," *Le Devoir*, 12 May 1936, p. 2; Omer Héroux: "Où?," *Le Devoir*, 18 November 1938, p. 1; Georges Pelletier: "Les Juifs d'Allemagne font déraisonner le Star.," *Le Devoir*, 26 November 1938, p. 1, editorial; Georges Pelletier:"Combien sont-ils?," *Le Devoir*, 21 December 1938, p. 1; Le Grincheux: Le carnet du grincheux, *Le Devoir*, 9 March 1939, p. 1; Georges Pelletier: "Etrangers.," *Le Devoir*, 5 April 1939, p. 1.

54. Le Grincheux: Carnet d'un grincheux, *Le Devoir*, 17 April 1936, p. 1.

55. Pamphile: Carnet d'un grincheux, *Le Devoir*, 9 December 1933, p. 1; Le Grincheux: Carnet d'un grincheux, *Le Devoir*, 5 March 1936, p. 1.

56. Mgr. Gfoellner: "L'internationalisme juif.," *Action nationale*, (June 1933), p. 381.

57. André Laurendeau: Partisannerie politique, *op. cit.*, pp. 60-61.

58. Joseph-Papin Archambault, s.j.: "Le cinéma et les enfants.," Action nationale, (January 1933), p. 58; "The Jew Crémieux said it in France, and Northcliff realised it during the Great War: "Take over the newspapers and the rest will fall into our hands.," Abbé Ph. Perrier: "Vingt-cinq années de journalisme.," Action nationale, (February 1933), p. 86.

59. Louis Dupire: "M. Roger Bason et le cinéma populaire.," *Le Devoir*, 13 April 1929, p. 1, editorial.

60. Roch: "Journaux jaunes, complices du crime.," *Le Devoir*, 8 January 1932, p. 1; Paul Anger: "Logique.," *Le Devoir*, 1 June 1936, p. 1.

61. Louis Dupire: "L'oiseau bleu.," *Le Devoir*, 23 December 1931, p. 1.

62. *Ibid.*

63. Paul Anger: "La taxe des divertissements.," *Le Devoir*, 22 January 1932, p. 1; Georges Pelletier: "Le jaunisme l'a tué.," *Le Devoir*, 28 February 1931, p. 1; Georges Pelletier: "Les "funny papers.," *Le Devoir*, 13 February 1935, p. 1; Georges Pelletier: "Un roi de presse.," *Le Devoir*, 22 February 1936, p. 1; E.B.: "Problème juif et antisémitisme.," *Le Devoir*, 29 November 1938, p. 1; Le Grincheux: Le carnet du grincheux, *Le Devoir*, 3 December 1938, p. 1; Le Grincheux: Le carnet du grincheux, *Le Devoir*, 18 August 1939, p. 1;

64. Paul Anger: "Il y a compensation.," *Le Devoir*, 30 May 1930, p. 1; Alvarez Vaillancourt: "L'industrie du cinéma.," *Le Devoir*, 20 October 1937, p. 10;;G. Pelletier: "Cinéma.," *Le Devoir*, 10 July 1934, p. 1; P. Anger: "Cinéma pourri.," *Le Devoir*, 13 July 1934, p. 1; G. Pelletier: "Leur départ.," *Le Devoir*, 30 January 1936, p. 1.

65. "…de la musique américano-judaïque,…, de la "…Rotten Music!" Le Grincheux: Le carnet du grincheux, *Le Devoir*, 12 August 1937, p. 1.

66. Paul Anger: "Il y a compensation.," *Le Devoir*, 30 May 1930, p. 1.

67. Pamphile: Carnet d'un grincheux, *Le Devoir*, 4 April 1934, p. 1.

68. G. Pelletier: "Si c'est cela l'art français.," *Le Devoir*, 28 February 1930, p. 1, editorial; On the controversy surrounding the Phi-Phi operetta: G. Pelletier: "Bonne presse et francophobie.," *Le Devoir*, 10 March 1930, p. 1; G. Pelletier: "Le théâtre d'exportation.," *Le Devoir*, 23 April 1931, p. 1, editorial

69. G. Pelletier: "Porto-Riche.," *Le Devoir*, 8 September 1930, p. 1; G. Pelletier: "Du travail.," *Le Devoir*, 24 November 1934, p. 1.

70. Paul et Jean: "Censure.," *Le Devoir*, 12 October 1932, p. 1.

71. Jean Labrye: "Serait-ce la crise?," *Le Devoir*, 20 July 1934, p. 1.

72. P. Anger: "Mussolini triomphera-t-il?," Le Devoir, 10 October 1929, p. 1.

73. P. Anger: "M. Savignac sait-il cela?," Le Devoir, 17 August 1936, p. 1.

74. Fr. Lemarc: "Nos villes d'eaux.," *Le Devoir*, 19 February 1930, p. 1.

75. René Monette: *Commerce juif et commerce canadien-français*, op. cit., p. 39.

11

SUPERMEN AND GODS

Consciousness of being right bred a righteousness which excesses would not destroy, but only confirm. Terrorism became the hallmark of plurality: 'There is nothing,' exclaimed St. Just, 'which resembles so much virtue as a great crime.' It seemed, indeed, as though great crimes were the only way to ensure justice: 'There is something terrible,' St. Just also said, 'in the sacred love of the fatherland; it is so exclusive as to sacrifice everything to the public interest, without pity, without fear, without respect for humanity...What produces the general good is always terrible.[1]

The eschatological aspect of Groulx's ideology reared up in all its sinister splendour. French Canada was close to death, a paschal lamb to be sacrificed on the altar of that high priestess of the forces of destruction—democracy. Was the situation absolutely hopeless? Groulx, a master at ideological conjuring tricks, now pulled a final card from his sleeve: millenarian Fascism. To counter the rot and disease plaguing French Canada, he offered a utopian vision of absolute purity. It effectively offset the nihilism and destructive despair permeating his nationalism.

Fascist thematic concerns and terminology cropped everywhere in Groulx's utopian vision: French Canada would reconcile itself with the soil and its ancestors, combining forces and converging in a powerful, unified beam (in French, "faisceau," the etymological root of "Fascism"). Utopian visions of this nature tended to be totalitarian, and ironically, Groulx and his fanatical devotees ended up promoting the mystique of both Fascism and Communism in French Canada; the important thing was to undermine democracy. Dictatorships were invariably the earthly embodiments of this kind of idealistic mysticism. Sometimes, like the regimes in Portugal and Ireland, they fell on the extreme right of the political spectrum, and they were almost always Fascist. Mussolini was roundly applauded. Hitler also received his share of praise for educative work and for his political platform. Dictators were depicted as brave rescuers, snatching the moribund nation from the gaping jaws of death and existential nothingness. Fascism was vastly different from our miserable little democracies, as Groulx so eloquently lamented.

The French state, corporatism, national education, mystique, spontaneous revolution—regardless of the formula, the goal was always the same: the establishment of a utopia which would provide a counterweight to democratic liberalism.

The creation of this paradise on earth required the expulsion of all Jews. Forget about pogroms, André Laurendeau cautioned, because they did not work. Instead, ghettos should be built, educational institutions should impose quotas, voting rights should be repealed, deportations to Palestine should be ordered, mandatory identification cards should be given to those living in Christian lands and economic boycotts should be instituted. These measures would take care of the "Jewish question." The solutions proposed by Groulx, l'Action nationale, Jeune-Canada and Le Devoir echo those found in Nazi race legislation. In April 1933, the Germans imposed "a limit on the number of Jewish elementary and high school students to reflect the percentage of Jews living in Germany;"[2] and in 1935, the Nuremberg laws reserved full voting rights for citizens of the Reich, as opposed to those who were merely domiciled in Germany.[3]

The Traitor would be permitted to tread on the soil of Paradise only after having gone through extensive national and political reeducation. As humanity was only possible in the context of nationhood, the French Canadian people would achieve human status by becoming a nation. Reeducation had other virtues as well: French Canadians would leave the sub-human realm of liberal democracy to become the supermen and Gods if the utopian dream.

FRENCH CANADA WAS OSCILLATING between survival and destruction. Cut off in the North American continent, it struggled "to live, in the most basic sense of the word which is to defend one's life from the forces of death."[4]

Superimposed on the life-death dichotomy were those of good and evil, nation and party, nationalist and traitor. Democracy, referred to by Groulx as "the tyranny of opinion," sets up "an immense battle between the forces of good and evil, between the powers of truth and error." The Traitor jauntily straddles the forces of evil and error. "The displaced and apathetic will always regard nationalists as doom-sayers and sharp-tongued Catos." There is, however, a glimmer of hope. "Our duty is to join this drawn-out battle and hope that national spirit will be able to emerge victorious over partisanship."[5]

Hermas Bastien remarks on the scope of the liberal. "On the other hand, liberalism has contaminated absolutely everything: our religious convictions, education, law, our institutions and our charities." He is under no illusions about "the effort required to straighten out a regime in which the forces of death seem greatly to outweigh the forces of life."[6]

For 60 years our lives have revolved around a ballot box. Surprisingly enough, before we shrank down to what we are today—a thin crust of partisan politicians—we were huge—a race of men, a French Catholic nation.[7]

Because "the time has come when we must either wake up or die," Groulx warns yet again, "we will have to unite all our forces together into a powerful beam."[9]

André Laurendeau recites the same Bible verses of national salvation. "No more partisan politics; the interests of the French Canadian people must precede those of a group of individuals." Anticipating a slogan often used by the Vichy government he concludes with the following words, "We must add: French Canada to the French Canadians."[10]

Groulx's brand of nationalism tended to divorce itself from daily concerns. In one of the most enigmatic declarations of his career, he voluntarily admitted as much, foreseeing:

> ...spiritual ascension, which will not provide practical solutions for every problem faced by our nation, but will allow us to reach a "doctrinal heaven," as Maritain would say, a united body of ruling truths hovering above the chance happenings of life, gathered at the source, and as such, eminently decent, which will illuminate our road and all the problems we encounter.[11]

Nationalism and the "body of prime truths" also included "the secret instinct, the blood and tradition flowing through our veins, the ancestors living within each and every one of us."[12]

It was the responsibility of "intellectual leaders and university professors" to disseminate national myths, those "strong, invincible reasons for living."[13] If national education permeated with mysticism had allowed "other, more down-trodden peoples, who had started lower down on the ladder, to rise up and claim power," would it not do the same in French Canada? With "a voluntary and virile education," the "mystique of effort," hammered into schoolboys' heads, "this watchword and haunting *leitmotif: to be masters in our own land,*" will sound the death knell of the "parlour knick-knacks" populating the province's "schools, convents and colleges."[14]

Starting with the simple premise that only a "French Canada with will-power and strength" could be considered truly alive, l'-Action nationale cursed schools which failed to do their part in saving the nation from existential nothingness. "A school which rejects nationalist principles is one which goes against the nation and commits treason."[15]

The propagation of a national mystique depended more on the providential actions of a leader, a Fascist dictator, than on any teacher. One year after the National Socialists took power in Germany, Lionel Groulx heaped praise on German dictators for their pedagogical talents. "The present dictators know full well that their first priority is to seize control of teachers and schools; not so much for purposes of teaching as for those of education." German leaders did not approach the task half-heartedly, Groulx enthusiastically observes.

> Was it not during the holidays which just passed that Germany's teachers, mobilized in special camps as if preparing for important pedagogical manoeuvres, heard their country's leaders express their plan for the national training of young Germans?[16]

The schools of Fascist Italy inspired Groulx in much the same way. "The name of a national hero is inscribed over the door of each classroom in Italy's schools...The Duce, who is a former teacher, understands how to mould the dough of human minds."[17] How removed all this was from our wretched little democracies! "Fortunate country whose schools are possessed of a soul! Fortunate countries to whom fate has delivered a leader!" Groulx exclaims. His reservations were timid and few. "Far be it from us to admire everything about Mussolini's government, as we do everything about Italian pedagogy." But how progressive it seemed compared to democracy.

> When we see the mediocrity of our miserable little democracies and hear the low level of public discourse, how can we convince ourselves that a nation can be happy and great while it is governed by several hundred yapping, empty-headed members of parliament?[18]

Groulx regarded Fascist Italy and the Soviet Union as two examples of revolutionary mystique, articulated by true leaders and diffused by systems of education. Under the guise of a pseudonym, Groulx quotes himself on just this topic. "The speaker (Lionel Groulx) cited Italy as a case in point. He demonstrated how, with the particular help of the school system, a firm-handed leader could create a new race of Italians in no time at all." The Duce received additional praise. "He might also have noted that the present strength of Il Duce's government is due to the generation of young Italians trained according to Fascist principles." The U.S.S.R. seemed to be Fascist Italy's worthy equal. "In the same vein, it does not take a genius to notice that the extraordinary and mysterious longevity of the Soviet regime is in large part due to the revolutionary mystique with which an entire army of masters inspired Russia's youth."[19]

French Canada would do well to emulate Communism's mystique. "In this regard, take Communism as an example. Its coarse materialism did not prevent it from grasping the fact that in order to stir up and mesmerize the proletarians it had to create a myth encompassing daily and future life." All French Canada had to do was follow in its footsteps. "Will it take appealing to the spirit and soul of our race, finding the non-materialistic impulses capable of propelling us into action?"[20]

Fascism promised rebirth to races heeding its call.

> Weak minds which believe in democracy at the expense of the Church and Christ react with horror to Fascism in all its shapes and forms. This, despite the fact that certain nations are currently very content, experiencing the most glorious kind of rebirth under this political system.[21]

Examples of the dictatorships of Italy, Austria and Portugal were used to silence chattering parliamentarians. "Our chattering members of the legislature might learn something about pulling a nation from the clutches of poverty and moral anarchy by considering the examples of Italy, Austria and Portugal."[22] What lessons these inept politicians would learn from Italy and Mussolini! "In Mussolini's country, for example, they would see how a real head of state goes about inculcating the taste and passion for greatness and resurrection in a moribund nation."[23]

The leader or dictator removed the threat of death under which his nation was cowering.

> Men, leaders breathe greatness into their nations and immediately these countries, long considered dead and gone, pull themselves free from their fear of death, and rediscover their direction and destiny as well as the passion necessary to live and re-shape themselves.[24]

Groulx marvels yet again at how the Duce and Dollfuss, two "true national agitators," managed to pull their people out of the moral quagmire into which they had sunk by invoking the past greatness of the blood flowing in their veins. "In 1922, Mussolini denounced the social and political abjection of the Italian people;

but he also reminded them that with the blood of Caesar running in their veins they could still revive themselves with palatine breaths," he writes with a fevered pen. Dollfuss was equally effective, the Canon continues, when "he reminded little Austria that for many centuries it was the heart and soul of a great empire and an important civilization." Using the myth of origins to thwart the possible death and the more immediate moral decay of a nation, Groulx concludes by reminding "the cowardly nation that is contemporary French Canada that they are the direct descendants of northern America's conquistadors."[25]

French Canada was badly in need of a leader, one who could point the way to its resurrection. Groulx was full of supplications.

> A man! A leader! Will he ever come our way? Unlike other more fortunate nations, our present crisis has not resulted in a real man stepping forth from the crowds, a man capable of pulling us out of the mire in which we are foundering...One is almost tempted to say, "Lucky nations which have managed to find a dictator!"[26]

Groulx even goes so far as to appeal to providence.

> Who will ignite us and take on the responsibility of spreading fervour and determination? Who will be our nation's leader? Who will be our Valera or Mussolini, whose policies may be debatable, but who have spiritually recreated Ireland and Italy in the space of a decade, just as Dollfuss and Salazar are in the process of reconstructing Austria and Portugal? Alas, we might as well admit that we do not have such a national leader. Will we ever have one?

> What should we do? Simply accept this uninspiring political resignation? God willing, and with hands on our hearts, we will ask Providence for help.[27]

Groulx reassured his readers that Providence would not abandon Quebec. "Because of the extreme danger we face, we can also count on Providence." How could fate turn its back on French Canada when it had helped out Portugal by allowing Salazar to step into power? "I've heard it said on occasion that 'Portugal had to wait 300 years for Providence to heed its cries. Isolated and hemmed in by ocean and a neighbour with an essentially similar civilization, Portugal could afford to wait." French Canada, on the other hand, was located on a continent dedicated to its demise, and was struggling to ward off death. It obviously merited a providential helping hand. "We cannot accomplish what Portugal has done, situated where we are and under constant threat."[28]

Are the French Canadian people worthy of redemption? Groulx, the nation's most ardent attacker of traitors, was not altogether convinced.

Whether the miracle of a saviour—for which we hope and beseech Providence—is granted today or tomorrow, we have to look realistically at our chances of developing a truly national policy. French Canadians know nothing about nationhood. They are a poor people with plenty of feeling, to be sure, but they have never attended any call beyond that of their stomachs.[29]

Predictably, l'Action nationale echoed Groulx's remarks. The latter's image of the "faisceaux" inspired Abbé Albert Tessier. "Once we decide to gather our scattered energies into powerful 'faisceaux' welded solidly together, we will be a healthy, respected people."[30] The magazine's staff implores Providence to provide them with "a leader, a true leader, moulded by our traditions, a visionary with determination and passion in his heart"[31] modelled along the lines of Salazar, who brought the past to life again,[32] or Mussolini, of whom Abbé Tessier writes, "his great work has been to rekindle the Italian nation's very soul."[33] Only a leader with "passionate determination" could rid the province of the "foreign yoke weighing it down" which "robbed it of its ethnic personality, the only remaining trace of its will to remain alive."[34]

André Laurendeau began to despair. "No matter how often I scan the horizon, I never find the nation's saviour...I search in vain for this tall figure, this man who will embody our hopes, expressing them heroically and definitively."[35] The more optimistic Paul Simard of Jeune-Canada believed he had identified a Saviour. There is "a man who, through his pride and intellectual independence, has been able to implant the seeds of love in our young peoples' souls." "A man who personifies the sum of our people's ambitions, desires and hopes, and who lives only for them." Who was this individual? "You can probably guess this man's name...Abbé Lionel Groulx! And why not?"[36]

Dictator-saviours tended to share very particular moments with their peoples.

Like myself, I am sure you occasionally reflect upon all those countries, both large and small, who have recently experienced their moments of awakening, exaltation and intoxicating reconstruction. Your thoughts take you to Italy, Ireland, Portugal, Austria and elsewhere. And you ask yourself, "Will the people of our province ever experience these same moments?"[37]

These moments constituted a complete, spontaneous revolution—the fruit of "an almost desperate effort to reclaim our people's soul, realign its orientation and reshape its destiny."[38]

French mystique was synonymous with "organic" revolution and the French State. "There can be no French State, no French nation without a French mystique. We should stop demanding action from our people when they possess neither the ideas nor the feelings to buttress it."[39]

History contained the seeds of destiny—self-evident to Groulx if not to his contemporaries—that would lead French Canada to political sovereignty. "If our history has any underlying meaning—and it does—our sole, legitimate and necessary destiny, and the logical result of 177 years of endeavour" is to build "a masterpiece of splendid human effort: a French Catholic State"[40] in North America.

Groulx's nihilism reared its head once again as he pondered whether the link between past and present might be illusionary. Perhaps it all boiled down to a series of isolated, contemporary, chance occurrences. Perhaps generations only followed each other chronologically, without passing along any vision of the future. Groulx created a mythical nation destined to form a French State in order to ward off the existential void underlying his ideology. With the creation of a French State, history was imbued with meaning and finality, and likewise, the French State derived its legitimacy and justification from history.

André Laurendeau predicted that this state, which he baptized Laurentie, would emerge with the inevitable disintegration of the United States. "The United States will break up (because Americans have no soul, and without a soul one cannot survive for long) and this wished-for country, this power we have been trying to build will rise out of the realm of desire."[41]

The French State described by Groulx had little in common with the conventional notion of a French-language state. "Our ideal should not be merely to conserve the French language, but to create a spiritual climate, a French culture, a French State."[42] He continues with a telling admonition. "Take care not to over-glorify the French language while shrinking the main issue: nationhood." Loyalty "to blood, to history and culture"[43] were more important.

The French State, an ineluctable by-product of history, represented the "legitimate and natural destiny"[44] of a community trying to achieve its "natural and national ends."[45]

Would it exist within or outside of the Canadian confederation? Groulx's answer was categorical. "Our one sure duty...is to work towards the creation of a French State in Quebec—within confederation if possible, outside of it if this proves impossible."[46] One Jeune-Canada member dreams of "secession," of "unshared political autonomy," while simultaneously admitting that at the present time, this was a "fanciful solution."[47]

Even though Jeune-Canada took Quebec's right to secede for granted, the geographic boundaries of this imagined new land were difficult to delineate. "How do we define Laurentie geographically? No one yet knows..." Jeune-Canada took a stab at outlining their beloved homeland. "Laurentie: an ill-defined country with contemporary Quebec at its heart, and tentacles reaching out into northern Ontario, New Brunswick and New England."[48] Laurentie was not so much a territory as the reverberation of "a sufficiently defined state of mind."[49]

L'Action nationale had a relatively clearer notion of the French State. "The province of Quebec can currently be labelled a state. It is possessed of a territory. Over three million men live within its boundaries, in permanent association under a single authority."[50] L'Action nationale's publisher, the Ligue d'Action nationale, tried to have St. Jean Baptiste Day (June 24) declared a national holiday[51] and the fleur de lis as the national flag. "Popular adhesion to the same national emblem will signal the beginning of spiritual unity amidst all our ridiculous divisions."[52]

Groulx felt that the national state would reconcile the "de jure country with the real country," a leitmotif copied word for word from Charles Maurras and his Action française. "Moreover, would you like to know exactly what I mean by a French State?...I mean a re-establishment of the link or identity between the 'legal country' and the 'real country.'" French Canadians would stop being "a race of subordinates and pariahs." The state could "put an end to the decline of our middle classes, re-establish a fair balance between rural and urban populations, prevent a handful of exploiters from exploiting the

masses and curb the appalling waste of our human resources."
Furthermore, exploitative foreigners would learn their place.

> Nationals will be able to speak in their native tongue anywhere
> without being looked at askance by civil servants, bar-room
> Negroes and foreigners, or by people they pass in the street who
> have not even had time to be naturalized.[53]

The aforementioned state was neither impartial, nor cosmopolitan; its primary concern was "to govern for the good of
the province's nationals, for the French Canadian majority of
the population."[54]

How did minority groups fit into this notion of statehood?
Groulx's tone became menacing on the subject "of a minority of
exploiters constituting perhaps six percent of the population—as
not all anglophones were exploitative—" who had claimed "the
right to prevent 2 500 000 people, or 80 percent of the
province's population, from living in freedom and dignity." It
would be better:

> even for the exploitative minority to opt for a just and peaceful
> solution rather than awaiting the predictable alternative—it may
> be the case that people will not unduly tolerate unacceptable
> regimes threatening to thwart their destiny.[55]

Groulx reiterates his warning to Jews and English speakers:

> It goes without saying that I am neither anti-English nor anti-
> Semitic. But I have noticed that the English are pro-English and
> the Jews are pro-Jew. I thus ask myself why French Canadians can-
> not be pro-French Canadian to a similar degree.

The sheep was getting ready to roar, and minority groups
would do well to heed the coming transformation.

> I will even dare ask whether the delays in redressing the situation
> benefit the minority. The key question can be formulated thus: will
> our people put up with the economic state of affairs currently
> prevailing in the province of Quebec, and can they put up with it
> indefinitely?[56]

Jews and foreigners who turned a blind eye to the problem, exclaimed Lambert Closse, simultaneously reminding his readers
of their ancestors' mettle, might encounter an enemy sporting as
powerful a symbol as the swastika. "Do not forget that our ancestors opened up this country with French axes which likewise
served as weapons to ward off dangerous enemies." Closse dis-
cerned a lesson here. "We should not be afraid to dig up the

French cultural axe. Its worth compares favourably to the swastika; if Jews or other foreigners fail to realize this, they will have to learn at their own expense."[57]

The Buy-At-Home campaign was an attempt to foster solidarity among French Canadians so that they might become just as unassailable and closed-off as Groulx accused the English and, most of all, the Jews of being. "In six months or a year our watchword will miraculously be understood and followed, and the Jewish problem will be resolved both in Montreal and across the entire province." Quebec would rid itself of the Jewish problem—or nearly. "Of the Jews, none would remain except those who could make a living solely off of their own people. The rest would scatter, or of necessity disband to make their living in sectors other than business."[58]

Expressions coined by Groulx often had ulterior meanings and, as it turned out, Buy-At-Home was more than a simple incitement to purchase exclusively or even predominantly from French Canadian institutions. Buy-At-Home should not be limited to "over the counter transactions," but should "be inspired by frank education as to national goals." Education would put an end to treacherous consumer behaviour. "The inconsistencies and disorder that continue to characterize our daily lives are due primarily to disorderly, treacherous minds."[59]

It was treason pure and simple: the vast majority of French Canadians frequented foreigners' shops or simply bought things without paying attention to the vendor's ethnicity.

Initially, l'Action nationale took the Buy-At-Home slogan at face value and supported it as "another efficacious means of fighting foreign trusts."[60]

The issue quickly became more complex. Should one, for instance, support French Canadian soft drink manufacturers appealing to national solidarity? L'Action nationale urged caution. "Is it one of those companies bandying about the words Ginger Ale and Cream Soda, when Gingembre and Crème would have done just as well?" The company's name and the street on which it was located, while French, were soiled with English influence. "They will find a way to anglicize things. They will write de Lanaudière St. instead of using the French 'rue.'"[61] Economic solidarity should not be exercised so blindly so as to encourage the Traitor, no matter how trivial his act of betrayal may seem.

Omer Héroux of Le Devoir threw himself recklessly into the fray surrounding the Buy-At-Home campaign. Excluding Jews was necessary to fortify anaemic French Canadian nationalism. "In a normal country of mixed ethnicity, customers roughly divide up according to affinities in language, customs and ordinary relations. As a general rule, people encourage their own." French Canada, however, was not a normal country because "everything has been turned on its head, and French Canadians do not possess the economic clout that is their rightful due." They are nowhere to be seen in the upper echelons of finance and business, and they avoid small operations because of "the pressure exerted by foreign business, and in particular Jewish entrepreneurs." Small French Canadian businesses allow themselves to be pushed around because their fellow countrymen "refuse to follow the example of non-French citizens— starting with the Jews—who habitually and often reflexively help each other out financially. Who can blame them?" The weakened French Canadian race's instinct would be strengthened by the publication of lists of French Canadian suppliers. Need it even be said that this measure "is not intended to be hostile?"[62]

The Buy-At-Home argument as disseminated by the Outaouais and Clarence Hogue was not softened in either content or tone. Hogue enjoined H.M. Caiserman, secretary general of the Canadian Jewish Congress who had denied that his people frequented only Jewish establishments,[63] to describe his personal buying habits. "Does Mr Caiserman himself purchase much from French Canadian or even English Canadian stores in Montreal?" The self-appointed inquisitor and defender of small businesses continued his attack. "Can he name a single French Canadian or English Canadian business in an exclusively Israelite neighbourhood, or elsewhere for that matter, thriving on an exclusively Jewish clientele?"[64]

Mr Caiserman reflects what would become of the country if "each of the 33 religious groups in Canada" fired its French Canadian employees "not because they were incompetent, but simply to make room for other staff sharing their bosses' ethnicity."[65]

Clarence Hogue shot back the following incredible response. "Is this not, for the most part, the way things are already?

French Canadian employees, whom Mr Caiserman obviously intended to threaten, often owe their employment to the fact that their services are considered irreplaceable." A French Canadian hired by a Jew as a clerk or "to lend his name so as to mislead the public into believing the business was French Canadian and not Jewish," was forced into playing "a potentially dishonourable role" because "he has to feed himself and his family," and Jews "simply cannot do without our people's services."[66]

The indefatigable Caiserman returned to the battlefield. "I cannot supply the names of French or English stores thriving in Jewish communities because there is no credible data available on this subject."[67] Clarence Hogue stubbornly insists on having the last word, informing him that he should simply have admitted "that Jews prosper because of the encouragement given them by other races."[68]

In addition to promoting Buy-At-Home, l'Action nationale proposed setting up dykes to stop the flow of foreign capital. "Let us erect dykes and rebuild the foundations of our economy within the familiar framework of our parishes and religion."[69] Monseigneur Gfoellner's lavish advice concerning the re-establishment of ghettos was also relevant.

> In days gone by, especially in the cities of Italy, Jews were assigned special areas or "ghettos" in order to fetter Judaism's spirit and influence as much as humanly possible. In our day, we no longer ban Jews from any country. It would, however, be a good idea to use legislation and government policy to erect a dyke to counter this intellectual muck, this wave of garbage associated primarily with Judaism, which threatens to flood the world.[70]

Quoting from Jacques Maritain, André Laurendeau writes that he is not in favour of pogroms which "have never resolved anything but have, in fact, done just the opposite," and argues for legislative measures. "Anti-Semitism extends beyond national borders, just as Jews do. Their presence creates a problem wherever they live: one which is properly resolved by "government measures."

Anatole Vanier describes these government measures in greater detail. He magnanimously concedes they "certainly have a right to exercise religious freedom and to enjoy all the privileges of new immigrants," but he is not one to get carried away by misguided generosity. "Their hosts are not obliged to give them absolute freedom in the political arena, especially if this freedom imperils their own political or economic independence." Host nations finding themselves so threatened "were entitled to regard and treat them as citizens apart."[72]

Among other measures designed to whittle away at the Jewish Canadians' civil and political rights, l'Action nationale suggests imposing a quota system in universities just like the ones in Europe and "well before Hitler's time, in a good number of universities, as exists moreover at the American border. It behooves us to introduce a similar practice in our institutions of higher learning, and elsewhere, in order to protect Catholicism and the expansion of French Canada."[73]

Another measure, more radical than the first, was suggested by the Three Rivers newspaper, *Le Saint Laurent*. L'Action nationale adopted it as their own, claiming the proposal was "entirely apt." "The way things are going, it is clear that many Jews will have to 'downgrade,' and exchange their offices and counters for manual labour jobs." The Jews began to solve the problem themselves by emigrating to Palestine. "There are reports that two or three hundred Israelites apply to Berlin's zionist offices every day, trying to get sent to Palestine as farm labourers. This is helpful both for the country and for the work that needs to be done."[74]

With uncharacteristic optimism, l'Action nationale predicted that whatever the means employed—government measures, ghettos,quota systems—the French Canadian body politic would triumph, sooner or later, over the Jewish virus. "How exactly will our people begin to heal themselves?" No one knew, Anatole Vanier wrote without expressing the slightest worry. "But Jews are provoking a visible, natural inflammation in the body of our people, and in this struggle the strong will overpower the weak."[75] Le Devoir also favoured forcibly deporting Jews to Palestine and issuing obligatory identification papers to those who insisted on remaining in Christian territory. In one of his editorials, Georges Pelletier justified these measures by appealing to an international Jewish conspiracy bent on fomenting insurrection. It was the Jews' fault that anti-Semitism "had erupted in so many countries like Germany, Poland and Romania," and, worse still, "it was due to the fact that Jews had become influential and powerful there. This was the case in Soviet Russia as well as in allied France."[76]

Georges Pelletier derives his belief in the Jewish peril from "the author of a recent book possessed of a moderate tone and filled with genuine quotations from the Talmud and various Jewish writers which are as strange as they are alarming." The misguided assumption underlying the book was that Jews conducted themselves collectively according to the letter of the Talmud. This study of the Talmud and Jewish scholars written by H. de Vries de Heekelingen suggested that the real problem had little to do with Jewish religion or economic power. "It is not the Jewish religion that most worries non-Jews any more, nor even Jewish economic clout..." What was the problem, then? "It is the knowledge that one is sheltering elements of an unassimilable nation whose object is world domination, and many of whose members are bent on fomenting revolution...Jews will increasingly turn up as noncommissioned officers in revolutionary political groups, if not as generals." What would become of this unassimilable people who dreamed of conquering the world? "In their exasperation, non-Jews will resort to atrocities or deportations." (Israël, son passé, son avenir, by H. de Vries de Heekelingen, pages 3 and 4.) What a sardonic prediction this turned out to be!

This state of affairs was inevitable because all past "solutions" had failed. "Neither persecution, deportation, emancipation, tolerance, nor even attempts to assimilate Jews scattered throughout the world had come even close to constituting a solution to the Jewish problem," he observes. The Jew would remain irrevocably, "biologically" Jewish despite all his signals (which could be deceptive to the uninitiated) that he was assimilating.

> The Jew who appears assimilated...remains Jewish in the depths of his soul. He remains Jewish first and foremost, to such an extent that if, at any point in time, he must choose between his adoptive country and the Jewish nation, his Jewish blood will force him to opt for ties which have existed for 30 centuries rather than those which date back only 10 years or so. (Israël, son passé, son avenir, p. 7)

One naive Canadian challenged this assertion. "How could the Jews of France not be considered French given the role they played in the French army during the war, dying by the thousands on the battlefield between 1914 and 1918?" The biological and religious aspects of Jewry were explained to him by a Collège de France professor, described without a trace of irony by Georges Pelletier as "absolutely non-racist, like so many European intellectuals." This unblemished academic writes that "The most intelligent and racially impartial cannot help themselves; at base, they are Jews. At the Collège de France I have many intellectually gifted Jewish colleagues." No matter how hard they tried, however, religious and biological determinism blocked their assimilation.

> They sincerely believe they have broken the ties that bind them to their race. They are no longer religiously observant. They are agnostics. But at certain times when you are talking with them they cease to follow you; they cannot seize or comprehend things in the manner of a French mind steeped in Christianity. Despite their best efforts, and no matter what they believe, their spirit is secular. This is the Jewish mind-set.

There were, however, methods to eliminate this mob. The first was deporting all Jews to Palestine. Jews would thus become true foreigners in every country except Israel.

> "The solution to the problem...is the existence of the zionist state, the recognition of this country as the Israeli nation, a distinct nation where Jews may congregate and become citizens. This would mean that outside Israel's boundaries, Jews would be foreigners."

To put it more succinctly still, there would be "Voluntary repatriation of some, mandatory deportation of others and the imposition of Jewish passports on all those wishing to live in countries outside Israel where they would be foreigners regardless of their birthplace."

Did Jews have any choice in the matter? Jews will have to choose between "correct, unadulterated zionism and fighting Aryan forces which are awakening and organizing themselves on the international front..." (Israël, son passé, son avenir, p. 240). Anti-Semitism would not die out until the day the Jews disappeared, allowing Christians to live in peace. "This and only this will extinguish the fires of anti-Semitism," a danger "which will only disappear the day Jews live in their own homeland." (Israël, son passé, son avenir, p. 242) H. de Vries de Heekelingen then adds, "And we can relax alone in our home, among Christians."

Following the lead of Georges Pelletier, Le Grincheux agrees wholeheartedly with these proposals. "Toronto has been advised to deport three young Jews. Why only three?"[77] Elsewhere he notes that "Zionist leader Vladimir Jabotinsky wants to move 7 million Jews to Palestine. If he cannot find enough, Baptiste will willingly hand his over."[78]

Wealthy capitalist and ardent Communist, set apart from the rest of the population by his religion, ideas and blood, the mythical Jew had to disappear before the perhaps not-so-utopian dream of a province where only Christians were full citizens could be realized. Real, flesh-and-blood Jews would pay dearly for the mythical Jew's crimes.

The day would come when French Canada, "cleared of foreign vegetation"[79] and freed from "all its loans to foreigners," would experience "the blossoming of the soul which is its legacy."[80]

Groulx's plans for the Traitor, inevitable accomplice of the Other, were inspired by one of the most sinister of totalitarian regime practices. Groulx starts off by repeating how resistant the people are to their devoted liberators. "The most dangerous and hostile enemies of the French State, as you might already have noticed, are not those who immediately jump to mind; they are your own French Canadian countrymen." This is so because "years of political and national enslavement have bowed our shoulders, accustomed us to servitude, turned us into a hesitant and pusillanimous nation." It follows that *before they can muster the simple courage to accept their future, French Canadians require political and national reeducation.*"[81]

André Laurendeau warns that the road will be so long and difficult that "martial training will be necessary, something akin to military training"[82] to create the New French Canadian Man.

The Jew would be forever excluded from the French State while the Traitor would be permitted entry only after a radical transformation. This alone distinguished the former from the latter.

Whether one's terms of reference were the French State or national education, what was at stake was always the struggle against the misdeeds of the Other and the Traitor. Bernard Hogue of Jeune-Canada swore that only national education would end "25 years of americanization" which had caused dangerous fissures to appear in "the moral structure which had taken centuries of virtue and courage to build." But national education had murderous, as well as purifying tendencies.

> It is the only accurate weapon we possess, and it alone will enable us to shoot down certain idiotic prejudices, foreign vermin and politicians who are not even worthy of the scaffold .[83]

In the French State, all the social evils formerly attributed to these two mythical figures would evaporate. Groulx predicts, "Our economic and social troubles, mortal perils which so threaten French life" will be "brushed aside, cured."[84]

"Sound minds in our country are worried," writes l'Action nationale. "We wholeheartedly condemn the abuses of the capitalist system, which is at once sensual and grasping."[85] Capitalism engenders "chaos in modern societies."[86] L'Action nationale believed a solution was within reach. Inspired by the encyclicals *Rerum Novarum* and *Divini Redemptoris*,[87] it declares that "Christian corporatism is in direct opposition to liberal economics."[88] Corporatism would sound the death knell for technology and machinery. "Just as competitive liberalism encourages quantity over quality, thereby creating a need for machines which run better than human beings, so corporations elevate the manufacture of the humblest object to the level of a work of art."[89]

The magic of corporatism would be able to quell the forces of capital, freeing the province from party discipline. "Odious and corrupt party discipline has turned most of our representatives into muzzled dogs..." But the wicked would lose out in the end. "The experienced, vibrant corporate voice" would successfully "thwart capital's shady, antisocial machinations."[90]

Anatole Vanier marvels that gallicizing would occur spontaneously in the corporate state. "Watchwords to encourage the reinstatement of French would no longer be necessary;" French Canadians would become rich and able. "Lucrative and strategic administrative positions, which belong to us by right, would fall into our hands. An unquenchable desire for competence and superiority would torment us." The Buy-At-Home ethic and Catholicism would be scrupulously honoured. "People would buy at home as a matter of course; Sundays and holidays would regain the religious aspect which our ethnic dignity and faith demand." But the best and biggest miracle of all was that Jewish electoral districts would be abolished. "Jewish preserves would disappear. What would be next?"[91]

André Laurendeau daydreams that "Artists will produce laurentian art for us" and the race will be strong and beautiful like it was in the days of New France. "Doctors, dentists and gymnasts will help build a strong, chaste race of handsome young men and beautiful young girls."[92]

Was it possible for such a paradise to exist on earth? L'Action nationale's Esdras Minville wrote that Nazi Germany embodied his own aspirations as well as those of Lionel Groulx and l'-Action nationale. He begins his article with a quotation from Gonzague de Reynold:

> If the National Socialists mean to restore the honour of, salvage, cultivate and even exalt everything German they must bring Germany back to its traditions and spirit, impart to it a sense of self, a sense of its own genius and faith in its destiny. If they mean to give it back its dignity, pride, independence, its love of living the German life, then they are doing wholesome, intelligent, deliberate work...I trust that I have interpreted their intentions correctly.[93]

Minville continues with observations of his own, pointing out similarities between German National Socialist intentions and those of Lionel Groulx and l'Action nationale. "What Gonzague de Reynold wished for Hitler and his brown-shirts in 1933, he could also have written, and could accurately write today, of Abbé Groulx and l'Action nationale's editorial board." Gonzague de Reynold could not have expressed our aspirations with greater accuracy, Esdras Minville reiterates, marvelling at the fortunate coincidence.

> A more succinct and perfect summation of their philosophy could not be written. They are hoping to, "restore the honour of, salvage, cultivate and even exalt" (will we make it this far?) everything French Canadian; bring French Canada "back to its traditions and its spirit, impart to it a sense of self, a sense of its own genius and faith in its destiny...its dignity, pride" and love of living the French Canadian life...

Minville could not resist repeating for a third time how happy he was to have stumbled across a philosophical soul-mate, and abruptly dismissed those who took offence at the innocent overlap between the two ideologies. "Despite claims made by those who would have us excommunicated, this is our ambition. Anyone who has followed the evolution of l'Action nationale since its foundation, or meditated on Abbé Groulx's latest work [Orientations] will be aware of this."[94]

Lionel Groulx harped on the idea that to be truly human one must belong to a nation that has evolved sufficiently to consider statehood.

> In the end, not every people has the right to form a state. A people may claim this privilege only if it is possessed of adequate material and spiritual resources, and sufficient political and moral capital to allow its nationals or citizens to develop their humanity and attain their civic aspirations.[95]

It was up to politicians to do "all they could to ensure the blossoming of national culture, which would in turn allow citizens to fulfil their human potential."[96] A "truly national" education organized within the framework of the French State would give French Canadians back the human dignity that had been so badly eroded by liberalism, the Traitor and the Other.

> We will possess our own art and literature when, through improving our pedagogy and education, and taking a firm and determined hold of our culture, *we cease to be a hollow shell of a nation, a shadow of all that is French and human, and become great French Canadians and great human beings.*[97]

The French State signalled the arrival of the first generation of living French Canadians; the dead generation—those of middle or old age—would be pushed out the door. "Regardless of whether we want it or not, our French State will establish itself..." despite the nay-sayers, "snobs, men of good intentions and defeatists." Groulx had chilling words for this bunch. "I and the entire younger generation answer them as follows, 'We are the generation of the living. You are the last generation of the dead!'"[98]

Among the country's young people were tomorrow's "saviours"[99] and "architects of the national resurrection."[100] The middle class could mend its ways by undergoing "religious rebirth, a complete renaissance whereby amidst all its other duties it will recognize its national commitment."[101] The people awaited its "redemptive orders."[102]

Citing Cardinal Villeneuve, Paul Simard declared that the French Canadian nation of the future would be "in the midst of a growing new Babylon, a modern-day Israel, the France of America, a sainted nation of light!"[103]

Lionel Groulx promised a "Nietzschean" destiny to the living generation, untainted by human frailty, which was working so hard to resurrect a chosen race.

Those young men and girls who have been smitten with an absolute ideal, eagerly pushing their personality development to the limit, will realize that their birth into the Catholic faith and a Catholic country accords them the immense privilege of possessing Christ's infinite perfection as a spiritual ideal. During the course of their spiritual development *this ideal can transform them, if they so desire, into supermen and Gods*.[104]

Notes

1. Élie Kedourie: *Nationalism*, p. 18.

2. François de Fontette: *op. cit.*, p. 83.

3. *Ibid.*, p. 84.

4. Lionel Groulx: *Orientations*, pp. 16-17; *Ibid.*, pp. 52-53; Lionel Groulx: *Directives*, p. 104.

5. Lionel Groulx: *Notre maître le passé*, tome 1, p. 22.

6. Hermas Bastien: "Corporatisme et liberté.," *Action nationale*, (April 1938), p. 313.

7. Lionel Groulx: *Notre maître le passé*, tome 2, pp. 19-20.

8. Lionel Groulx: *Directives*, p. 87; *Ibid.*, p. 135 et p. 213; Lionel Groulx: *Orientations*, p. 219; Lionel Groulx: "L'éducation nationale et les écoles normales.," *Action nationale*, (September 1934), p. 25.

9. Lionel Groulx: *Orientations*, p. 116.

10. André Laurendeau: *Partisannerie politique*, in: Les Jeune-Canada: *Politiciens et Juifs*, p. 61; Pierre Dansereau: *Politiciens et Juifs*, in: Les Jeune-Canada: *Politiciens et Juifs*, pp. 6-7.

11. Lionel Groulx: *Notre mystique nationale*, p. 1.

12. Lionel Groulx: "Notre destin français.," *Action nationale*, (March 1937), pp. 130-131; Lionel Groulx: *Notre mystique nationale*, p. 2, pp. 6-7; Lionel Groulx: *Orientations*, p.18, p. 208 et p. 260.

13. Lionel Groulx: *op. cit.*, p. 184; On educators and mysticism: *Ibid.*, pp. 267-268, p. 299, p. 301.

14. *Ibid.*, pp. 104-105; Lionel Groulx: *La déchéance incessante de notre classe moyenne*, p. 16; Lionel Groulx: *Directives*, p. 94; Lionel Groulx: *Notre maître le passé*, tome 2, p. 20.

15. "L'éducation nationale," *Action nationale*, (November 1936), p. 154, editorial.

16. Lionel Groulx: "L'éducation nationale et les écoles normales.," *Action nationale*, (September 1934), p. 15.

17. André Marois (pseudonym of Lionel Groulx): "Pour vivre," *Action nationale* (May 1937)., p. 313.

18. *Ibid.*, p. 313-314; Lionel Groulx: *Orientations*, p. 232.

19. Jacques Brassier(pseudonym de Lionel Groulx): "Pour qu'on vive.," *Action nationale*, pp. 204-205.

20. Lionel Groulx: *Directives*, pp. 161-162.

21. André Marois (pseudonym of Lionel Groulx): "Pour vivre.," *Action natio-nale*,(May 1937), p. 311.

22. *Ibid.*

23.*Ibid.*

24. Lionel Groulx: *op. cit.*, p. 221.

25.Lionel Groulx: "Vivre.," *Action nationale*, (November 1934), pp. 175-176.

26. Jacques Brassier (pseudonym of Lionel Groulx): "Pour qu'on vive.," *Action nationale*, (January 1934), p. 52.

27. Lionel Groulx: *Orientations*, p. 218; On the leader: Lionel Groulx: *L'ensei-gnement français au Canada*, tome 1, p. 265; Lionel Groulx: *Orientations*, p. 296-299; Lionel Groulx: *Notre maître le passé*, tome 1, p. 11; Jacques Brassier (pseudonym of Lionel Groulx): "Pour qu'on vive.," *Action nationale*, (October 1934), p. 139.

On Louis-Hippolyte Lafontaine: Lionel Groulx: "Un chef de trente-trois ans.," *Action nationale*, (May 1935), p. 266-276. Reproduced in: Lionel Groulx: *Notre maître le passé*, tome 1, p. 180-187.

On the literary construction of the leader: Lionel Groulx: *L'Appel de la race*, p. 95-97, p. 100-102, pp. 108-109, pp. 114-115, p. 137, p. 155, p. 158, p. 160, p. 162; Alonié de Lestres (pseudonym of Lionel Groulx): *Au Cap Blomidon*, p. 1, p. 14, p. 19, pp. 24-25, pp. 27-28, p. 30, p.32, p. 40, pp. 92-93, pp. 114-115.

28. Lionel Groulx: *Directives.*, p. 249.

29. Jacques Brassier (pseudonym of Lionel Groulx): "Pour qu'on vive.," *Action nationale*, (November 1934), p. 205; Lionel Groulx: *La bourgeoisie et le natio-nal*, p.125.

30. Albert Tessier, Abbé: "Pour une politique nationale.," *Action nationale*, (May 1937), p. 260.

31. *Action nationale*, (January 1935), p. 4, editorial.

32. Arthur Laurendeau: "La situation est-elle acceptable?," *Action nationale*, (February 1937), p. 73.

33. Albert Tessier, Abbé: *op. cit.*, p. 259.

34. *Action nationale*,(January 1935), p. 3, editorial.

35. André Laurendeau: *Qui sauvera Québec?*, in: Les Jeune-Canada: *Qui sauve-ra Québec?*, p. 52.

36. "Les Jeune-Canada au Monument national.," *Le Devoir*, 9 April 1935, p. 8.

37. Lionel Groulx: *Directives*, p. 86; Lionel Groulx: *Orientations*, p. 212.

38. Lionel Groulx: *Ibid*, p. 85; Guy Frégault: "Où est la révolution?," *Action na-tionale*, (February 1937), p. 82-89.

39. Lionel Groulx: *Orientations*, p. 266-267.

40. *Ibid.*, p. 215; *Ibid.*, p. 48; Lionel Groulx: *Directives*, pp. 128-129, p. 204; Lio-nel Groulx: "Notre destin français.," *Action nationale*, (March 1937), p. 138.

41. André Laurendeau: *Notre nationalisme*, pp. 50-51; Lionel Groulx: *Notre maître le passé*, tome 2, p. 304.

42. Lionel Groulx: *Orientations.*, p. 233.

43. Lionel Groulx: *Directives*, p.216.

44. *Ibid.*, p. 165.

45. *Ibid.*, p. 167.

46. *Ibid.*, pp. 121-122.

47. Les Jeune-Canada: *Qui sauvera Québec?*, pp. 3-4, Introduction; "Laurentia, we who are now twenty-five, will we live to see you in your maturity? Before our eyes close forever here on earth, will you become a political entity, a State?" André Laurendeau: *Notre nationalisme*, p. 50; Paul Simard: *Notre idéal politique*, in: Les Jeune-Canada: *Qui sauvera Québec*, p. 23; Gilbert Manseau: "État et nation.," *Le Devoir*, 10 July 1933, p. 2.

48. André Laurendeau: *op. cit.*, p. 45.

49. André Laurendeau: *Qui sauvera Québec?*, in: Les Jeune-Canada: *Qui sauvera Québec?*, p. 56; "In effect, nationality is inseparable from the individual, which the State is supposed to fully develop." Gilbert Manseau: *Les Canadiens français et le régime anglais.*, in: Les Jeune-Canada: *Sur les pas de Cartier.*, p. 34.

50. Maximilien Caron: "Pour une politique nationale.," *Action nationale*, (January 1937), p. 5; Hermas Bastien: "Politique et éducation.," *Action nationale*, (June 1937), p. 322.

51.Anatole Vanier: "L'État du Québec," *Action nationale,*(December 1939), p. 262; "La Saint-Jean-Baptiste.," *Action nationale*, (May 1933), pp. 3-4.

52. "Pour le drapeau national.," *Action nationale*, (March 1936), p. 3, editorial; "Arborons notre drapeau national.," *Action nationale*, (June 1935), pp. 3-4, advertisement, "Le scandale des drapeaux.," *Action nationale*, (May 1937), p. 3, editorial.

53. Lionel Groulx: *Directives.*, pp. 169-170.

54. *Ibid.*, pp. 109-110; *Ibid.*, pp. 242-243.

55. *Ibid.*, p.111-112; *Ibid.*, pp. 217-218.

56. *Ibid.*, pp. 65-66.

57. Lambert Closse: *La réponse de la race.*, p.498.

58. Jacques Brassier(pseudonym of Lionel Groulx): "Pour qu'on vive.," *Action nationale*, (April 1933), pp. 242-243.

59. Lionel Groulx:*op. cit.*, p. 105.

60. Anatole Vanier: "Discours en l'air," *Action nationale*, (January 1935), p. 122; E.M.: "Si l'on voyait clair.," *Action nationale*, (April 1933), pp. 248-249; "Un devoir patriotique," *Action nationale*, (November 1934), pp. 2-4, editorial; Les Jeune-Canada: Thuribe Belzile: *Nos déficiences, conséquences, remèdes.*, p. 27.

61. "La vie courante," *Action nationale*, (December 1933), p. 272.

62. Omer Héroux: "La maison est à l'envers.," *Le Devoir*, 19 January 1934, p. 1, editorial; Omer Héroux: "M. Joseph Cohen et la Saint-Jean-Baptiste," *Le Devoir*, 5 January 1934, p. 1, editorial; Omer Héroux: "De quoi donc se plaint M. Joseph Cohen?," *Le Devoir*, 17 January 1934, p. 1, editorial.

63. H. M. Caiserman, Letter to the editor, *Le Devoir*, 3 July 1935, p. 2.

64. Clarence Hogue: "Politique de suicide.," *Le Devoir*, 6 July 1935, p. 8; The World Jewish Conspiracy being what it is, the situation is the same in Ottawa: Outaouais: "Le procès Freiman-Tissot.," *Le Devoir*, 25 June 1935, p. 1.

65. H. M. Caiserman, Letter to the editor, *Le Devoir*, 3 July 1935, p. 1.

66. Clarence Hogue: "Politique de suicide.," *Le Devoir*, 6 July 1935, p. 10.

67. H. M. Caiserman, Letter to the editor, *Le Devoir*, 26 July 1935, p. 3.

68. Clarence Hogue: "Nos prétendus sophismes.," *Le Devoir*, 27 July 1935, p. 6; Sur la polémique Caiserman-Hogue: Clarence Hogue: "Nos prétendus so-

phismes.," *Le Devoir*, 29 July 1935, p. 6; Clarence Hogue: "Nos prétendus sophismes.," *Le Devoir*, 30 July 1935, p. 6; Clarence Hogue: "Pour clore un débat.," *Le Devoir*, 10 August 1935, p. 8; Clarence Hogue: "Pour clore un débat.," *Le Devoir*, 12 August 1935, p. 6.
On the Buy-At-Home campaign in Le Devoir, see appendix F., French edition of this book.

69. Maurice Tremblay: "Régionalisme.," *Action nationale*, (May 1937), p. 277.

70. Mgr Gfoellner: "L'internationalisme juif.," *Action nationale*, (June 1933), pp. 381-382.

71. André Laurendeau: *Notre nationalisme*, pp. 26-27.

72. Anatole Vanier: "Les Juifs au Canada.," *Action nationale*, (September 1933), p. 19.

73. *Ibid.*, p. 9.

74. "Encore les Juifs.," *Action nationale*, (December 1933), pp. 277-278.

75. Anatole Vanier: "L'antisémitisme.," *Action nationale*,(February 1934), p. 87.

76. Georges Pelletier: "L'antisémitisme, péril grandissant.," *Le Devoir*, 17 April 1937, p. 1, editorial. The following three paragraphs are quoted from the same editorial.

77. Le Grincheux: Carnet d'un grincheux, *Le Devoir*, 4 September 1936, p. 1.

78. Le Grincheux: Le carnet du grincheux, *Le Devoir*, 8 February 1938, p. 1.

79. Lionel Groulx: *Notre doctrine*, p. 8.

80. Lionel Groulx: *Méditation patriotique*, pp. 15-16.

81. Lionel Groulx: *Directives*, p. 122. Author's italics.

82. André Laurendeau: *Qui sauvera Québec?*, in: Les Jeune-Canada: *Qui sauvera Québec*, pp. 64-65.

83. Bernard Hogue: *Comment chacun de nous fera de l'éducation nationale.*, in: Les Jeune-Canada: *Qui sauvera Québec?* , p. 72.

84. Lionel Groulx: *op. cit.*, p. 241.

85. *Action nationale*, (May 1933), p. 307, editorial.

86. *Action nationale*, (January 1938), pp. 24-25, introduction.

87. *Ibid.*, p. 25; Gérard Picard: "Association professionnelle et corporation.," *Action nationale*, (May 1938), pp. 386-387; Wilfrid Lebon: "Corporatisme social et corporatisme politique.," *Action nationale*, (September 1938), p. 43.

88. Hermas Bastien: "Corporatisme et liberté.," Action nationale, (April 1938), p. 307.

89. *Ibid.*,p.310.

90. Maurice Tremblay: "Régionalisme.," *Action nationale*, (May 1937), p. 280.

91. Anatole Vanier: "La méthode anglaise.," *Action nationale*, (April 1935), p. 244.

92. André Laurendeau: *op. cit.*, p. 48; Lionel Groulx: *Directives*, pp. 225-227; Lionel Groulx: *Notre maître le passé*, tome 1, p. 10.

93. Esdras Minville: "Ce que nous voulons.," *Action nationale*, (October 1935), pp. 96-97.

94. *Ibid.*, p. 97.

95. Lionel Groulx: *Orientations*, p. 249; *Ibid.* p. 63.

96. Lionel Groulx: *Directives*,p.107.

97.*Ibid.*, p. 98. Author's italics; Ibid., pp. 159-160; Lionel Groulx: *Orientations*, pp. 265-266; Lionel Groulx: *La bourgeoisie et le national*, pp. 124-125; André Marois (pseudonym of Lionel Groulx): "Pour qu'on vive.," *Action nationale*, (June 1935), p. 372.

98. Lionel Groulx: *Directives.*, pp. 222-223.

99. *Ibid.*, p. 225, p. 227, p. 243.

100. *Ibid.*, p. 249.

101. Lionel Groulx: *La bourgeoisie et le national*, p. 119.

102. *Ibid.*

103. Paul Simard: *Notre idéal politique.*, in: Les Jeune-Canada: *Qui sauvera Québec?*, p. 30.

104. Lionel Groulx: *Orientations*, p. 113.

A SAD EPILOGUE

THE BEST THING that can happen to a doctoral student is to have some of her original hypotheses *not* borne out by her investigations. Tripping on your own academic shoelaces really is the spice of research life! At the beginning of my studies, starting from known theories on racism and studies about anti-Semitism, I had posited as my hypothesis an antithetical relationship between the Jew and the French-Canadian, i.e. that each was the fictional opposite of the other, each serving to define its contrary. But as I began to analyze the material available, it became clear that my comfortable hypothesis was full of holes and sinking fast. The "French Canadian" was also a symbol: shameful, loathsome, and vituperated just as the "Jew" and for the same reasons. Their linking to the evil totality was complete, in the minds and writings of the subjects of my work.

The "evil totality" was the second surprise of this research. I had anticipated its presence, but without foreseeing the intensity of the nihilist furore expressed through it. This universe populated by sub-humans and ravaged by cankers, microbes and viruses, as the writers I studied painted liberal society, was unequivocally similar to Nazi ideology. I had thought that I would find elements of extremist right-wing nationalism of the ilk of Charles Maurras, but I also found myself knee-deep in Maurice Barrès, Fascism and National socialism.

Nazi ideology, through the publication of Julius Streicher's "Der Stürmer," castigated the Jew as a powerful microbe,[1] an approach followed by the subjects of my research. The Nazi affirmation that the "press, art, literature, the cinema, the theatre are all areas where the young Hitler sniffed out the Jews who "behave like the worst bacilli and poison our souls"[2] has an awfully familiar ring to it. This Jew, that my subjects described, repulsive and dirty, revolting, stinking, crooked-fingered and big-nosed, who soils the public parks, is he not lifted directly from Nazi symbolism?

Haven't we constantly seen here the opposition between the city and the countryside, about which Pierre Sorlin wrote in his work on German anti-Semitism: "The banal opposition between the urban and rural worlds takes on another colouring: one side represents health, the other, sickness."[3]

And didn't Hitler deliver this warning: On 30 September 1939, he promised to punish "international Jewry" if it succeeded, "in Europe or elsewhere, in precipitating the nations into a world war,"[4] so similar to the preoccupations of Groulx, Jeune-Canada and Le Devoir?

Wasn't the association of the Jew with capitalism as well as Communism, made constantly by all these writers, one of the most-employed strategies both of Nazism and of extremist right-wing nationalism?

> The equation propounded by Nazism between democracy one the one hand and Communism or "Jewry" on the other, became one of the most popular "ideas" of National socialism. It doubtlessly enters into the identification made by some (Ernst Nolte in particular) of l'Action française to Fascism.[5]

And all these references to the "rise of the new Germany," to the forces that must be made to converge into a powerful "beam," to counter the forces of "dissolution" hard at work; all this sympathy for Hitler and Mussolini, who are valiantly trying to stop the Jews? So that finally can resonate the voice of the soil and the dead? Lionel Groulx, l'Action nationale, Jeune-Canada and Le Devoir pick up, to different degrees, the themes and the slogans not only of extremist right-wing nationalism, but also of Fascism and National socialism. The demarcation line between these three ideologies is not always so clear: I built my interpretation from existing works and my uncertainties reflect in large part those of current research. This also is a part of the rewards of scholarship.

Approached from the angle of the evil totality and its two agents, the Traitor and the Jew, the nationalism of Lionel Groulx, l'Action nationale, the Jeune-Canada and Le Devoir ceases to be a defense mechanism protecting a Catholic and French identity which feels threatened in North America, as conventional interpretation has it. For this very identity means little to them except as a pretext to abuse their compatriots whenever they forego Sunday Mass in favour of the cinema or whenever they give English names to their businesses. Most of their energy is given over to denunciation and descriptions of undefinable evils and sins: the "Americanization" which has nothing whatsoever to do with the United States, the urbanization which has nothing to do with the city, the anglicization which has only very distant connections to the English language, and all of this in the name of an equally-undefinable identity, as being French Canadian seems to having nothing to do with being born in Quebec of French-speaking and Catholic parents. Their discourse is hardly a pastoral symphony, typical of the country-side, sympathetically anachronistic: on the contrary, it is a nihilistic and delirious tautology. The Traitor and the Jew are jejune accomplices, but also the cruel masters of a universe in full-fledged decay, ravaged by fevers and poisons. There are no crimes, even of the most trivial kind, that cannot be laid at their doorstep.

The undeniable influence that European ideologies of the radical contestation of liberalism had on the discourse of Groulx, l'-Action nationale, Jeune-Canada and Le Devoir put to rest, in my view, another myth which is popular in Quebec. According to this myth, there reigned prior to 1960 in this province a period called the "great obscurity," where this innocent North American village evolved as a kind of recluse, in a virginal ignorance of all the torments of the planet and of the century. Several years ago, when I was still braying this foolishness without giving it much thought, my future doctoral thesis director, Professor Jacques Zylberberg made the following remark: "And what about the thousands of French Canadian missionaries who travelled about the world? They never wrote to their families or their friends, to relate events that they had been witness to? Did they never mention the political struggles and reversals of governments in Africa and elsewhere? Be serious!" he roared. Well, of course. Lionel Groulx and company were quite knowledgeable about Salazar, Dolfuss, Mussolini, Hitler and the other dictators of the age under whose spell they fell; Georges Pelletier travelled to Europe in order to study "the Jewish question;" during the twenties, Le Devoir reproduced large excerpts from La Libre Parole, the paper of France's best-known anti-Semite, Edouard Drumont. In other words, the knew all about these European ideological movements and felt right at home with them

In the manner of the ideologies that Fascism will copy in some respects, Groulx, l'Action nationale and Jeune-Canada call for the establishment of a dictatorship and a leader who will save the nation.

> The onslaught on bourgeois society went hand in hand with the wholesale condemnation of liberal democracy and parliamentarian government, for one of the ideological tenets common to this whole vast protest movement was the reforming of all institutions in the authoritarian mould. The call for a leader, a saviour embodying all the virtues of the race, was to be heard throughout Europe, at the end of the century.[6]

And doesn't Groulx's ideology share its "Nietzschean ecstasy"[7] with European Fascism? And its millenarianism?

> The Fascist revolution built upon a deep bedrock of popular piety and, especially in Germany, upon a millenarianism that was apt to come to the fore in times of crisis. The myths and symbols of nationalism were superimposed upon those of Christianity—not only in the rhythms of public rites and ceremonies (even the Duce's famed dialogues with the masses from his balcony are related to Christian "responses")—but also in the appeal to apocalyptic and millenarian thought. Such appeals can be found in the very vocabulary of Nazi leaders. Their language grew out of Christianity; it was after all, a language of faith. In 1935, at Munich's Feldhernhalle, where his putsch of 1923 had resulted in a bloody fiasco, Hitler called those who had fallen earlier "my apostles," and proclaimed that "with the third Reich you have risen from the dead." Many other examples spring to mind, as when the leader of the Labour Front, Robert Ley, asserted that "we have found the road to eternity." The whole vocabulary of blood and soil was filled with Christian liturgical and religious meanings—the "blood" itself, the "martyrdom," the "incarnation."[8]

Pierre Milza mentions "...the will to break by "Fascist custom" with the "negative" model incarnated by the previous élites, and proposes to substitute for it the model of the New Man, "dynamic and virile," standard-bearer of the hopes of millenarian Fascism."[9] The healthy race formed by French-Canadian hygienists will obliterate the memory of pot-bellied politicians dripping Scotch from their lips.

And then, only then, will Paradise Lost reappear:

> This mystical, romantic, anti-rationalist Fascism was as much a moral and aesthetic system as a political philosophy; it constituted a complete vision of man and the community. Usurping the place occupied by revealed religion, its aims were to create a world of

fixed criteria, a world freed from doubt and purged of all foreign accretions; to give back their authenticity to man and the community; and reestablished the compromised unity of the nation. Once all this had been achieved, all the members of the national community, being of one body with it and existing through it alone, would react as one man and respond identically to the problems confronting it; and once this unanimity had been forged, political and social problems would be reduced to matters of details.[10]

This mystical unanimity derived from Catholic metaphysics which had the good sense to keep it to the hereafter characterizes the utopian project of Groulx, l'Action nationale and the Jeune-Canada. If Le Devoir is less loquacious in this respect, its attacks on "political partisanship" and its enthusiasm for nationalist extremists who think "in a national way," the applause it showers on dictators who take on the International Jewish Conspiracy as well as its Buy-at-Home campaign which would reduce Jewish shopkeepers to impoverishment, its virulent attacks against capitalism, democracy and modernity all of which let loose the destructive actions of the Jew, its avowed desire to only live among Christians, all the above leads us to believe that it would not have objected to the establishment of a society of absolute purity inhabited by supermen and Gods. All of these commentators express the same wish, at heart: via dictatorship, by the re-education of the Traitor and the expulsion of the Jew, the chaos and decay which surround us will end.

It is a truism to write that it took a sea of blood to quench the thirst of this twentieth-century secular mystique. In his frenzied despair to arrive at a social order incandescent with purity, Groulx neither hesitates to cast sidelong glances at Communism. The philosopher Isaiah Berlin wrote in his last book:

...the search for perfection does seem to me a recipe for bloodshed, no better even if it is demanded by the sincerest of idealists, the purest of hearts. No more rigorous moralist than Immanuel Kant has ever lived, but even he said, in a moment of illumination: "Out of the crooked timber of humanity no straight thing was ever made." To force people into the neat uniforms demanded by dogmatically believed-in schemes is almost always the road to inhumanity.[11]

The perfection sought by Groulx and company, finally, does not stand so much on a series of dogmas as it straddles the high-tension wire of their delirium. The French Canadians, hardly more than an insult to humanity in a liberal society, will become supermen in the coming utopia. But just as Evil is undefinable, so is perfection. It is easy to imagine, under these conditions, an endless re-education, with new crimes constantly compromising an endlessly-delayed state of perfection. This infernal logic only ends when no one is left to be a victim. It is not hard either, to imagine the price that real human beings would have paid for this institutionalized delirium had Groulx and his ideological clients taken power. Parked in ghettos, deprived of their political rights, deported to Palestine, given special passports, assembled in re-education camps, living under a dictatorship, Jews and French Canadians would have expiated the crimes imputed to their accursed doubles.

The last happiness that can be accorded to a doctoral student is to measure, during her research, the road left to travel. If much has been written already on the subject of totalitarianism, National socialism, Fascism, extremist right-wing nationalism, anti-Semitism and racism, even more remains to be understood. I plead only for one thing: a plurality of interpretations. Mine has its own strengths and its weaknesses. One day, someone else will pick up the same subject, enlarging or narrowing the focus, looking at it in a different light, and will see what I may have missed, bringing a knowledge of studies which had not yet been made at the time I constructed my interpretation. This latter has benefitted from those writings that came before, sometimes if only to disagree. These are the rules of the game, and applied in the proper way, they should flatter any author who is singed by the impertinent researcher's fire.

One last word: research has no other goal than to assuage the intellectual curiosity of the scholar who undertakes it. If the principal motivation of the giddy-headed is to change the world, this desire is not enough to sustain his interest over the course of the thousands of hours spent going through microfilms or combing the library stacks. No prophetic vocation can resist this arduous task. And yet I sometimes think that if this research had the indirect and unforeseen consequence of making sure that there would never again be a "Traitor," or a "Jew," in Quebec, it would give me a certain amount of satisfaction.

Notes

1. Pierre Sorlin: *L'antisémitisme allemand.*, Paris, Flammarion, 1969, p. 79 (Coll. Questions d'histoire).

2. François de Fontette: Le racisme., Presses universitaires de France, 1984, p. 74, (Coll. Que sais-je?).

3. Pierre Sorlin: *op. cit.*, p. 79.

"Anti-urbanism, or at least anti-metropolitanism is not found in all Fascist movements but is often an important element." Juan J. Linz: *A Comparative Study of Fascism.*, dans: Walter Laqueur, ed.: *Fascism: A Reader's Guide.*, Berkeley and Los Angeles, University of California Press, 1976, p. 20.

4. Pierre Sorlin: *ibid.*, p. 77.

5. Colette Capitan-Peter: *Op. cit.*, p. 166.

6. Zeev Sternhell: *Fascist ideology.*, dans: Walter Laqueur, ed.: *op. cit.*, p. 323.

7. George L. Mosse: *Masses and Man. Nationalist and Fascist Perceptions of Reality* , New York, Howard Fertig, 1980, p. 175.

8. *Ibid.*, p. 167.

9. Pierre Milza: *op. cit.*, p. 279.

10. Zeev Sternhell: *op. cit.*, p. 349.

11. Isaiah Berlin: *The Crooked Timber of Humanity. Chapters in the History of Ideas.* New York, Alfred A. Knopf, 1991, pp. 18-19.

BIBLIOGRAPHY

RACISM

Banton, Michael: *Race Relations*. London, Sydney, Toronto, Tavistock Publications, 1967.

Knight De Reuck, Julie: *Caste and Race. Comparative Approaches*. London, J. and A. Churchill Ltd., 1968.

Dumont, Louis: *Homo hierarchicus*. Chicago, The University of Chicago Press, 1970.

Delacampagne, Christian, Girard, Patrick, Poliakov, Léon: *Le racisme*, Paris, Seghers, 1976, Coll. "Point de départ."

Delacampagne, Christian: *L'invention du racisme*. Antiquité et Moyen-Age. Paris, Fayard, 1983.

Duchet, Claude, de Cormarmond, Patrice (publié sous la direction de): *Racisme et société*. Paris, Maspéro, 1969.

Flem, Lydia: *Le racisme*, Paris, M.A. éditions, 1985, Coll. "Le monde de…,"no.5

Gabel, Joseph: *Sociologie de l'aliénation*. Paris, Presses Universitaires de France, 1970. Bibliothèque de sociologie contemporaine.

Guillaumin, Colette: *Idéologie raciste: Genèse et langage actuel*, Paris, La Haye, Mouton éditeurs, 1972.

Guiral, Pierre , Temime, Émile: *L'idée de race dans la pensée politique contemporaine*. Paris, Éditions du C.N.R.S., 1977.

Memmi, Albert: *Le racisme*, Paris, Gallimard, 1982, Coll. "Idées."

Mosse, George L.: *Toward the Final Solution. A History of European Racism*. New York, Harper and Row, 1978.

Olender, Maurice (édité par): *Pour Léon Poliakov. Le racisme, mythes et sciences*. Bruxelles, Éditions Complexes, 1981.

Poliakov, Léon: Le mythe aryen. *Essai sur les sources du racisme et des nationalismes*. Paris, Calmann-Lévy, 1971.

Poliakov, Léon: *Hommes et bêtes. Entretiens sur le racisme*. Paris, La Haye, Mouton éditeurs, 1975.

Poliakov, Léon: *Ni Juif ni Grec. Entretiens sur le racisme*. Paris, La Haye, Mouton éditeurs, 1978.

Poliakov, Léon: *Le couple interdit. Entretiens sur le racisme*. Paris, La Haye, Mouton éditeurs, 1980.

Simpson, George Eaton, Yinger, Milton J.: *Racial and Cultural Minorities: An Analysis of Prejudice and Discrimination*. New York, Harper and Brothers,1953.

Snyder, Louis L.: *The Idea of Racialism*. Princeton, Van Nostrand,1962.

Taguieff, Pierre-André: *La force du préjugé. Essai sur le racisme et ses doubles.* Paris, Éditions La Découverte, 1988.

Van des Bergh, Pierre: *Race and Racism. A Comparative Perspective.* New York, John Wiley and Sons, 1967.

Wagar, Warren W.: *European Intellectual History since Darwin and Marx.* New York, Evanston and London, Harper Torchbooks, 1967.

Zylberberg, Jacques: "Fragments d'un discours critique sur le nationalisme.," Anthropologie et Société, vol.2, no.1, Québec, 1978.

Zylberberg, Jacques: *La régulation étatique des minorités religieuses.* In: Pierre Guillaume, Michel Lacroix, Réjean Pelletier, Jacques Zylberberg: *Minorités et État.* Bordeau, Presses Universitaires de Bordeaux, 1986.

ANTI-SEMITISM

Abella, Irving, Troper, Harold,: *None is too many.* Toronto, Lester and Orpen Dennys, 1983.

Arendt, Hannah: *The Origins of Totalitarianism.* New York and London, Harcourt, Brace Jovanovitch, 1973.

Bernstein, Peretz: *Jew-Hate as a Sociological Problem.* New York, Philosophical Library, 1951.

Byrnes, Robert: *Anti-Semitism in Modern France. Prologue to the Dreyfus Affair,* Vol. 1, New Brunswick, Rutgers University Press, 1950.

Chevalier, Yves: *L'Antisémitisme. Le Juif comme bouc-émissaire.* Paris, Éditions du Cerf, 1988, Coll. "Sciences humaines et religion."

Cohn, Norman: *Warrant for Genocide.* New York, Harper and Row, 1966.

De Fontette: *Histoire de l'antisémitisme,* Paris, Presses Universitaires de France, 1982, Coll. "Que sais-je?"

De Fontette, François: *Sociologie de l'antisémitisme,* Paris, Presses Universitaires de France, 1984, Coll. "Que sais-je?"

Faye, Jean-Pierre: *Migrations du récit sur le peuple juif.* Paris, Belfond, 1974, Coll. "Eléments."

Friedländer, Saul: *L'Antisémitisme nazi. Histoire d'une psychose collective.* Paris, Éditions du Seuil, 1971.

Girardet, Raoul: *Mythes et mythologies politiques.* Paris, Éditions du Seuil, 1986, Coll. "L'Univers historique."

Glock, Charles Y., Stark, Rodney,: *Christian Beliefs and Anti-Semitism,* New York and London, Harper and Row, 1966.

Graeber, Isaacque, Britt, Stewart Henderson: *Jews in a Gentile World. The Problem of Anti-Semitism.*,New York, MacMillan, 1942.

Herszlikowicz, Michel: *Philosophie de l'antisémitisme.* Paris, Presses Universitaires de France, 1985.

Hertzberg, Arthur: *The French Enlightenment and the Jews. The Origins of Modern Anti-Semitism.* N.Y., Schocken Books, 1968.

Isaac, Jules: *Genèse de l'antisémitisme.* Paris, Calmann-Lévy, 1985, Coll. "Agora."

Katz, Jacob: *From Prejudice to Destruction. Anti-Semitism 1700-1933*. Cambridge, Massachusetts, Harvard University Press, 1980.

Katz, Jacob: *Out of the Ghetto. The Social Background of Jewish Emancipation 1770-1870*. New York, Schocken Books, 1978.

Langmuir, Gavin I.: *Anti-Judaism as the Necessary Preparation for Anti-Semitism*. Viator, vol.2, 1971.

Leschnitzer, Adolf: *The Magic Background of Modern Anti-Semitism. An Analysis of the German-Jewish Relationship*. New York, International Universities Press, 1956.

Lovsky, François: *L'Antisémitisme chrétien*. Paris, Éditions du Cerf, 1970.

Massing, Paul W.: *Rehearsal for Destruction. A Study of Political Anti-Semitism in Imperial Germany*. New York, Howard Fertig, 1967.

Montuclard, Maurice: *Conscience religieuse et démocratie*. Paris, Éditions du Seuil, 1965.

Morin, Edgar: *La rumeur d'Orléans*. Paris, Éditions du Seuil, 1969.

Mosse, George L.: *The Nationalization of the Masses*. New York and Scarborough, New American library, 1977.

Nikiprowetzky, Valentin: *De l'antijudaïsme antique à l'antisémitisme contemporain*. Lille, Presses Universitaires de Lille, 1980.

Parkes, James: *Anti-Semitism*. Chicago, Quadrangle, 1963.

Parkes, James: *The Emergence of the Jewish Problem. 1878-1939*. Westport Connecticut, Greenwood Press Publishers, 1970.

Pierrard, Pierre: *Juifs et Catholiques français. De Drumont à Jules Isaac*. Paris, Fayard, 1970.

Pinson, Koppel(edited by): *Essays on Antisemitism*. New York, Conference on Jewish Relations, 1946.

Poliakov, Léon: *The Weapon of Anti-Semitism*. Dans: Beaumont, Maurice (éditeur): *The Third Reich*. N.Y., Frederick A. Praeger, 1955.

Poliakov, Léon: *Les Juifs et notre histoire*. Paris, Flammarion, 1973, Coll."Science.."

Poliakov, Léon: *Histoire de l'antisémitisme*. Tomes 1 et 2. Paris, Calmann-Lévy, 1981, Coll. "Pluriel." (The History of Anti-Semitism. Oxford, Oxford University Press, 1985).

Poliakov, Léon: *Bréviaire de la haine*. Bruxelles, Éditions Complexes, Bruxelles, 1986 (Harvest of Hate: The Nazi program for the Destruction of the Jews in Europe, New York, Holocaust Library, Schocken Books, 1987).

Pulzer, Peter: *The Rise of Political Anti-Semitism in Germany and Austria*. New York, London, Sydney, John Wiley and Sons, 1964.

Reichmann, Éva G.: *Hostages of Civilization. The Social Sources of National Socialist Anti-Semitism*. Westport Connecticut, Greenwood Press, 1970.

Rodinson, Maxime: *Peuple juif ou problème juif?* Paris, Maspéro, 1981.

Sartre, Jean-Paul: *Réflexions sur la question juive*. Paris, Gallimard, 1954, Coll. "Idées."

Sorlin, Pierre: *La Croix et les Juifs*. Paris, Grasset, 1967.

Sorlin, Pierre: *L'Antisémitisme allemand*. Paris, Flammarion, 1969, Coll. "Questions d'histoire."

Sternhell, Zeev: *Maurice Barrès et le nationalisme français*. Paris, Fondation nationale de science politique, 1976.

Sternhell, Zeev: *La droite révolutionnaire*. Paris, Éditions du Seuil, 1978, Coll. "Histoire."

Trachtenberg, Joshua: *The Devil and the Jew. The Medieval Conception of the Jew and its Relation to Modern Anti-Semitism*. Cleveland and New York, Meridian books and The Jewish Publication Society of America, 1963.

Verdès-Leroux, Jeannine: *Scandale financier et antisémitisme catholique. Le krach de l'Union générale*. Paris, Le Centurion, 1969, Coll. "Sciences humaines."

Weber, Eugen: *The European Right. A Historical Profile*. Berkeley and Los Angeles, University of California Press, 1966.

Weber, Eugen: *The Nationalist Revival in France*. Berkeley and Los Angeles, University of California Press, 1968.

Wilson, Stephen: *Ideology and Experience. Anti-Semitism in France at the Time of the Dreyfus Affair*. Rutherford, Madison, Teaneck, Fairleigh Dickenson University Press, London, and Toronto Associated Press, 1982.

Winock, Michel: *Edouard Drumont et Cie. Antisémitisme et fascisme en France*. Paris, Éditions du Seuil, 1982.

Winock, Michel: *Nationalisme, antisémitisme et fascisme en France*. Paris, Éditions du Seuil, 1990, Coll. "points Histoire."

Whiteside, Andrew G.: *The Socialism of Fools. Georg von Schonerer and Austrian Pan-Germanism*. Berkeley, Los Angeles, London, University of California Press, 1975.

NATIONALISM AND ANTI-SEMITISM IN FRENCH CANADA

Anctil, Pierre: *Le Devoir, les Juifs et l'immigration. De Bourassa à Laurendeau*. Québec, Institut québécois de recherche sur la culture, 1988.

Anctil, Pierre: *Les Juifs de Montréal face au Québec de l'entre-deux guerres. Le rendez-vous manqué*. Québec, Institut québécois de recherche sur la culture, 1988.

Bélanger, André-J.: *L'Apolitisme des idéologies québécoises. Le grand tournant 1934-1936*. Québec, Presses de l'Université Laval, 1974.

Brunet, Michel: *Trois dominantes de la pensée canadienne-française*. Dans: *La présence anglaise et le Canada. Études sur l'histoire des deux Canada*. Montréal, Beauchemin, 1964.

Caldwell, Gary: *L'Antisémitisme au Québec*. Dans: Anctil, Pierre et Caldwell, Gary: *Juifs et réalités juives au Québec*. Québec, Institut québécois de recherche sur la culture, 1984.

Dumont, Fernand, Hamelin, Jean, Montminy, Jean-Paul (sous la direction de): *Les idéologies au Canada-français 1930-1939*. Québec, Presses Universitaires de Laval, 1978.

Linteau, Paul-André, Robert, Jean-Claude: *Histoire du Québec contemporain. De la Confédération à la crise. 1867-1929*. Montréal, Boréal Express, 1979 (Quebec: a history 1867-1929. Toronto, Lorimer, 1983).

Linteau, Paul-André, Robert, Jean-Claude, Falardeau, Jean-Charles (édités par): *Essais sur le Québec contemporain*. Québec, Presses Universitaires de Laval, 1953.

Felteau, Cyrille: Histoire de La Presse. Tome 1, Le Livre du peuple, 1884-1916, Montréal, Les Éditions La Presse.

Fortin, Gérald-Adélard: *An Analysis of the Ideology of a French-Canadian Nationalist Magazine: 1917-1954*. A Contribution to Sociology of Knowledge. Ph. D. Thesis, Cornell University, 1956.

Frégault, Guy: Lionel Groulx tel qu'en lui-même., Montréal, Leméac, 1978.

Gaboury, Jean-Pierre: *Le nationalisme de Lionel Groulx. Aspects idéologiques.* Ottawa, Éditions de l'université d'Ottawa, 1970.

Gingras, Pierre-Philippe: *Le Devoir.* Montréal, Libre Expression, 1985.

Groulx, Lionel: *Mémoires.* Tomes 1 et 2, Montréal, Fides, 1972 et 1973.

Groulx, Lionel: *Mémoires.* Tomes 3 et 4, Montréal, Fides, 1974.

Hamelin, Jean,Gagnon, Nicole: *Histoire du catholicisme québécois. Le XXième siècle 1898-1940,* Tome 2, Montréal, Boréal Express, 1984.

Handler, Richard: *Nationalism and the Politics of Culture in Quebec.* Madison, The University of Wisconsin Press, 1988.

Pelletier, Réjean, Hudon, Raymond (sous la direction de): *L'engagement intellectuel. Mélanges en l'honneur de Léon Dion.* Sainte-Foy, Presses de l'Université Laval, 1991.

Hughes, Everett C.: *Rencontre de deux mondes.* Montréal, Boréal Express, 1972 (French Canada in Transition, Chicago, University of Chicago Press, 1943).

Jones, Richard: *L'Idéologie de l'Action catholique. (1917-1939).* Québec, Presses Universitaires de Laval, 1974.

Langlais, Jacques, Rome, David: *Juifs et Québécois français, 200 ans d'histoire commune.* Montréal, Fides, 1976, Coll. "Rencontre des cultures."

Laurendeau, André: *Ces choses qui nous arrivent. Chronique des années 1961-1966.* Montréal, HMH, Collection aujourd'hui 1970.

Monière, Denis: *Le développement des idéologies au Québec. Des origines à nos jours.* Montréal, Éditions Québec-Amérique, 1977(Ideologies in Quebec: The Historical Development, Toronto, University of Toronto Press, 1981).

Monière, Denis: *André Laurendeau et le destin d'un peuple.* Montréal, Québec/Amérique, 1983.

Oliver, Michael Kelway: *The Social and Political Ideas of French Canadian Nationalists. 1920-1945.* Ph. D. Thesis, September 1956, McGill University.

Robertson, Susan (Mann): *L'Action française. L'Appel à la race.* Thèse de doctorat, Février 1970, Université Laval.

Sherrin, Phyllis: *The Devil, the Word and the Flesh.* Ph. D. Thesis, York University, 1975.

Téboul, Victor: *Antisémitisme: Mythe et images du Juif au Québec.* Dans: Voix et Images du pays, Montréal, Presses de l'Université du Québec, 1980.

Wade, Mason: *Les Canadiens-français de 1760 à nos jours.* Tome 2, Ottawa, Cercle du livre de France, 1963. (The French Canadians 1760-1967, Toronto, MacMillan, 1975-76).

Wade. Mason: *The French-Canadian Outlook. A Brief account of the Unknown Americans.* Westport, Conn., Greenwood Press, 1974.

Wilhelmy, Jean-Pierre: *Les mercenaires allemands au Québec du XVIIIième siècle et leur apport à la population.* Belœil, Maison des Mots, 1984.

EXTREMIST RIGHT-WING NATIONALISM, FASCISM, NAZISM

Ayçoberry, Pierre: *La question nazie. Les interprétations du national-socialisme 1922-1975.* Paris, Seuil, 1979, Coll. "Points Histoire."

Bernstein, Serge: *Le nazisme.* Paris, MA Éditions, 1985, Coll. "Le monde de..."

Capitan-Peter, Colette: *Charles Maurras et l'idéologie d'Action française.* Paris, Éditions du Seuil, 1972, Coll. "Esprit."

De Felice, Renzo: *Interpretations of Fascism.* Cambridge, Massachusetts and London, England, Harvard University Press, 1977.

Gregor, A. James: *The Ideology of Fascism. The Rationale of Totalitarianism.* New York, The Free Press, 1969.

Hamilton, Alastair: *The Appeal of Fascism. A Study of Intellectuals and Fascism 1919-1945,* New York, Macmillan, 1973.

Hobsbawn, Eric, Ranger, Terence (edited by): *The Invention of Tradition.* Cambridge, London,Cambridge University Press, 1983.

Kedourie, Élie: *Nationalism.* N.Y., Frederick A. Praeger, 1960.

Laqueur, Walter (edited by): *Fascism: A Reader's Guide.* Berkeley, University of California Press, 1976.

Michel, Henri: *Les fascismes.* Paris, Presses universitaires de France, 1983, Coll. "Que sais-je?."

Milza, Pierre: *Les Fascismes.* Paris, Imprimerie nationale, 1985, Coll. "Notre siècle."

Mosse, George L.: *Masses and Man. Nationalist and Fascist Perceptions of Reality.* New York, Howard Fertig, 1980.

Nolte, Ernst: *Les mouvements fascistes. L'Europe de 1919 à 1945.* Paris, Calmann-Lévy, 1969.

Nolte, Ernst: *Three Faces of Fascism. Action française, Italian Fascism, National-Socialism.* New York, Holt, Rinehart & Winston, 1966.

Sternhell, Zeev: *Ni droite, ni gauche. L'idéologie fasciste en France.* Paris, Éditions du Seuil, 1983.

Weber, Eugen: *Peasants into Frenchmen.The Modernization of Rural France 1870-1914.* Stanford, Cal., Stanford University Press, 1976.

THEORETICAL RECONSTRUCTION

Boudon, Raymond, Bourricaud, François: *Dictionnaire critique de la sociologie.* Paris, Presses Universitaires de France, 1982.

Gabel, Joseph: *Réflexions sur l'avenir des Juifs.* Paris, Méridiens Klinsieck, 1987.

Tajfel, Henri: *Differentiation Between Social Groups*. London, New York and San Francisco, Academic Press, 1978.

Tajfel, Henri: *Human Groups and Social Categories*. Studies in Social Psychology. Cambridge, Cambridge University Press, 1981.

Weber, Max: *Economy and Society*. Vol. 1. Berkeley, Los Angeles, London, University of California Press, 1978.

METHODOLOGY

Bordeleau, Yvan: *Comprendre et développer l'organisation*. Montréal, Les Éditions Agence d'Arc, 1987.

Yvan Bordeleau: *Comprendre l'organisation*. Agence d'Arc, 1982.

Freund, Julien: *Sociologie de Max Weber*. Paris, P.U.F., 1968.

Gauthier, Benoît (sous la direction de): *Recherche sociale*. Montréal, Presses de l'Université du Québec, 1984.

Grawitz, Madeleine: Méthodes des sciences sociales. Paris, Dalloz, 1984.

Holsti, Ole R.: *Content Analysis for the Social Sciences and Humanities*. Massachusetts, California, London, Don Mills, Ontario, Addison-Wesley Publishing Company, 1969.

Krippendorf, Klaus: *Content Analysis. An Introduction to its Methodology*. Beverley Hills, London, Sage Publications, 1980. Coll. "The Sage Commtext Series.

Weber, Max: *Essais sur la théorie de la science*. Paris, Plon, 1965.

Weber, Robert Philip: *Basic Content Analysis*. Beverley Hills, London, New Delhi, Sage University, 1986.